GOD IN THE PITS

GOD IN THE PITS

*Confessions
of a Commodities Trader*

Mark A. Ritchie

Macmillan Publishing Company
New York
Collier Macmillan Publishers
London

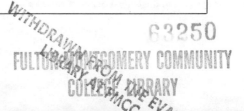

Macmillan Publishing Company
866 Third Avenue, New York, N.Y. 10022
Collier Macmillan Canada, Inc.

The author gratefully acknowledges the permission of Little, Brown
and Company to reprint the poem "The Kitten" from *Verses from
1929 On* by Ogden Nash, copyright © 1940 by Ogden Nash. It first
appeared in *The Saturday Evening Post*.

Library of Congress Cataloging-in-Publication Data
Ritchie, Mark A.
  God in the pits: confessions of a commodities trader/Mark A.
  Ritchie.
      p. cm.
    ISBN 0-02-603531-6
    1. Business ethics.   2. Wealth, Ethics of.   3. Ritchie, Mark A.
  4. Brokers—United States—Biography.   I. Title.
  HF5389.R58 1989
  332.6'2'092—dc20   89-2610   CIP
  [B]

Macmillan books are available at special discounts for bulk purchases
for sales promotions, premiums, fund-raising, or educational use.
For details, contact:

Special Sales Director
Macmillan Publishing Company
866 Third Avenue
New York, N.Y. 10022

10 9 8 7 6 5 4 3 2 1

Printed in the United States of America

To the unusually outstanding
Reedsport Union High School
Class of '66,
with apologies

Contents

Preface

"May I humbly suggest that we buy one fifth of the grain crop for the next seven years."

—Joseph, commodity trading adviser
to the pharaoh, 2000 B.C.

I never intended to write a book, especially one with a self-contradictory title. Yet the common stereotype is that integrity and commodities trading go together like Al Capone and Mother Teresa. While they are seldom accurate, neither are common stereotypes completely erroneous. Standards of conduct at all levels of our culture have come under considerable strain lately. And in the United States, it is almost considered un-American to allow anyone to impose his standard on anyone else. Individual freedom is the supreme American right; tolerance of everybody's standard of conduct is the supreme American obligation.

A story is told on one of the exchanges about a successful trader who solicited an exchange employee to perform a certain sexual favor for him in the elevator. They stopped the elevator between floors and were so caught up in their sexual encounter that they did not notice the elevator slowly descend to the next floor, where the doors opened to a crowd of impatient people, involuntarily coerced to observe new ways to ride—an elevator, that is.

The exchange was in a spot. Naturally, all the exchanges maintain the prestige of membership by requiring each member to uphold the "high standards of the exchange," or words to that effect. But how does an exchange legally enforce its code of morals in a society that anxiously defends an individual's right to violate them? Does there exist somewhere a code of morals that could give definition to our "high standard," some members wondered (but not out loud)? Naturally, the exchange is not staffed by philosophers who received their Ph.D.s in ethics. It was reported in this case that a $25 fine was levied for dress code violation.

In the time it took the offending member to walk to the pit, the news of his escapade had circulated far and wide. He stepped to the top of the pit to a rousing cheer from his peers.

Maybe we are, as some have feared, a society cast adrift like a deflated life raft on a sea of illusions. Or maybe we are a society with laws that define right and wrong behavior. What body of lawmakers could pass enough laws in sufficient detail to prevent every improper act—indeed, to even restrict the activity of two consenting adults in an elevator? And how many tax dollars would we have to pay our legislatures to pass such laws and our court system to attempt to decide on their constitutionality?

And even if a universal standard of kindness could be defined and put into law, we would insist on our individual rights to be free to disagree with it and violate it. Fundamental human freedom owes us that much. If a demagogue forced us into obedience, we would still find legal and illegal ways to skirt the laws—thereby providing "60 Minutes" with another decade of material.

Nevertheless the question remains: Is there any virtue in obeying these laws of kindness even if they never could be put on the books? If yes, who says so? If no, maybe I should wait in line at the elevator door for my turn. Rumor has it that the short-term thrill was worth both the fine and the fee.

I have chosen to write this story not because I know the answers to these questions, but rather because the experiences I have endured have jammed them into my face at every turn. I think that many readers will identify with my struggles even though, like myself, they have never quite felt the freedom to mention it. And even now I derive that freedom merely by virtue of the safe separation from my audience that the printed page allows.

I must say up front that these "confessions" are anything but exhaustive—that would require a multivolume work of boring proportions. I expect that there will be some government agents who will read this book hoping to get the goods on the worst of the commodity thieves. There may be some thieves who might browse these pages looking for their names. I remind both groups that the word "confession" is used only when a person recounts his *own* shortcomings. There are a myriad of other terms to denote the telling of stories on others.

I fear that I may disappoint some of my business friends for certain uncomfortable disclosures. My thesis that the public ought not to be in this business at all will most certainly earn me the wrath of the entire branch of the industry that relies on the public.

I also fear that many friends (and former friends) may say, "He left out the time he shafted me!" To all these I extend the warmest personal invitation to drop me a line and say so. The hope for resolve may not yet be gone.

But what I fear most is the wrath that could befall me from my wonderful friends inside the Church for my willingness to plead guilty to that ancient charge that the Church is full of hypocrites. Anyone who has been inside the Church knows full well that the worst that can be said about the charge is that it is a slight exaggeration. But why, some will ask, would I want to publicly bare the dirty undies? Because it is the refusal to admit the obvious that gives the charge such validity. Never has there been a time when we have been so desperate for a standard of conduct that is practical and useful. The Church claims to have a standard—love God and neighbor, for example—by which it judges all outsiders. When insiders, often leaders, are found to be incapable of living by the standard, the Church attempts to preserve its credibility by covering it up. The presumption is that the spiritually enlightened and outsiders are made of different stuff. This presumption is fatal.

All the stories herein are true. All the conversations actually took place. A number of names have been changed, however, in the interest of privacy.

I used to think that authors and editors loved to hate each other. Now I know why. This uninteresting fact, coupled with one honest editor's description of flinging my manuscript across the room (in almost-holy anger) only serves to highlight the unselfish suffering of my two new editor-friends, Lela Gilbert and Steve Wilburn.

CHAPTER 1

Shortages: Silver and Purple Pencils

East down Jackson Boulevard, the morning sunlight had just begun its day over Lake Michigan when I turned right and walked into the Chicago Board of Trade with an optimistic step. And why not? Any day that you're not belly-up is a good day in this business.

September, 1979: At 8:54 A.M. I caught an overcrowded express elevator to the fourth floor, where I swapped my coat at the coat-check station for a tan trading jacket. It looked and sounded pretty much like an ordinary day when I passed the guard station at the entrance to the trading floor.

Just the sight of the room inspires a little awe. The morning light was streaming through the three-story-high windows that watch LaSalle Street traffic slowly move north all the way to the gold coast. Either side of the three-quarter-acre room is lined with massive electronic quote boards that extend the full three stories to the ceiling. The trade checkers called out names of people they were looking for to verify yesterday's trades. At 8:55 everything looked and sounded pretty ordinary. These sights and sounds can be deceiving.

I walked over to the soybean pit to find my trade checker, hoping he would tell me that all my trades had cleared without any misunderstandings.

1

As always, I climbed the five steps to the top of the soybean pit, a point from which I could see the entirety of the largest trading floor in the world. The pits, scattered around the room, rise four feet up from the floor and then form a shallow bowl with steps descending gently toward the center. Around the perimeter of the room are the phone-order desks, each one jammed with phones that would soon pour orders into the market for execution. Even now, at 8:56 A.M., with the market not yet open, they had already begun to ring.

The soybean pit was the largest, maybe fifty feet across, with eight tiers descending gently toward the middle. In another half hour it would be packed with hundreds of traders facing each other, ready to make bids (a price at which one is willing to buy) and offers (selling price). It is the world's finest example of free trade in action.

"Good morning, how's things?" I asked the trade checker when I located him.

"All right, I'll tell ya," he answered. "You're out this trade with Eddie. You're trying to buy twenty-four lots a couple of dollars lower and he doesn't know it. It'll cost you about five grand if we don't find it." The trade checkers have the thankless job of settling all discrepancies that might arise between traders. In this case, I had bought twenty-four lots from Eddie and the central computer that sorts all the trades did not show that Eddie had sold me anything at that price.

"He sold me the twenty-four," I told him. "I remember it. It's a good trade."

"Well, we haven't seen him and his trade checker doesn't know anything about it."

"I'm telling you, it'll turn up. I've never had an out-trade with Eddie. He probably went home with a card in his pocket." A common oversight that prevents trades from getting punched into the computer.

It was 8:58 when I headed over to the silver pit where the bell would begin the trading in only two minutes. I had been introduced to the commodities business in this very pit only a few years before, but I had not traded there since then—until a few months ago, when my partners and I had purchased silver just below $6 an ounce. When we sold it at $7.25, it was the biggest profit we had ever made on one trade. It now stood at double that price. Whoever could have imagined such a tremendous rise in the price?

I could feel the tension in the air when I stepped to the top of the silver pit and waited for the opening bell. I was especially curious about silver today because rumors were rampant concerning yesterday's meetings of the exchange. Oil baron Bunker Hunt and a group of his wealthy family members had been buying silver for months, placing the most established giants of the silver world in severe financial straits. There was simply not enough of the stuff available to meet the short-term demand (contracts due for delivery over the next six months).

It was a textbook example—this market was cornered. Someone (or group) had, over a period of months, been buying silver and not selling it back. Any trader, like myself, who does not actually have a use for a commodity will always sell it back. If he doesn't, the person who sold the silver will have to deliver it. It was a real-life example of the purple-pencil shortage in Mrs. Hample's second-grade class.

For a reason I couldn't remember, I had agreed to come to Mrs. Hample's class and tell them about my occupation. I had racked my brain for days trying to figure out how in the world I would explain commodities to a bunch of second-graders. After all, it is an occupation that almost everyone is either fascinated with, ignorant of, or both.

I finally came upon what I thought was a brilliant idea. I passed out a pencil and ten pennies to each child. "These pennies and pencils are yours to keep," I explained. "But if you want, you can sell your pencil to anyone of your friends. Or you can buy their pencil if you want. So, if you want pennies, you will be a seller of your pencils; if you want pencils, you will be a buyer. If you just like trading, which I know you kids do every time you open those lunch boxes, you can buy and sell pencils until you run out of pennies. Okay, is everyone ready to start trading?" I saw a bunch of heads nodding up and down so I said, "Go."

The room was transformed into a madhouse; hands waving, bodies jumping, little voices calling out prices all over the room, colored pencils (mostly yellow) being swapped for pennies, half of which rolled on the floor and were chased and retrieved by sellers anxious to get on to the next transaction. Any other second-grade teacher would have reprimanded the entire class, sent me to the principal's office, and never invited another commodities trader to come talk to her class. Not Mrs. Hample. She seemed to be aware that her students were behaving like real investors . . . or maybe the entire industry acts like a bunch of second-graders. I was as surprised as she at how quickly these kids learned that they could make or lose money depending on how they traded.

It took both of us a while to restore order. They all seemed to have just one more deal that *had* to be made. One girl who wouldn't be denied caught my attention when she told me she would pay me thirteen cents for a purple pencil I held. It was the highest price bid for a pencil—far higher than the going rate among the kids. "Why do you want to do that?" I asked. "I'm offering to sell this yellow pencil to anyone for three cents."

"I don't want the yellow pencil for three cents," she answered. "I want a purple one and the kids who have 'em won't sell 'em."

A kid in the back perked up. "We've got tons of yellow pencils. Nobody wants any more of 'em, and there aren't enough of those bright purple ones to go around." I could see out of the corner of my eye that Mrs. Hample was smiling at this odd turn of events, and I was about to say something about the law of supply and demand, but why should I confuse the issue? We all just heard the kid explain it better

4

than any economics prof ever had. "Look," I said to the group, "I'll sell anyone a purple pencil for thirteen cents."

"But you only have one," a child properly observed.

"That's right, so I'll make a deal with you to bring some more a week in the future. That's why we call it a 'futures' market. And between now and then, I'll try to buy the purple pencils somewhere for less than thirteen cents."

"What if you can't find 'em?" he said.

"Then I'm in trouble, aren't I? But even if I have to pay a dollar for each pencil, I'll have to buy them and sell them to you for thirteen cents. Because that's the deal we made. Mrs. Hample, I think you've got some financiers here."

Apparently, some silver dealers had sold silver for future delivery at exhorbitantly high prices, believing they would have no problem buying silver from the producers, and thereby making a huge profit. Now, with the price soaring, they were in big trouble. If they couldn't get the silver to deliver, they would have to neutralize their selling obligation by buying from a seller who would then face the same dilemma.

Rumor had it that the buyers owned more silver than could be delivered, leaving the sellers only one option: liquidate their short positions (an obligation to deliver at a set time and price) by buying from someone who doesn't know any better—and these people were becoming very scarce. It began to look as if the buyers could just about name their price (a little like me getting a high price for that purple pencil because no one else was willing to sell theirs).

"Cornering the market" might be the object of a card game, but in the real world of commodities it is totally disruptive, potentially catastrophic, and also illegal. And in this instance there was little doubt about who was in control. The Hunt family had a grip on the market's most sensitive parts. The only question that remained was how hard they would squeeze.

By 8:59 A.M. the tension was nothing like what usually greets the morning bell: butterflies, tension headaches, bodies shoving for space. No, this morning there was real live genuine fear in the air. For the first time in my life I was thankful that I was not a player in the silver market.

I stepped to the top of the pit only a few feet to the left of the largest silver trader. I was little more than an observer since I was a trader in the soybean complex, but a lot of silver traders would become "observers" today and for a lot of days to come.

At 9:00 A.M. the bell rang and a few trades of little import were made as the pit established an opening price for each delivery month. Then a gruff voice next to me yelled, "Sell a hundred April limit-down!" (Limit-down is the lowest permissible price for that day.) The pit paused. It was an incredibly bold way to open a market: a huge order to sell limit-down! A contract for delivery in April didn't trade that much because April was still a long way off. And the gap opening! Normally, the market opens at approximately the level at which it closed the day before. But it doesn't have to. If the first trader with the courage to speak up wants to move the market, it's up to him.

But down the limit!? Did he know something that we didn't about yesterday's committee meetings?

Everyone recognized the voice. Bob Roland, a flamboyant Rolls-Royce owner, never had any trouble getting the attention of the silver pit. Undoubtedly the biggest silver trader on the board of trade and considered by many to be the best, he commonly would use his huge trading numbers to bully the market around, which is what he was doing in this case.

There was a pause while the pit absorbed the size and implication of his offer. If someone yelled, "Sold," and purchased Bob's offer, the buyer would make a slick $300,000 profit when the price moved back to where it had closed the previous day. But what if it didn't?

Still, the April contract had to be worth more than limit-down. I knew that, and I wasn't the only one who knew it. But who would step up and buy even a little five or ten lot in the face of this intimidating hundred-lot offer? So Bob's words were met with an awed, two-second hush.

A trader down in the bottom of the pit broke the silence. "I'll take fifty." It created another hush as everyone realized that one major force had been met by another, the second being half the size, maybe much smaller. I looked down into the pit. It was my brother Joe. Now a four-year veteran of the board of trade, Joe had gained quite a reputation as a trader. He was willing to buy any amount he could afford if he felt the price was too low. This price was clearly too low and the seller may not have really wanted to sell even a few of the hundred he offered. He may have just wanted to force the price down to a level where he could buy some. Who could guess his strategy? That's the beauty of this business. Everyone is dying to know what the next guy is up to: Is he bluffing? Covering his tracks? Does he have hidden motives?

Joe never cared about any of it. If the price was too low, he bought. If too high, he sold. That's the optimum way to make money in this business.

It wasn't always easy being Joe's brother. A friend sitting behind me in high school English class used to console me when the teacher occasionally mentioned Joe's academic achievements, thinking that it would motivate me to work closer to my potential. I had followed him into the business and though we were partners, we generally worked different pits. I stuck around a few minutes more to watch the silver trade before I had to go settle my trades from yesterday and get ready for the soybean opening at 9:30; I was curious about the outcome of the price of April. Traders began bidding for April, but no trades were being made because no one was willing to sell. By the time I left for the bean pit, they had bid the price up twenty cents (a $50,000 profit) and it was still rising. It was the kind of trade a person dreams about and then is always too faint of heart to execute when the opportunity comes.

I made my way back to the soybean complex to prepare for the opening. As I had predicted, Eddie knew my trade. Like the vast majority of people in the grain pits, he is honest, and I knew he had made the trade with me. If he had tried to duck the trade (renege on a bad trade), then my "buy" would be no good and I'd lose $5,000.

From my spot between the soybean meal pit and the soybean oil pit, I could see my trading partner on the top step of the soybean pit. Again I felt the tension mount while we all watched the clock tick toward 9:30.

9:29:54, :55, :56, :57 . . .

Someone in the bean pit yelled out a bid that was met by bids and offers from the entire pit. The trading day was under way; the roar drowned out the sound of the bell three seconds later. I calculated the beans to be a half cent too high in relation to the meal and oil, so while I bought the meal and oil, my partner sold the beans. A few moments later, when the beans dropped half a cent, he bought them back and I sold back the meal and oil. A half-cent profit on ten contracts of soybeans is a profit of $250. Not a fortune, but if we could do it often enough, well. . . .

This was not to be a great year for soybeans, but silver was making history. The wild opening this morning proved to be only the beginning of a market that forced the price of silver to unimaginable levels. And all this amid widespread speculation that some of the major silver dealers could be broke—on paper anyway.

"How in the world," I recalled asking Joe, only a few years before, when he initiated me to the fast world of commodities, "can anyone go broke 'on paper'? Is it possible to be less broke than flat broke?"

"You will be amazed at how much common sense you'll

have to drop in order to understand this business," he told me. "Let me give you a quick summary: When an individual or a firm—let's say a silver user like a jeweler—buys a contract of silver at the Chicago Board of Trade, they don't actually transfer the commodity in exchange for cash. Instead, the jeweler enters into a contract with a seller—say a silver mining company—to exchange silver for cash at some future date. Hence the term 'futures market.' The board of trade acts as the guarantor to both parties."

"So what do they need the board of trade for?" I asked, showing my ignorance.

"They don't *need* the CBT. If the buyer and seller can get together on their own and arrange their own terms, delivery time, place, price, quantity—all that stuff—they don't need the board. All the board of trade does is bring all the buyers and sellers together at the same time in order to make as efficient a market as possible. They set standard contract sizes and delivery points. All the parties have to do is agree on price. In any case, almost none of these contracts ever result in the actual delivery of product for cash."

"You're kidding. What's the point of it all?"

"The point is for both the jeweler and the silver mine to be able to proceed with their businesses without having to worry about what the price will be six months down the road. When the time actually comes that they need the silver, the jeweler will buy it on the open market from the most convenient source and at the same time sell the silver contract they bought at the CBT. If the price of silver rose over the six-month period, the extra cash they will have to lay out will be offset by the profit earned at the board of trade."

"And where does that money actually come from?"

"The money comes from the silver mining company who originally sold it to them."

"I don't suppose they're too thrilled about the whole deal."

"Well, they make up the difference when they sell their silver on the open market at the increased price. The point is that both the seller—or the producer, whatever you want to call him—and the buyer—the user—protect themselves against price moves by locking in a price for a future date."

"Sounds to me like it's nothing more than a great big bet-hedging operation," I said.

"That is exactly what it is; nothing more."

"Okay," I said. "Now explain what it all has to do with being broke on paper?"

"All right, look. This is the most confusing thing about this business and people just will not understand it. Say you're a jeweler or a speculator or just some innocent person who listens to a fast-talking broker—it doesn't matter who you are—if you buy silver, you only have to put up a little money as margin, and that means if the price goes down—below what you've bought the silver at—you've lost money, right?" I nodded. "So you now have to deposit in your account the difference, the amount your account shows you've lost on paper. That money goes to the CBT and is paid to the seller; he's short, the market went down, he makes money."

"And if the market goes back up the next day?" I asked.

"Then you get your money back, and if the price goes higher, you get more money. At the close of every business day, cash moves between the buyers and the sellers in accordance with the price movement for that day. It's a simple way for some of the money to change hands before the actual delivery date. It's known as the infamous 'margin call.' If the price suddenly explodes in the wrong direction and you don't have the cash to meet the margin call, you'd be broke on paper."

"Sounds to me like it's just straight broke."

"Well, it might be hard for a commercial producer to go broke that way because he has the actual, physical silver, which increases in value every time the price rises. But a speculator, who sells a contract expecting the price to fall, could find himself broke on paper if the price continues to rise beyond his ability to meet his margin calls."

"Just how much silver could a speculator control?"

"He only has to put up, let's say, about one twentieth of the value of the contract. So he could buy a whole bunch if he wanted. Naturally, the more he buys, the easier it will be for him to be wiped out if the price goes against him. Normally, when a speculator runs out of money, his positions are liquidated, but it has been known to happen that people will allow him to maintain his positions in the market even with a debit on the books. Why in the world they would do it, I'll never know."

"Sounds just like a person is flat broke only if he is forced to pay his bills," I said.

"That's right. As long as his creditors carry him, he is only broke 'on paper.' And you know how some people value their assets, a pure figment of their exaggeration. Why, they might not even be broke on paper."

"So 'broke on paper' means he's only broke if you prevent him from lying about the value of his assets or force him to keep his word by paying his bills?" I asked with the usual cynicism that accompanies these conversations.

"And who would be so cruel?" he responded in kind.

I recalled this conversation as I heard rumors that some major New York silver dealers might not be able to meet their margin calls. What would happen if the exchange had to step in and force the shorts to liquidate? It's not inconceivable that the entire exchange could be broke—on paper anyway.

October 3, 1979: Silver is trading at $17 an ounce—up $6 in the last month; a price mysteriously inconsistent with the common knowledge that it could be mined and delivered for less than half that.

I couldn't recall a day in the past month that silver hadn't been limit-up or limit-down. Yesterday it hit both limits, a $1.20 range. Everyone knew it was due to crash. No one knew when. A situation of this sort produces a market that is characterized by panic-driven neuroses. The moment the price starts to move down, the pit is immediately filled with sell orders and not a fool in sight that is willing to buy. The market will drop the daily limit in almost no time.

An hour later, when some buy orders enter the pit, the same panic occurs in reverse; all buyers and only an occasional fool willing to sell. The market will move up the daily limit just as quickly as it fell.

And that is precisely what happened on October 2. The market traded both limit-up and limit-down. The limits are imposed on some commodities by the exchange to restrict how far the price can move in one day, thus avoiding a panic collapse of a market. The upper limit places a ceiling on how far the price can rise from the previous day's closing price; the lower limit places a floor on how far it can fall. It is extremely rare for a price to hit either the up or down limit. But when a price moves to the upper limit and then back down to where it started and then falls to the lower limit, you know you have made some history—serious cocktail party material.

I promised myself yesterday that when it hit the limit again, I would get in the market—buy if it went limit-down, sell if it went limit-up.

All you need, I told myself, is enough courage to buy when it hits limit-down and put an order in to sell when it goes back limit-up. It was that easy—except you could lose a fortune if it never goes back up. It could just continue on down, which everyone knew it would do sooner or later.

On this morning, October 3, 1979, the bell rang and silver opened only a little higher than yesterday. The market was not nearly as orderly as it used to be. The price moved with treacherous speed, making it very difficult to liquidate a losing trade. Huge price swings had already caused the daily limits to be increased from twenty cents to sixty cents.

From my position in the soybean meal pit, I kept an eye on the big quote board. It wasn't long before silver took an enormous drop, just like yesterday, to limit-down, sixty cents lower than yesterday's close. This is your big chance, I told myself. Get over there and buy yourself some of that cheap silver. I struggled with the clear risks involved. Surely it would go back up as it had for so many previous days in a row. But what if it didn't? I'll be in over my head.

But I had promised myself that the next time it went down the limit I would buy. So I walked over to the silver pit. Everyone there was trying to sell silver limit-down. It's difficult for a commodity to look very valuable when everyone in the pit wants to sell it at the lowest allowable price and there's not a buyer in sight.

I watched for a moment and then walked away as if I didn't really have any interest. No sooner had I returned to the bean complex than some buy orders came in and rallied the price all the way back up to where it had closed yesterday.

You total idiot, I told myself. Why in the world didn't you buy ten lots? You shot your mouth off about how you would buy the next time it went limit-down. That was $30,000 you would have just made. I really read myself the riot act. Next time you tell yourself you'll do something, just do it (you big dope). It doesn't help to talk to yourself if you don't listen. All right, all right, get off your back, you. Next time it goes limit-down, I'm buying and that's final.

While I inflicted myself with this bit of personal penance, the sell orders began pouring into the silver pit, and when I glanced up at the big board, there it was, offered limit-down again.

Okay, supermouth! What will ya do now? I walked back to the silver pit filled with fear and trepidation, telling myself, "No guts no glory," and all those things that might get me to do what I promised I would, which might also end my already short career. I stepped up into the pit and bought ten lots as quietly as I possibly could from a broker who was as shocked as I was.

I left the pit telling myself how big a fool I was to follow my own advice. I knew I couldn't stick around the floor watching the agonizing seconds tick by, waiting for each one to be the moment that might start silver moving back up again. At least I knew it couldn't go any lower today.

There's nothing I can do to help myself now, I thought. I'd better get out of here. But just in case silver rallied back up, I placed an order at the desk to sell ten lots of silver as soon as the market moved limit-up. I then headed for the doorway, strode past the guard station, and took an express elevator to the first floor. Walking out into the sunlight on Jackson, I turned right toward the lake and a few blocks later crossed State Street and proceeded on over to Carl Fischer on Wabash, where I buy all my music. I browsed for a few minutes without any luck of getting silver off my brain.

I crossed back over State and walked north a block to Wards, still trying to kill time before I had to go back for the closing of the soybean market. By noon curiosity was killing me, and I headed across the square in front of the post office and back into the CBT building to discover the outcome of my fate.

Just as I had expected, silver had moved up from limit-down and was back to yesterday's level. I had pocketed a quick $30,000. Now if it would only continue to rally until it got up the limit and my sell-order could be filled, I could liquidate a $60,000 profit. Not wanting to get too close to the situation, I stayed in the soybean complex and traded my usual small lot sizes while keeping my attention on the silver prices posted on the big quote board.

Then it happened, just as I had assured myself that it would: a buying frenzy overtook the market and, within a short minute or two, the buyers had bid the market limit-up. Pure, exhilarating ecstasy. There it was, 17.53B all over the board, and the other contract months were limit-up as well. The "B" following the price told the world that every contract for sale at that price was bought and there were more buyers willing to pay that price—maybe even higher—except they would have to wait until tomorrow since 17.53 was the highest price allowable today. I should get over there, I told myself, and make sure my order was filled. But then I realized that I didn't know who held my order. If I sold the ten lots myself and later found out that the broker who held my order also sold ten lots, I would end up oversold in a market exploding on the upside.

I signaled to the clerk at the order desk to check on my order. As he left I noticed that silver had come off the limit and the price began declining again. But what did I care now. I had pulled off the greatest trade of my life. I was out of the market with sixty grand. Now I could wait for another big drop and try the idea all over again.

A minute later the clerk returned with the broker who held my order. But all I got was double-talk about why he hadn't sold my ten lots. WHAT!!!! I shouted to myself. You oversized liar!!

"How could you possibly not have sold this order?" I asked in disbelief, and trying to maintain my calm. "The market was bid there for at least thirty seconds."

"It was too hectic and I couldn't fill it," the broker told me. I had seen him trade and I knew he wasn't incompetent. He was a big guy, good looking, outgoing, well liked by everyone, a colorful personality who held positions on the pit committee and other committees of prestige. And it was certainly well within my right to ask if he was even in the pit at the critical time the order should have been filled, but the question could hardly be asked without being accusatory. Certainly no one can responsibly fill orders if he is not even in the pit, and he couldn't have been in the pit or he would have filled the order. A number of brokers had been trying to buy silver limit-up.

What a *shaft!* I finally hit it big and some jerk has wiped out my profit. Any honorable broker would sell the ten lots and pay me the difference in cash. But I was a lowly freshman at this institution, so what could I say? "See ya at arbitration," maybe? But what chance would I have against him—all his friends on the committee. So I went home with a ten-lot buy position in my account and tried to sleep.

The next day silver opened limit-down and stayed there all day. Everyone, myself included, was trying to sell and there were no buyers. So I sold my ten lots the following day, losing $85,000. Naturally, fate being the kind of satirist that it is, the market turned around after I sold out and resumed its erratic climb toward $20 and higher.

How could God let a thing like this happen to me? Wasn't he supposed to protect me from unscrupulous people? Maybe I should have stayed in seminary where I belonged? This is probably the punishment I get for leaving.

December 26, 1979: Silver trading at $25 an ounce. Soviet tanks and troops pour across the border into Afghanistan, fueling the market into a merciless climb toward the stratosphere. Merciless to those who had sold, of whom there were many, but to the longs (the buyers) it was the same euphoric blessing that I had felt for those fleeting moments. All the while concern spread; concern not only for the occasional broker who might take a bigger loss than he could afford (like one who ended up emotionally collapsed in the hospital without a dollar left), but also concern about the stability of the major market forces in New York.

"We've got ourselves an interesting one here, don't we?" I mentioned to Pat one morning while we chatted about the situation. A wealthy self-assured veteran of many years in the business, Pat had traded his way through many a crisis in commodities. He was a handsome family man, owned a gorgeous home in Chicago's classiest suburb, and sat on exchange committees that would handle such matters. Yet he wasn't in the least pretentious. He had made me feel welcome when I was a beginner.

"I've never seen anything like it in all my years around here," he told me. "There is not a professional in this business who could have anticipated this situation!"

"What are the possible outcomes to this thing?" I asked.

"Right now it appears that the Hunts and other silver buyers are holding massive positions in the March contract. If they should do the unthinkable and decide to take delivery, we'll see an unprecedented bloodbath. I'm not even sure there's enough silver to make those deliveries. People who have sold that March contract, like those New York silver guys, with the idea that it's way overpriced, which it certainly is, will have to pay ridiculous prices to liquidate. We'll see a lot of bankruptcies."

"How can the price of silver go so much higher than silver is worth?"

"It's not silver per se. It's silver that can be delivered in March that is unavailable. If they had another year to get it out of the mines and refined—maybe. But for March—there's only a limited amount. We'll have ten people fighting to buy five items. There's no way! I wouldn't doubt that we'll see some political finagling by the time that happens."

"Well, what kind of politics could solve this?" I asked while we stood there looking at the massive board, which showed silver now just over $25.45 an ounce.

"You back someone into a corner, which is exactly where the Hunts have them, and there's no telling what they'll do. The Hunts seem to have completely forgotten that the New York silver people control that exchange out there. What if they can't deliver the silver? You know they can't buy it anywhere. They're the ones who are supposed to have it!" he said, laughing at the ridiculous thought. "Do you honestly think they'll hand over all their money to some heir of an oil fortune from Texas just because he's cornered the market?"

"What options do they have?"

"Don't worry, in the face of real live bankruptcy, they'll come up with something. Look," Pat said, getting down to business, "we know that these huge purchases belong to the Hunts. No one else is crazy enough to hold big positions in this market. They could just leave the Hunts with huge paper profits and no way to collect them. Or better yet, they could pass an exchange rule that would prohibit the Hunts from taking delivery."

"Just change the rules of the exchange in the middle of the game?" I responded. "They couldn't do that in a million years!"

Pat laughed again. It was the laugh of a mentor at his naive novice. "When the real world sticks it to you, you'd be surprised what they can do." I shook my head. We both laughed at the thought. It was unbelievable!

So the speculation was that the country's major silver dealers might not have enough silver to deliver all they had sold and there was no one who could sell them any more. The price continued to rise with no end in sight. Open interest, the sum of the contracts that had been bought (and sold) for future delivery, totaled far more than the available silver on hand. Exactly how much of that open interest was held by the Hunt family was a matter of pure guess.

December 31, 1979: Silver is up an unprecedented $4 to $34 an ounce—a history making move; so high in the cash (nonfutures) market that the price on the exchange (for futures) had been limit-up four days in a row and still lagged behind the cash price by $5. President Jimmy Carter admitted publicly his ignorance of Soviet intentions in Afghanistan—it was the sort of statement that urges people to look elsewhere, anywhere, for their security. There was a general feeling that the Hunts were serious buyers and might actually take delivery of the physical stuff. The people obligated to deliver the silver had to be sweating more than just perspiration. With the open interest at well over 30,000 contracts, the shorts had to come up with over $150 million in margin money each day the price went limit-up. And it now had five more days to go limit-up just to get even with the cash price. Some year-end prayers were offered for a cooling-off period in silver.

January 2, 1980: Silver makes another historic rise of $4.50 in the cash market to almost $39 an ounce. The year-end prayers went unanswered. The cash market now stood almost $9 over the limit-up price of the March contract on the Comex.

"What on earth do you suppose these people are up to?" Pat asked me during a quiet spell in the soybean meal pit. It was a continuing dialogue that had begun months earlier as we all watched the silver developments with fascination. "They've got their hands directly into the bank accounts of the wealthiest people on the Comex. Is there anything to the rumor that they have some vendetta against them?"

"I have no idea what they're up to," I told him, shaking my head. "You can be sure a few people in New York would pay us a small fortune if we could answer that question. It's possible that they just want a hedge against inflation. Y'know Carter hasn't exactly held the lid on it."

"Then why aren't they buying gold?" He asked the obvious question.

"Who knows. It's far undervalued compared to silver. But the Hunts have never been accused of being overadvised in this industry."

"That's for sure, but nobody's this dumb. Gold is dirt cheap compared to silver. It just doesn't make sense."

"Y'know," I added, "the Hunts have a reputation for being conservative born-again Christians. It's possible that they want some protection against an economic collapse, a third world war, the Armageddon-style tribulation preached by the doomsayers."

"Still, it's an idiotic way of going about it," he observed. "They could get plenty of silver and gold at reasonable prices if they exercised a little patience. Someone has taken total leave of his senses. This $35 silver is big-time moron stuff."

"That's for sure." I nodded agreement. "We wrote the Hunts once, y'know . . ."

"You're kidding! Really?"

"Yeah. It was after they lost a fortune in their last commodities debacle here in soybeans. Who could forget the chaos they helped create in that '77 bean market?"

"I hope you weren't complaining. You guys made a fortune in that market."

"Everyone did—except the Hunts. No, we had heard that they used their money for certain charitable goals that were similar to ours. So we thought they might have some interest in a team effort. We never heard from them. We were just beginners, why should they listen to us?"

"Look," Pat said to me, "tell me why an upstanding Christian would want to hoard the world's supply of silver?"

"I can assure you categorically, Pat, there is no *good* reason why!"

"But doesn't it look like that's what they're doing?"

"Sure. It looks like simple market manipulation. And I don't understand it. Maybe there's something to the rumor that he's got it in for the boys in New York. You remember that they were forced out of soybeans by the rules regulating the quantities they could buy." Pat nodded and I added, "So one of the young geniuses probably said, 'Look Bunker, in silver there's no rule that says you can't buy all you want.' So maybe he took his money to play in greener pastures."

"Well, whatever they're up to," Pat said, "they sure have this market by the tail."

January 7, 1980: Silver is limit-up eight days in a row and still not high enough to equal the cash market price. Predictions abounded of hundred-dollar silver. These were dampened only by rumors that the Comex was considering requiring the Hunts to liquidate, just as Pat had suggested. It was unbelievable, unthinkable! "How in the world could they ever make a thing like that stick?" I asked him.

"You got me, but that's what they're saying. Like I told you, when your back's against the wall, you can make any rule you need to."

"Are you saying that you think there are silver shorts sitting on the committee making the rules?" I asked him.

Pat thought for a moment. "Well, I hate to just repeat the cheap rumor that all the shorts are on the committees and they're trying to force the Hunts and the other longs to sell.

I'd think anybody would know better than to try that. What I'm saying is that there could hardly be a trader at the Comex who is unbiased. It's not just the shorts who are in jeopardy here. The entire exchange could collapse."

January 8, 1980: The Comex announces position limits on silver. The ruling limited all speculators to a maximum position of 2,000 contracts.

"Well, if it's the Hunts that have all the longs, which we have always assumed, this oughta force them out and kill the bull market," Pat told me that morning. "It's not fair, but you had to know they would do something like this. You just can't buy what nobody's got."

The cash price dropped $4 in a panic sell-off. It was the first day since Christmas that the shorts did not find themselves looking for a $100 million total in margin money. The reprieve was short-lived—one day to be exact—then new buying came into the market. Over the next week and a half the cash market climbed another unprecedented $18, sending the shorts on a daily vigil to any lender with a new version of that old song, "Buddy can you spare a hundred mil."

January 17, 1980: The cash market in silver rallied another $3 to almost $49 an ounce. The March contract locked limit-up at $39.50. It was the fourteenth limit-up move in the past sixteen days and the shorts paid up at least another hundred million to cover the margin on their positions. Even with all the limit-up moves, the March contract still lagged more than $9 behind the actual cash price. The shorts knew that in nine more days the price of the March and other futures contracts would be allowed to rise the daily limit, forcing them to cough up another billion dollars even if the cash price didn't rise any further.

January 18, 1980: The cash market in silver hit its zenith as it rallied to over $50, accompanied by concern over a boycott of the Olympic Games. As rumors continued to fly that the Comex would somehow stop the longs from taking delivery,

21

the price dropped back to $46. The March contract was limit-up again, and again the shorts were forced to come up with another hundred mil or more.

January 20, 1980: The hostages in Iran and the Soviets in Afghanistan had already stimulated demand for all precious metals. So while the shorts had a weekend's relief from the daily hundred-million margin calls, President Carter announced a boycott of the Moscow games. This could only make a bad situation worse.

January 21, 1980: On Monday morning word on the floor was that the silver market in New York would delay its opening. We all gathered around giving out our usual free speculation on the subject. "Even if they had enough physical silver to cover all their shorts," Pat told us, "they still have to borrow against it to cover their margin calls. That's why interest rates are in excess of 20 percent. But the key point is . . ." He bent forward as if to give out the last word on the subject, the ultimate secret that was common knowledge. "The key point is that they don't have that much silver and *everybody knows it.*"

"There's little doubt that the shorts have had enough of this," another trader suggested. "They'll have to require liquidation."

"They could never make it stick," a couple of others voiced everyone's sentiment.

"What else can they do when the cash market tells you that it will be limit-up for the next nine days. A blind man can read this handwriting." The opening was delayed repeatedly, and when it finally opened, the cash price dropped $3 in anticipation of possible forced liquidation.

January 22, 1980: Finally it happened; the unthinkable, the unimaginable rumor became fact. The news seemed to permeate the corridors of the building: The Comex had announced a for-liquidation-only order. That meant that the huge holders of long positions would now be forced to sell.

I hurried onto the floor to get in on the buzz of excitement. "It looks like they've finally done it," I said to Pat. "The longs will be forced to sell now."

"Boy you're not kiddin'. They made sure of it. Have you heard what the order actually said?" I shook my head. "Well, it said that they will allow new sellers in the market if they can make delivery, but they won't allow new buyers."

"You're not serious? You can't be serious!"

"Unless I don't understand English, that is exactly what it said." We shook our heads in disbelief.

"Unbelievable! You can sell, but you can't buy. A new concept in free enterprise." We laughed at the thought. Was this a joke? "That ought to remove any doubt about whether or not the committee members are biased in one direction." We laughed even harder.

"I wonder if they put a footnote at the bottom of the resolution saying, 'By the way, this resolution was passed by traders who hold no positions in silver.' " We laughed some more.

"Anyone wanna guess what will happen to the price this morning?"

I made my way through the trade checkers over to the silver pit. The factors of supply and demand had given way to the political power of certain committees of the exchange. All sane traders, recognizing the possibility of political manipulation, were by now out of the market.

At the top of the silver pit I waited for the market to open. But there would be no free trade this morning. None of the major traders were even here. Everyone knew what would happen—a total market collapse.

Broker Irwin Smith, a respected veteran in the silver pit, handled the whole thing by himself.

"Sell it at $44!" he yelled as the bell sounded. No one responded. "At 43! At 42! At 41!" I used to trade this commodity by the half cent, I told myself as I felt a chill run down my back. Now it's falling at a dollar a crack and not even trading. The fabric on which the industry is based had been stretched. I was watching it begin to tear.

Only a fool would step out and buy this (and there were a few fools). "At 40!" Irwin continued. "39! 37! 35!" A couple more lots traded and the price stabilized in the low thirties. Within two months it would drop another $20, straining the financial stability of the country.

The great silver market was over, but it ended not by any free-market factors of supply and demand. What I saw wasn't a market collapse. It had already collapsed by edict the day before. I had just seen Irwin adjust it back to a level more suitable to some people. There was no way the Hunts could find buyers who were willing to pay these unreasonably high prices for the silver they were now forced to sell.

It was the beginning of the end for the Hunts, who did indeed have something by the tail; they just didn't realize how it could bite. And bite it did.

No doubt the issue will end up in the courts, I imagined as I stepped down from the pit and made my way through the trade checkers toward the soybean complex; in which case it will be resolved in the eighties, nineties, or maybe even the next millennium.

CHAPTER 2

Baseball, Boats, and Baksheesh

It was late August 1978. The grain market, active earlier in the year, had quieted to the point of boredom. Along with our partner, Ron Bird, Joe and I had worked the soybean "crush" (an arbitrage between soybeans and meal and oil) for five months. But when the trade dried up, our crushing team disbanded. Joe was trading at the Mercantile Exchange, Ron was on vacation, and I was by myself working the soybean complex.

I entered our small, badly overcrowded office space at the close of the trading session. We had half a dozen desks and a couch jammed into three rooms on the fifteenth floor of the Board of Trade Building. I hung up my trading jacket and was ready to split for the day when our secretary approached me. Through her excellent work over the years she had become a trusted friend. I recognized the look on her face though I couldn't remember where I had seen it before. I was about to ask, "What went wrong this time?"

With trembling hands and a shaky voice she answerd my unspoken question. "Your father," she started to say, but then began to cry, "has been killed." Dad was in the most remote corner of Afghanistan and I knew that the fastest communication took days to arrive.

I went into a tiny private office, sat down, and tried to absorb it all. Money had changed a lot of things for me, but some things it could not affect. I knew what the pain of loss felt like. It felt the same now with money as it had without.

While waiting for Joe to return from the Mercantile Exchange, I reflected on my life with Dad. He was as far away from me as anyone could get. You could return from the moon faster than you could get home from Herat, a corner of Afghanistan almost forgotten even by the Afghans. They wondered why anyone would want to help "those" people.

And we were separated by more than time and distance. He chose to use his training as a twentieth-century engineer to construct an eye hospital in a thirteenth-century setting. I bought and sold more commodities in one day than his entire district was worth. My friends live in Lake Forest and Barrington—two of the wealthiest suburbs of Chicago. His friends are the poorest of the poor. His goal: Do God's will by serving them. My goal: Buy low and sell high.

I'd come a long way from my early years in Oregon, then Texas, then four years in Afghanistan, and back to Oregon to finish junior high and high school. It had been a long road to get where I am: an independent trader on the largest exchange in the world. But none of it seemed to matter so much now. Residents of Herat and Lake Forest are equally dead when they die.

My faith had come a long way, too. But could it sustain me in this time of grief? Really sustain me, with something more than the clichés, "All things work together for good," and so forth.

There had been military unrest when my parents went to Afghanistan the year before, and over the year the situation continued to worsen. A family friend in Washington, D.C., had received the news from the U.S. State Department. I called him to find out what had happened. The information he had received was packed with all the detail one might expect from a State Department telegram: "Dwight Ritchie killed,

Winifred Ritchie in critical condition." Yet our friends had been able to acquire some details. An automobile accident had occurred halfway between Herat and the capital city of Kabul. Dad was killed and Mom was in the hospital; her condition was impossible to determine.

To call anything in Kabul a hospital would be to pervert severely the definition of the word. And to call anything in the towns outside of Kabul a hospital would be an obvious distortion of truth.

The seventy-two hours that followed were an intricate maze of confusion. Since we had no knowledge of precisely where Mom was or what sort of medical attention she was receiving, we felt we had to go to Afghanistan; we had to find her and make sure everything possible was being done. Joe had a passport and left that day on a route that took him through Paris. I waited for Nancy, my wife, and Dani, our three-year-old son, to get emergency passports and we left the following day on the only flight we could get, which took us through Copenhagen to New Delhi, India. This was Nancy's first time off the North American continent.

When we arrived in Copenhagen we had reservations to Delhi but no tickets. At the ticket counter in Copenhagen where I purchased our tickets, the agent told me Dani's fare was half price if he was under three. When I informed her that he was not, she repeated the information, graciously allowing me the opportunity to recompute his age. I said something to the effect of how convenient it might be if he were younger, but I didn't know any way to achieve it. "No," she said again, obviously thinking I was having trouble with her English, "if he's under three, he's half price." She paused patiently, waiting for me to tell her he was under age three.

What reason could I possibly give for refusing to take a hundred dollars from an airline to which I had no obligation? My logic, my philosophy, my education failed me. I recalled Dad saying, "Mark, what if everyone behaved like that?" But in this case that argument didn't work. Everyone *was* behaving like that. So much so that I was considered odd for not doing it, too.

I debated the issue for a moment. I'm probably only having this struggle because Dad's memory and his religious legalism, which I thought I had rejected, were so strong on my mind right now. I could almost hear him saying, "It's wrong because God says it's wrong," his favorite appeal to a creator of an arbitrary moral code. Other than Dad, who would say this is wrong? Obviously the ticket agent saw nothing wrong with it.

"It's all right," I said, and I showed her the birth date on his passport. "We'll pay the full fare." She shrugged as if to say that it wasn't her fault that I had an I.Q. problem. That look on her face stuck with me while I sat with Nancy and Dani waiting for our flight. After all the years of struggle I had become a legalist myself. I looked around me to see if anyone else noticed. This is ridiculous, I thought. There had better be a God somewhere approving of this, I thought, or at least some SwissAir stockholders (even if their children might be under three when they ride on other airlines).

Somewhere between Copenhagen and Delhi I began to wonder if this resurgence of morality was just a passing fancy, a leftover of my father's influence. Maybe it will fade when all the grieving is over. I'll be able to remember him with fondness without being haunted by his moral code.

I started to cry. All the things I had failed to learn would no longer be repeated. All the years I should have enjoyed with him but didn't would now never happen. But thank God for the memories. While Dani slept between us, I stared into the clouds 35,000 feet over Eastern Europe and drifted back twenty-five years to a romantic little town.

Reedsport is located on the Oregon coast in the middle of a forty-mile stretch of breathtaking sand dunes. This quiet town was the sort of place a teenager runs from for lack of excitement in his teenage years, then runs back to in his twenties for just the opposite reason. There was not a better place for an adventurous three-year-old with a mind of his own to go exploring—and I did. Around and under the maze of blackberry brambles behind our little house, I imagined myself a character in all sorts of fantasies.

A winding path led precariously down to the slough, where I was strictly forbidden to go—it was "too dangerous." Still, I had a vision in my mind of what it was like. I saw a place where bad boys went, a place like the one where Pinocchio threw mud and chopped up furniture. Visiting the slough sounded like a lot of fun to me and I planned to escape there someday with my four-year-old brother and sister, the twins, Joe and Joanna (called Janny), and the tagalong baby of the family, my little two-year-old brother, Danny.

The four of us shared a record player that played little records with big holes in the middle. Together we listened to all sorts of stories. My favorite was the one about Pinocchio. I always cried when Pinocchio turned into a donkey and then got eaten by the whale. I loved that little wooden critter. To me, he seemed almost like a real boy right from the beginning, especially with his friend Jimminy, the cricket. I understood Pinocchio because I had a kind of Jimminy Cricket, too, just like the one Pinocchio had. Mine irritated me just like Jimminy did Pinocchio, and I didn't always listen, either.

One day my father seeded a small, bare section of lawn with grass seed. This was quite an involved process. He dug up the soil, broke the dirt clods, and smoothed it until it was flat soft soil. Then he spread the grass seed and enclosed the area with a string.

"If any of you go in there, you're gonna be spanked," he warned us.

All went well for a few days. But I had this boat—a flat-bottomed, ferry boat—and it desperately needed a flat, smooth, soft surface to run on. A surface just like that seeded area. My ferry just didn't work in the grass.

I listened to my Jimminy Cricket for a few long days, but

this was an irresistible situation. At last I took my ferry boat in hand, crawled under the string, and pushed it around on the smooth dirt. It wasn't quite as much fun as I thought it would be, so I didn't stay but a few minutes.

"Who's been in the dirt where they're not supposed to be?" my father asked everybody in a gentle voice when he got home from work. He was calm, but that didn't mean I would escape the reaping of my reward.

"Not me!" I volunteered right away.

"Mark did it!" everyone shouted before I was finished with my two-word denial.

"I did not."

My father delivered on his promise that day. And during the trauma of that spanking I promised him that I would never be bad again. While being punished, I said anything that might shorten the process. And I really meant it. I had no desire to ever be bad again.

Jimminy Cricket didn't even laugh at me. I knew very well that I would have been better off if I had listened to him. That dirt had looked so attractive. Yet I was amazed after I got into it how little fun it really was.

Not long afterward I found my mother's can of white paint on the back porch. I loved to watch her paint things around the house. It made things look so new even though they weren't, and I longed for the day I would be big enough to make things white and new like she did. She knew that oil-base paint and three-year-old boys did not mix, so she never let me paint and always tightly secured the lids on the cans. This time she was careless. It would be my day.

"You're gonna get in trouble," Janny warned me. She spent most of her time being good. Jimminy Cricket whispered the same thing, though it really seemed as if I was just talking to myself.

And I answered them both the same way, "I know what I'm doin'." And just about anything that wasn't more than three feet off the ground got some paint on it that day. That old swing set was in desperate need of a fresh coat of paint.

Many things were clearly wrong and I knew most of them. But no one had ever told me not to paint the car. It was an old car, definitely needed a newer look. No doubt I'd forgotten the promise I had made in the heat of that ferry-boat spanking.

I was never punished for my creativity with the paintbrush. My parents reasoned that I should have known I was doing wrong, was probably warned by my siblings, but nevertheless had not been specifically prohibited from playing in the paint. So even though the net effect of my action was far more damaging than my boat-in-the-dirt infraction, I walked away without a scratch. I alone knew what I had done.

I really did want to be good. But it just kept getting in the way of having fun. And having fun was always more fun.

My parents were devout Christians. Fundamentalists. So the issue of being good often came up when it was time to say bedtime prayers. In my case it was especially critical. My mother explained to me that if a person was truly sorry for his bad behavior, he could tell God how sorry he was and then ask Jesus to "come into his heart." Having Jesus "live inside" would help any little boy to be good. So at my bedtime prayers the night after the painting, I said something very different. "Jesus," I prayed, "I'm sorry that I'm not a good boy. Please come into my heart and help me be good." I hoped this would help me be a better boy and cut down on the rather frequent use of the spanking stick.

The all-important truth that anyone who does not invite Jesus Christ into his heart as his "personal savior" goes to hell raised a simple and obvious question that we regularly asked Mom.

"If only people who know Jesus go to heaven, what about all the people in the world who never hear about Jesus in their whole lifetime?" The question seems to be asked with surprising regularity by children and adults alike.

"It's still the same, if they don't know Jesus, they go to hell."

"But that's not fair," I objected along with Joe and Janny.

"They never had the chance to hear."

Actually, my mother did have an answer. She told us that, in fact, everyone in the world had an opportunity to hear because Noah told his children and they passed the word along to their children. If everyone had continued to do this (pass the word on to their children), everyone would know.

It's difficult for a four-year-old to tell his mother that she doesn't make sense. As I hit my teen years it got a lot easier; in fact, it became a downright habit. But at the age of four, it's tricky to make the objection stick. Nevertheless, I found this argument quite unconvincing and continued to press my mother on the fairness of our God. She would point out that the real question is not a matter of God's fairness but a matter of our obligation. If we meet our obligation to tell everyone in the world about the Christian message, there will no longer be the excuse of ignorance.

The obligation was not one from which my parents would shrink. When I was still four years old, Dad left his promising career as a construction engineer in Reedsport to study for a masters in theology at Dallas Theological Seminary, a fortress of conservative Christian thought. So it was that we all said "good-bye" to Reedsport and headed south.

The matter of having Jesus living inside was not a magic solution to the problem of being good. Though I never gave it much conscious thought, it must have been quite obvious to my mother when one day she found me in the beautiful Texas sun peppering the little old lady next door with dirt clods. This lady was such a wimp, so easily intimidated. I had her pinned behind her screen door and would let fly with a clod each time she got the courage to poke her gray head out. The more she scolded, the more euphoric I became.

Then suddenly I found myself hanging from my left arm, feet swinging, desperately trying to reach the ground as my saintly mother hauled me back into our yard and toward the house. I had never been told not to do this. I hadn't actually hit the lady, it was after all a first offense, and, anyway, I thought Jesus was supposed to keep me from doing these things. It was tricky to make these points when the first priority was to keep my left arm in its socket. Somehow I knew my pleading would fall on deaf ears. Ol' Jimminy Cricket had been on my case even more actively since that little prayer some time back, so I was better informed than I wanted to be about what was right and wrong.

They were sweet years, those years in Texas, in spite of the occasional strain on my left arm, which was always so well deserved. We didn't have much—precious little, in fact—and we knew it. Our neighbors watched neat things on their TVs and rode in new cars. We had everything we needed, never went hungry, but when a father of four is a student, there is never much left over for the extras.

I longed for a baseball glove, a real glove that would catch a real ball. Mommy would seal a business-size envelope, cut the end off, stick my hand into it, and use a ball to form a pocket in the section of the envelope that covered my palm. Outside I went to play catch with my ball and disposable glove. Each night I would open the Sears and Roebuck catalogue to the picture of the bat, ball, and three-fingered glove that sold for $4.99. I saved my allowance forever to order that bat, ball, and glove.

One day Mom told me that I had saved enough to buy it. It couldn't have been true because our ten-cent-a-week allowance combined with my inability to save would have prohibited me from ever amassing that kind of money. She had no doubt been supplementing my nickels and dimes.

It was a great day when the order for the bat, ball, and glove was finally mailed, and an even greater day when, on Christmas Eve, the delivery man from Sears knocked on the door with a package for Mark Ritchie. A real ball, a real bat, and a glove made out of leather. So I spent Christmas day playing catch with Dad in the driveway, and life with Joe and Danny began to center around baseball.

Being poor wasn't fun, but it never kept me from having fun. It just made me sad sometimes to know that it was so. That's why when Dad got rid of our seventeen-year-old Studebaker, appropriately named "Old Smokey," and replaced it with a six-year-old Nash, which he was able to buy for $300, we kids thought we had a brand-new car.

Danny was the one character who added color to our family. When he didn't do something outlandish himself, fate did it to him. In the bean-picking season, Mom and we kids worked the fields with the migrant workers. We weren't big enough to pick much, but what little money we made was a lot to us. Danny was too little to help, however, so Mom left him with a friend, Mrs. Brown. On one particular morning, there was no one awake at the Browns' home when we arrived, so Danny got into the backseat of their car parked in the driveway to wait for Mrs. Brown to get up.

By the time Mr. Brown came out to drive to work, Danny was sound asleep. Mr. Brown, not in the habit of checking his backseat for strays, was later puzzled when his coworkers returned from lunch saying there was an upset little boy sitting and crying beside his car. Although he knew our family, Mr. Brown didn't know what Danny looked like, and Danny could not yet talk plainly. Danny kept saying, "I'm Anny Itchie. I'm one of four." At the end of the day, Mr. Brown took the little boy home with him, only because Danny seemed convinced that he belonged in Mr. Brown's car. They returned to a confused Mrs. Brown, who assumed that Danny's parents had kept him in the hot bean fields for a day.

One day Danny was counting the money he had saved over as long a period as either of us could remember and he had actually been able to put enough change together to acquire a dollar bill. I had never been able to save enough to have a piece of paper money; even when I had saved for so long for that glove, I never actually saw a real dollar bill. It was such an attractive piece of money, a whole paper dollar. I couldn't imagine how he had ever saved that much money.

So a few days later, when Danny damaged the ramp on my ferry boat, I insisted that he do something to make it right. We all agreed, Joe and Danny and I, that a ferry boat with a broken ramp was no longer worth the $4 that our parents had paid for it.

"I think that a dollar would make up for it," I said, knowing that this would be a fair way to settle the problem and also gain me that paper money that looked so good. "I still won't be able to fix it, or get another one," I added to further enhance my bargaining position. It seemed fair to all of us, so my five-year-old brother, feeling so bad about the damage, was sadly willing to part with the dollar that it had taken him a lifetime to save. I was thrilled to get that dollar and I knew it was all done fairly. I hadn't even needed to steal it.

A few days later Mom learned about the negotiation. She did not share our opinion about the fairness.

"That's not right, Marky," she told me. "Danny has been saving his small allowance for a long, long time to be able to have that dollar. You've been spending your allowance on candy and pop and now just because you want something he has, you made him feel like he owes it to you. That dollar is all Danny has and now you have taken it away."

Danny was sitting quietly listening to Mom paint me into this corner of selfishness. I knew that every word she said was true, and there was my little victim right in front of me. Tears of remorse came into my eyes. I pulled the dollar from my pocket.

"Here, Mommy, you take it." She took that new dollar bill and handed it back to Danny, sitting so quiet, so vulnerable, so defenseless; having only his Mommy to protect him from the likes of me. Glad as I had been to get it, I was even happier to get rid of it.

By the time Dad finished his degree in theology, he was too old to be a missionary, even though his greatest concern was for people who had never heard about Christianity. So he took a job as a professor of engineering in Kabul, Afghanistan, in spite of that country's strict rules against proselytizing. The Afghan government, being Muslim, would not allow anyone to enter the country with any religious intentions.

We spent a week in Karachi getting acclimated to our new world, which really meant learning to run to the toilet at top speed, the result of having drunk the dangerous water they'd warned me about. Sometimes these bathroom "runs" got me there in time. Sometimes not.

It was an ordinary Asian day, hot and sunny, when we boarded an old twin-engine DC-3 and began the climb up into the Hindu Kush mountains of Afghanistan. There were now seven of us, counting the addition of the five-month-old baby, James. After a stopover in Kandahar, the plane followed the mountain range northeast toward Russia. (I asked Joe if he thought the Russians might shoot us down.) Emerging from atop the steep jagged mountains we descended to the Kabul River valley below.

Kabul, Afghanistan, would provide a matchless introduction to the way the other half of the world lives. Early morning sounds alone identify the locale. The mullah's song calling the people to prayer competes with the rooster. Both precede the sun. Donkey bells clang as the country's beasts of burden put the first action into the day. Bleating sheep are herded through the streets toward market as stray dogs bark and harass them.

There were a number of American families in Kabul, all working in some phase of our aid to that country. A boy named Bill from one such family came over to meet us and took Joe, Danny, and me for a walk around the neighborhood and through the bazaar. Every yard was completely surrounded by an eight-foot, mud-brick wall making a network of walls that covered the entire block.

"What's that awful smell?" I asked Bill as we walked by a breach in the wall that extended all around the block.

"That's the public bathroom."

"Are you kidding? It's yucky." It was an area about eight feet wide by thirty feet long, surrounded by walls on three sides yet completely open to the street. The ground was covered by several pools of human waste.

"You'll get used to it," Bill told us. A few blocks later we were in the heart of the bazaar.

Beggars take their places in the busiest section of the marketplace—their ability to bring in money determined by the amount of sympathy they can generate on sight. One need not be blind or crippled to beg, however. We were immediately surrounded by a group of children about our age with their hands extending as far toward our faces as possible, all repeating the same word.

"Baksheesh! Baksheesh! Baksheesh!" they all yelled. We looked at Bill, wondering how to respond.

"Try to ignore them. If you give just one of 'em anything," Bill warned, "they'll never leave you alone." They were so different, so dirty, so distasteful.

A shopkeeper finally struck one of them and yelled. They scattered like frightened animals.

"He swore at 'em," Bill told us. "They'll be back around us in a minute. Don't worry. You'll get used to it."

We meandered throughout the bazaar and Bill showed us how to bargain for anything we wanted to buy.

"How much is this kite?" he asked a shopkeeper in Farsi, and interpreted for us. "He wants ten afs for it. That's about twenty cents." Bill shook his head and laughed.

"Five afs. I sell for five," the merchant responded. Bill just kept shaking his head. "Well, how much you pay then?"

"Half. Half an af."

"Aw!" The shopkeeper made an awful face. "Buddo! Buddo!" He told us to "Get lost. Beat it." We turned to leave.

"Stop, stop. Come back." Now he seemed almost conciliatory. "Three afs. I'll sell for three afs."

"One. I'll give you one," Bill responded. "That's all."

"Come, come." The man now sounded like he really wanted to get down to business. "Give me your top price, absolute highest you can pay."

"Top price?" Bill asked. "You want the highest price I will ever pay? Okay. One and a half afs. That's it, my top price."

The man's face again showed his total displeasure. "Two and a half afs. That's my lowest price."

"Look, here's what I want you guys to do," Bill said, turning to the three of us and speaking English, which the shopkeeper didn't understand. "We will all turn around and begin moving toward that shop over there where this guy knows there are more kites. Just pretend like this visit is over." We all said good-bye in our broken Farsi and began moving on.

"Wait, wait!" he said after we had taken about three steps. "It's yours for an af and a half." Bill took an af and a half out of his pocket while we stood there amazed that he could buy a twenty-cent kite for three cents.

"Two afs," the man said as the exchange was being made. "I really need to get two afs for it." Bill ignored the plea and took the kite. It was completely different from any kite I had ever seen, diamond in shape with a crosspiece that bowed from the left and right corners up into the top of the diamond.

"This kite is ten times better than the kites we have in the States," Bill told us. "This flexible crosspiece makes the kite go anywhere you direct it. That's how we have kite fights." Then he found some kite string, a special string that has finely ground glass glued into it. "This string makes it possible to cut the strings of the other kites." He went through the same bargaining routine over the string and we were on our way out of the bazaar. As we passed a beggar, Bill put an af into his outstretched hand. Later, he taught us how to fly the versatile kite; how to maneuver it, cross another kite's string, and cut it down.

On our bikes we explored the neighborhoods around Kabul. Foreigners weren't always the most popular people.

"Why do these kids throw rocks at us?" we asked Bill. "We haven't done anything to them."

"Well, we're rich, so they like to throw rocks at us."

"Us, rich?" I reacted, recalling how I had always thought myself to be the poorest kid on the block.

"If you were one of them, you'd think we were rich." This situation often resulted in an adversary relationship between most foreigners and Afghans. Bill, unusually mature for a twelve-year-old, was never interested in fighting back and knew how to avoid any serious confrontation.

About six months after we arrived, Bill and his family returned to the States, and we began to answer the rock throwers with a few rocks of our own. Sometimes we even hated them, and everywhere we went, we took our big German shepherd for protection. But generally, these rock fights were quite harmless clashes between different classes of children.

I knew these people were to be pitied. And I did pity them. They were so devoid of hope. The children my age spent their days in the streets gathering manure for fuel, went home to overcrowded, one-room mud houses, and slept on dirt floors. Winter was an especially difficult time. The need for manure was greater, but the street supplied less. The infant mortality rate was 65 percent—that was the official statistic—but I also knew there was no one keeping track of the number born to each family. That would have been an impossibility even if someone had cared enough to do it. Life here is just not that valuable.

On one occasion our family was in the humble home of some Afghans. Because of the economic gulf that existed between foreigners and the Afghan people, such a visit was almost unheard of. The mother had lost her first four babies and the one she was now holding was two years old and badly malnourished. He was the same age as my little brother James, who could run and play and was generally healthy enough to keep chaos ever present in the family. Her child, though, having never eaten anything except mother's milk, still looked like an infant.

My parents and others discussed the permanent damage to this child's physical and mental development. I was losing my appetite just looking at him. I couldn't help wondering why my brother James was born into our family and this innocent little fellow into his hopeless circumstances. Things could have been reversed. And I could have been one of the older siblings that didn't make it. Maybe they were the lucky ones. That was the kind of country it appeared to be: the survivors lived in misery; the luckier ones were dead.

The concern expressed by the adults over the condition of this child was all the more depressing because it made me realize that there were thousands more just like him. Helping him could hardly make a difference. But they did.

I got that same feeling every time my father tried to help someone. If you want to help the miserable, I thought, there is an unlimited number out there just waiting. What good does it do to help only one, I asked?

Danny was the first member of our family to become a trader. At the age of eight, he began raising pigeons. These were not the birds that one usually finds in big cities. These were an Asian strain, colorful birds with a variety of markings. It was common in Afghanistan for a young boy to collect and raise them, though they were not always cheap. A bird's value was determined by the uniqueness of its colors and markings, so there was a lot to learn in order to buy them intelligently.

Danny began by spending his allowance on a pigeon he found in the bazaar. The next thing we knew he was bartering for every pigeon he came across, trading pigeons with the local pigeon owners, and developing for himself quite a flock of birds.

Each day after school, Danny came straight home, got his pigeons out of their pen, and flew them around the neighborhood. From the top of the maze of walls that surrounded the block, Danny would direct his pigeons with a huge net as they circled the neighborhood. The purpose of this was to attract any strays or even a pigeon from another flock. He would clip the wings of any new pigeon for about a month until it became accustomed to its new home and could be trusted to fly with the others. Plucking feathers would achieve the same result, but if the feathers grew back too soon the pigeon might be tempted to fly off to another flock. Danny preferred to play it safe and wait until he was sure the bird was well adjusted to the others before he would allow the feathers to fully grow back. Then it would fly off with the rest to attract more pigeons.

Danny bargained for pigeons with the shopkeepers in the bazaar. He would decide what he was willing to pay for a pigeon, put that amount of afs in his right pocket, and proceed to try to strike a bargain. When all else failed, he reached into his right pocket, pulled out all the money, and looked at it as if to say, "Well, look at this, it's all the money I have." On many occasions the shopkeeper, thinking he didn't have another af to his name, would sell the pigeon at Danny's price. If not, he was off to the next shop. (It is amazing what an eight-year-old can learn from a bunch of Afghan boys.) Dad soon became known around the neighborhood as the father of the pigeon trader.

So it was, through common activities like Danny's pigeon raising, that we encountered the fragrance of another culture. They were four deeply impressionable years. But when Dad's term was over, we would pack up and return to the little town where we started.

We moved back to Reedsport immediately following my

seventh grade year, arriving early enough in the summer for Joe, Danny, and me to check into the local baseball teams and begin playing in earnest. And they were good teams. Danny played third base on a team that had a pitcher who could blaze the ball. I didn't know a baseball could be thrown that hard by a twelve-year-old. But Jimmy Brandow was an exception, as I would find out on the football field in the fall. It was a brand-new beginning for us, being back in the land of the free and the home of the chocolate shake. The future looked good, but the present was wonderful.

The screech of our tires on the Delhi runway brought me back to the present. We were over two hours late, one minute too late—according to the printed schedule—to catch the only connecting flight to Kabul, and dead tired on the second morning of our trip. We had telegraphed from Copenhagen to Delhi to ask if they could please delay their flight a few moments so that we could connect.

Stepping off the plane we were met by hot, humid, heavy air—the sort that makes you lift your arms up to keep them from contacting your body. It never works when you're carrying luggage.

Nancy and Dani had never experienced weather like this; it was only the beginning of culture shock for them.

I should have remembered how time in the Eastern world works. The connecting flight we should have missed was delayed the major part of a day. We entered an all-concrete waiting area with a high ceiling from which was hanging a slowly rotating four-bladed fan. We didn't notice it circulating any air. The place was right out of a Bogart movie, except he didn't have air that was thick with humidity.

We moved our bags from the main waiting room into a back room where an Indian man was selling a few concessions. Dani sprawled out on some of our things but couldn't sleep for the heat and humidity. It was early morning, and after covering twelve time zones, we could have used some sleep.

Under the slowly turning fan in the middle of the room, a man changed his clothes. Nancy pretended not to notice.

I bought a couple bottles of Coke, hoping it would help cool us down. The soda was room temperature, which was awfully warm, and contained far less carbonation than in the West. By the time the next flight arrived in Delhi, three hours later, we had drunk all they had. The flight was from Germany, and who should get off but my brother James. Refreshment to a sad soul is the sight of a familiar face in a strange land. Two more hours of exhausting delays and we were all on our way to Kabul.

As soon as Nancy and Dani tasted the food served on Arieana Afghan Airlines, they forgot all about the miserable Delhi weather. "Eu, yuck, Dad! What is this stuff?" Dani asked, spitting out his first bite. Nancy concurred with his taste.

"Don't worry," I told them. "You're gonna love Afghan food."

Aireana Airlines no doubt buys their jets on the used market at tremendous savings. Nancy found little comfort in my recollections of how much worse those flights of the fifties were in worn-out, beat-up DC-3s. I tried to take her mind off the left wing, which was flopping in the turbulence, by telling her stories about how many times I used to throw up in the old DC-3. "Why, I remember the time I filled the air sickness bag so full the stewardess had to take it away and bring me an empty one." Unfortunately, it wasn't taking her mind off of anything. She kept peeking through tightly closed eyes at the wing while at the same time clenching my arm with power that neither of us knew she had.

The country of Afghanistan is striking from the air. If you like the color brown, it can even be beautiful. Why anyone would really want to live here is a mystery to me. My parents were here to serve the people, of course, and thereby doing the work of God. Yet was this the glorious end to which God brings his children, I wondered, to be killed in the middle of the most desolate, barren, worthless piece of real estate on his globe? I imagined for a moment how incredibly different things would be if God asked me to run his world. All the improvements I would make. My goodness, I wouldn't even know where to begin.

As our wheels finally touched down, Nancy breathed an enormous sigh of relief. "We're down," she said.

Yeah, I thought, and of all the unbelievable places, right on the runway. Out the window of the plane was the setting of my boyhood memories. Nothing changes in this part of the world. Nothing. Would this trip back in time bring me the comfort I needed now? Maybe I'd find out for myself, now that I was back on my home turf, just how warm the theoretical love of God might be when the weather turns foul.

CHAPTER 3

God Murders Everybody Once

We were met at the airport by a wonderful British doctor and his wife, who drove us through the familiar streets toward the hospital where our mother struggled with her injuries after being moved from Kandahar. This was a trip back in time; twenty years back for me, a thousand years back for Nancy. The sights and sounds brought such strong memories. But even more powerful were the smells. Sights and sounds of the region have been captured on film and enjoyed over the years, but the special odor of this country is duplicated nowhere else in the world. The horse-drawn carriage, or *gawdi*, so common around the city, mixed the smell of fresh manure with so many other odors; the bazaar, animals, people and their clothing, fresh handwoven carpets. It wasn't a graceful fragrance, but it was a powerful message: One breath of air and I was again in my childhood.

Driving through Kabul with our British hosts, we heard all the details of the accident. Mom and Dad had completed half of the long trip from Herat to Kabul. Not far from Kandahar a bus driver raced toward them at the normal wild speed to pick up the stranded passengers of a broken-down bus. Between the blunt-nose Toyota van that Dad was driving and the

45

fast-arriving bus was a sight common to the country: camels being herded along the shoulder. Usually they stay on the shoulder, or even farther off the road in the sandy desert. As the bus driver approached, he laid on his horn and kept coming—the usual method of handling animals on the road. (If one slowed for every animal, traffic would never get anywhere. Camels especially, because of their value and size, have enough influence to claim as much right to the highway as anyone.) When a few startled camels jumped out onto the pavement, the camel driver was unable to restrain them. The bus swerved to avoid the camels, struck the Toyota head on, and sent it rolling down the road. When Mom came to, she was lying beside Dad in a little clinic in Kandahar. She could hear him breathing. But he never woke up.

We learned how God had protected her through the perilous injuries and enabled her to survive the extremely limited, if not nonexistent, medical facility in Kandahar until she could be airlifted to Kabul.

I should have been ready for this uncanny way of viewing reality that says all positive things that occur are attributed to God and all negative things are explained by some set of natural causes. I wondered if there was a diplomatic way to tell these new friends that there had been another person in the vehicle. But even when bad things happen, these people attribute it to God's goodness that they weren't worse. As to the dead man, did God somehow miraculously spare him from being more dead? There's some humor here somewhere, but it's not funny.

Fundamentalists have a low appreciation rate for humor anyway; they sometimes confuse it with cynicism and designate it as such. And I was well aware of the theological theory: "Precious in the sight of the Lord is the death of his saints." But his "precious" opinion is not always shared by his emotionally involved beginner-saints.

It all reminded me of the words of one of my atheist mentors, who wrote, "God murders everybody once." That seemed to be a point well worth considering as we moved through horn-honking traffic and saw the soldiers and Soviet tanks, some of which had been destroyed and burned during the overthrow of the Afghan government. My father's death was not the only death in this place.

As we drove to the hospital I saw two young women without veils making their way through the crowds, and I realized I had never seen an Afghan woman's face. The Afghanistan of my childhood was characterized more by stability than by anything else. The Islamic world might tolerate a few slight alterations, but not drastic changes. A clash with their faith could turn these peace-loving people into the fiercest of ideologues. There is no record of any citizen holding any faith other than Islam—for very long, anyway. In the fifties, an Afghan student had become a convert to Christianity while studying in the United States. Upon his return, he spoke of his faith and was killed within twenty-four hours.

The country that never changed was about to. The family that ruled for centuries had been violently overthrown, but the worst was still to come. It would be another year before the Russian invasion would teach Jimmy Carter more about Soviet intentions in a week than he had been able to learn in a year of high-visibility talks. The Soviets had always been here though, and their intentions were common knowledge to the average schoolboy with eyes. We used to ride our bikes out to the enormous Russian grain silo, a joke that sat empty for twenty years. We laughed at the thought that Afghan agriculture could ever produce enough grain to fill it.

Not to be outdone by Russian "generosity," the United States brought in sacks of grain for the poor. But because, in this country, that meant everybody, the grain was sold in the bazaar. It is doubtful that anyone knew what happened to the proceeds. The Russian silo was now full of grain to feed Soviet troops.

Joe, having arrived the previous day, met us at the hospital where our widowed mother lay recovering from her injuries.

"How's she doing," I asked him.

"She's holding on. She's tough."

We started up a flight of stairs toward her room. The building was just what one might expect to see in an old Asian-set movie—exposed concrete, concrete block, reinforced concrete stairs, concrete floor tiles.

"Is she getting the best care possible?" I asked as we walked up.

"Well, considering where we are," he said, "it's the best possible. It's kept her alive so far. Sanitary conditions aren't the best. I used the only bathroom available, that's it there"—he pointed to a door at the top of the stairs—"and her room is down this way. That bathroom serves all the patients on this floor. When I flushed the toilet the human waste and toilet water ran out from all around the bottom of the bowl. It was going nowhere but on the floor." Yet this hospital was the best, the one to which my mother had been airlifted so she could receive modern and sanitary treatment!

James and I entered her room, walked around her bed, and embraced a woman we barely recognized. I muttered the words, "I love you, Mommy," and fought back the tears. We sat on either side of her bed, each holding a hand. We wanted to hear her story, but it was obvious that she didn't have the strength to talk. So we sat in silence.

We listened to the sounds from our childhood coming through the open window; the crack of the *gawdi's* whip, the clanking of the animals' bells, the continuous beeping of traffic. The minutes passed, and passed. And we sat silently. It had now been precisely three days since the fatal meeting on the highway. Being a Christian person, I considered myself to be a child of the creator of the universe. Is this the end to which I would come if I were to follow in my parents' footsteps and be "faithful to God"? Would I wind up in some back corner of the world, stripped of my life's best friend, totally helpless and at the mercy of the most unsanitary, disease-ridden excuse for a medical institution known to man?

The questions were nothing new. I'd been asking them since I was thirteen; 1961, the year we left Afghanistan and returned to Reedsport. Now I could rehearse it all again, this time to the tune of an Asian street, while staring into a face that had just endured a seventy-two-hour struggle to avoid facing the creator that Dad had already met.

Same questions. New scene.

It had been a brand-new beginning for us, being back in Reedsport. The future had looked so good. And the present had been wonderful.

Summers on the Oregon coast were especially beautiful. It rarely rained and the coastal breezes kept the temperatures comfortably below eighty degrees. Almost every day was, in the words of the immortal Ernie Banks, "a beautiful day for a ball game."

Sports were everything to me and my brothers. And that being the case, we could not have lived in a better town than Reedsport. The high school baseball field was three blocks from our home. All we had to do was walk out our front door, turn one block east to Mr. Severson's Dairy Queen at Highway 101, travel one block south, and one more block east and we were in the only spot we ever wanted to be, the baseball diamond. Coming off a four-year drought of ice cream cones and shakes, Severson's Dairy Queen was ideally located. Mr. Severson was a large man, no doubt a result of the quality of food and ice cream he served. He helped coach baseball and his son played on my team. Not before or since I lived in Reedsport have I ever seen anyone serve a larger ice cream cone for a nickel than did Mr. Severson.

Danny took all his savings and bought a new three-speed bicycle similar to mine. Being a year and a half younger than me and three years younger than Joe, he found himself left out of most of the athletic endeavors that Joe and I had always shared.

Now that he had a bicycle of his own, Danny and I were suddenly spending a lot more time together. There was hardly a back street that didn't lead into a trail through the woods. And we had plenty of off-road cycling experience from our days in Afghanistan. It was during these early days around Reedsport that I began to develop a lasting friendship with those isolated places of privacy that nature provides.

One particular day, however, I was neither playing ball nor walking through the woods. It was a normal beautiful summer day in late July. There was a pony-league baseball tournament running all day, which meant that Danny would be playing in a number of ball games. Joe and I played in the Babe Ruth League.

I was helping Mom with some household chores when Mr. Severson drove up to the house in a big hurry. It was strange for Mr. Severson to be in a big hurry, indeed it was rare for anyone in Reedsport to be in much of a rush, Mr. Severson especially, because he was such a large man. And another thing I noticed, he was driving his car. I had never before seen anyone drive a car to go only one block. But Mr. Severson had actually driven his car one block from his Dairy Queen.

There I was on the front step of our home shaking out a rug for my mother when Mr. Severson came driving the one block to our home and rushed from his car to the front door ignoring me completely, which was not at all like Mr. Severson. He stuck his head in the door and said something to my mother. He could not have spoken to her for more than two seconds before he returned to his car at the same hurried pace. Without a word, she followed immediately, got in the car, and drove off with him. I knew that the status quo had taken a turn for the worse.

It was not difficult to surmise what had happened. Highway 101 carried all the coastal traffic, and with Danny playing in a tournament today, he'd be going back and forth repeatedly. I knew exactly what to expect. There had been some kind of accident. I walked one block east to the Dairy Queen on Highway 101. As I rounded the corner I saw that a crowd had begun to gather. Traffic was beginning to back up. I walked down the block across from the Fir Grove Motel, and there saw what would change my life—all of our lives: the first major tragedy to hit our family.

Danny was lying in the middle of the northbound lanes between Twenty-second and Twenty-first streets. His bicycle was off to the side, one wheel demolished and the other still turning. There was a stream of blood flowing from his body across the highway, meeting the curb at mid-block, and running down to the corner where it fell into the gutter. With all the traffic blocked, I stood in the middle of the four-lane highway attempting to absorb the sight.

I don't know how long I stood there. Not long I suppose. Then I ran home with a whole range of strange new thoughts in my head. What might it be like to live with a paralyzed or invalid brother? How long would it take him to recover from this? Could it actually be serious enough to be fatal? That final thought seemed too horrible to think.

The house was empty. My older brother and sister were a block away at the local Vacation Bible school. Suddenly Mom arrived home. She immediately sat me down at the kitchen stool and began cutting my hair. I guess people in shock do unlikely things. Sometimes a trivial little thing like the need for a haircut can take the focus off a reality that is too much to bear. Maybe the shock of reality had not yet hit her.

"How bad is it?" I asked. Up to that moment my emotions were fear and uncertainty about the future.

"Danny's gone."

The crisp finality of her words stuck me through like a blade. I blurted out a horrible cry of pain and started bawling. It's incredible, I thought. I have lived with this brother all of my life and until this moment I never knew how much I cared. In fact, it's never occurred to me that I cared at all. I had heard about people feeling regret, after a loved one died, for the way they had treated him. It never occurred to me that I was just such a person. It was too late now to make up for the harsh words spoken, the offensive things done.

I had heard my parents talk about people in other families who fought all the time. "Oh, they really love each other," I remember them saying. "They just have a strange way of showing it." Show it? I didn't even know it! I had no idea that I loved him. Much less had I felt it necessary to treat him as if I did. This brotherhood on which I had put no value whatsoever, this relationship that I had taken totally for granted, was over. Finished. I would never make any of it up to him now. It was too late, I thought. That phrase, "too late," only served to accent the grief.

This is the kind of thing that happens to other people. Why would God let this happen to us? I had never before experienced the emotion of grief. I had no concept of how synonymous it is with pain. But it was. And this pain had no location. A guy didn't know where to grab.

A time of tragedy turns one's thoughts, even those of a thirteen-year-old, toward the heavier questions in life: Where did Danny really go? And who am I? Where did I come from? Where am I going? I know I'm substantially different from the other works of nature I've been encountering—trees and animals. I have such a real awareness of myself. I know there was more to Danny than just the body that got killed. There was a real person there, and a person can't just disappear.

"Is Danny going to heaven?" I asked, as my mother continued clipping hair. In the normal everyday life of a boy whose primary goal is to get a hit his next time up at bat, the issue of heaven and hell seemed minuscule. At best a distant concern. Other than obligatory Sunday school and Sunday worship services and occasional family prayer time, the subject seldom came up. But now, suddenly, sitting at the kitchen table with my hair being trimmed and tears falling off my chin, theology and reality were having an overdue encounter. All this talk about the sweet by and by, the meeting in the air, goin' over Jordan, and on and on, was now a matter of paramount importance. It seemed to be the only thing that mattered.

"Yes, Danny was a Christian," she told me. "He had accepted Christ as his personal savior. We'll see him again someday." There was that troublesome theology again. As the old preacher put it: "Thems that knows Jesus Christ as their personal savior goes to heaven, thems that don't, don't." Where do the others actually go then? Well, they go to that other place, down under, weeping, wailing, smashing of teeth. That's the way I thought of it as a boy.

There is no question that the whole concept did help relieve the pain. No question about it. But is it really true, I wondered?

The rest of the day was a living nightmare. I did anything to make the present reality disappear. I walked over to the ballfield where Danny's tournament was being played. Almost no one in town knew me except for a few fellow ball players. And some, I remember one in particular, Joel Young, came to express his condolences. It was nice, to be sure, but he couldn't possibly know the pain. I was completely numb, only there because I had to be somewhere, just trying to escape the present.

My relationship with the surrounding forest grew deeper. There had to be some roots there, some stability, some answers, some continuity for life itself, some higher power, a creator maybe who could be summoned for help. I wandered for hours with a lump in my throat. I had heard about lumps in throats, but I thought it was something they only wrote about in stories. I had no idea how painful one could be. It wouldn't go away.

Mealtime was the worst. Each of us four children had a place at the table plus a high chair for the "baby," James, now four years old, not old enough to comprehend the gravity of the situation. The four of us children always fit neatly around a table, two on each side. Now things didn't fit right. There was no way to put anything in the space of the chair where Danny sat and still make things look normal. This disaster wasn't going to go away. They say time heals. But it doesn't heal really, it just takes the problem away—and so awfully slowly, about the speed of a ticking clock. Over the next year I would often find my mother in the kitchen crying. Going about her duties quietly crying.

If my parents are right that those who don't know Jesus are going to that other place, you know, hell, then those who do know Jesus are under a great deal of pressure. Because anyone who thinks this way is obligated to rescue his friends by making them aware of their need to know Christ. All the enigma surrounding this thinking is resolved once one sees the major premise: Those that know Christ go up, those that don't go down. Having understood this, it is easy to see why a man would stand on a street corner and preach hellfire and damnation to anyone passing by who is careless enough to come within earshot; it is out of kindness and a feeling of responsibility that he so inform them. My saintly parents could hardly shrink from such a grave responsibility.

All this was far removed from my world, the ballfield, until this moment. Now, wandering aimlessly from place to place, it all seemed very important. I certainly didn't want to go to hell myself and didn't enjoy the thought that my younger brother might be there. But since my parents were convinced that Danny did actually know Jesus Christ as his personal savior, that settled the issue. It was sort of a silver lining to the terrible storm we faced. If only all the stuff was true.

Jimmy Brandow, the fireballing pitcher from Danny's team, and another player came to the funeral. Over the years that followed, I would play a lot of football and baseball with them.

*   *   *

Five weeks after Danny's funeral, as the new school year began, there was a buzz of activity in Mrs. Dixon's eighth-grade homeroom. Ours was a secondhand school, magnificently old and picturesque with long, steep steps ascending from the drive to the massive front doors. Reedsport Junior High was a hand-me-down from the high schoolers who had moved into a modern new facility. Inside, the ceilings were so high no one would even think about writing on them, the doors were heavy, and the halls had that antique hollow echo.

Junior high school is "owned" by the eighth grade, and these eighth graders were ready to take their rightful place. Mrs. Dixon's homeroom students felt they were the indisputable cream of the grade. For convenience of scheduling, all band members were placed in this particular homeroom, and they believed they were special—a problem of pride that was aggravated somewhat by a certain element of truth.

Mrs. Dixon did nothing to stifle the situation. And the buzz of camaraderie took on a different pitch when the new kid—me—walked through the door. "Where in the world did he come from," was the first thought that came to mind. It was my jeans with the four-inch cuffs and the wavy hair that was the tipoff. Hot stuff in the fifties, but way behind the times now.

"He's got a horn," one boy whispered to his buddy, "so he must be in the right room."

"Yeah, I'm afraid he is," he whispered back. "Just look at that getup, will ya."

One of the kids leaned to the classmate in front of him and the word passed immediately around the room: "That's the guy whose brother got killed. He came from Afghanistan." Everyone had already figured that I had come from somewhere very far away.

I was lucky that morning that I couldn't read the minds of my peers. When everyone who's anyone knows everyone, the new kid stands out even more. And if newness wasn't enough to make me conspicuous, my appearance completely settled the matter. Who could have guessed what a difference four years would make.

To a normal eighth grader, acceptance is everything. Could I be accepted in this new and different world? By whatever means it might be achieved, whether on the athletic field, in the classroom, or attracting the opposite sex, the overriding goal was acceptance. I already had a number of strikes against me and I knew it.

First, I was the "new kid from far away." The "in" crowd, which seemed to be almost everyone, was having a great time getting used to being eighth graders, the kings of the school. I knew no one. The years in Afghanistan had in no way equipped me for life in what was about to become my hometown. The simplest of activities could create great anxiety in me—for example, the fear of approaching a water fountain and not knowing how to turn it on. Seems simple enough for anyone familiar with it, but to the uninitiated outsider who is shy and self-conscious, it can be a very threatening matter. One could find himself the object of considerable ridicule in no time at all.

The second strike against me was my religious convictions—were they really mine? Just how much validity there could be in the convictions of a thirteen-year-old was quite beyond me. Are they really mine or merely an extension of the adults who influence me?

Fall was a special time of year in Reedsport. It was a time when kids put on football pads and the men were separated from the boys. We had lots of manhood that needed proving, and in this town it was done on the athletic field. So eighth-grade football marked the beginning of five memorable years that would turn Reedsport into my hometown. To my immense relief, my classmates showed an amazing willingness to take in this newcomer from who-knows-where. These were formidable years and there could hardly be a nicer town in which to be formed than Reedsport, located in the beautiful center of the Oregon coast just far enough away from everything.

My love of sports sent me to the football field that first week in eighth grade, and we began knocking heads in earnest. And on the football field there was one guy I knew from summer baseball, Jimmy Brandow.

In all my years in athletics, both in high school and college, I don't believe it was ever my privilege to play with a finer athlete than Jimmy Brandow. Even at the young age of twelve he possessed a blazing fastball and a curveball that none of the pony-leaguers could hit—even when Jimmy was able to put it over the plate. As far as football went, our team developed an offense based around a two-play attack: On first down we ran Jimmy Brandow over the right tackle, and on second down we ran Jimmy Brandow over the left tackle. That was usually good for the first down, at which time we would confuse the defense by starting out with Jimmy over left tackle and then back to right tackle. As soon as they got smart and stacked up the tackles, we sent Jimmy around the end.

I did a little quarterbacking that year and found out how simple a job it is with a runner like Brandow in the backfield. He was big, strong, quick, fast, had excellent athletic instincts, and a fierce competitive spirit.

In addition to football, there were other activities by which a newcomer could get acquainted. The most critical social activity of eighth grade was dancing. Anybody who was anybody in the big world of junior high school demonstrated or at least attempted to demonstrate his all-around coolness on the dance floor. Now, Fundamentalism and dance floors go together like oil and dance floors. For the serious Christian to allow himself to be caught on the dance floor would be a grievous sin of the highest magnitude.

The arguments waged against dancing were legion, and I was capable of making them as convincingly as anyone. I recall one such discussion in which I made my point to an unsuspecting peer. "Dancing all by itself isn't wrong, but it leads to kissing!"

"What's wrong with that?" he asked. I explained that kissing leads to heavy necking.

"What's wrong with that?" he replied. I responded that heavy necking leads to petting. I wondered if he might be as curious as I was to know who coined the word "petting." He was.

"What's wrong with that?" he replied. "Who thought up that word 'petting' anyway? Really, just imagine what would happen if a bunch of us guys misunderstood that CHILDREN'S PETTING AREA sign at the zoo. Might get interesting, huh?" I tried to explain that petting leads to premarital sexual intercourse.

"Don't be ridiculous," he said. "Nobody around here would ever do anything that gross." Ah, the joy of spinning out deep intellectual conversation on the junior high level—or well below.

In any case, I had a significant problem. On the one hand, there was no good way to gain any reasonable acceptance with my peers without engaging in the activity of dancing. On the other hand, if one was as shy as I was, and as unsure of himself in a new cultural setting, it was all but impossible to carry on any meaningful dialogue with a member of the opposite sex. In short, you just couldn't meet a girl without dancing. Even if you could meet her, you couldn't hold her attention for more than a few minutes unless you were willing and capable of dancing with her. In addition to my conviction that dancing was morally questionable and my accompanying feelings of guilt when contemplating the need to engage in the activity, there was the additional problem that I had never danced a step in my life.

This set the stage for the making of a fool and I was well prepared to accommodate. Fortunately for me, the kind girls of my eighth-grade class were totally unwilling to take "no" for an answer or accept "I don't know how" as an excuse. I soon selected the girl I considered to be the most beautiful, mature, and intelligent in my class and proceeded to fall head over heels for her.

Jo Lynn was a brilliant person, the most formidable academic competitor I had up to this point in my life. So we danced our way as far into each others' hearts as is possible for a couple of eighth graders. The Halloween party that year was really nothing more than a dance, but I referred to it as a "party" when speaking to my parents. They would not have allowed me to attend a dance but a "party" was different.

My parents assumed that when eighth graders had birthday parties, they were similar to the parties that had always been thrown during the early preadolescent years. A certain amount of naïveté can be considered virtuous, but one thing is certain, conservative parents were not alone in their ignorance of what their kids were up to.

Jo Lynn knew that these dancing parties were a considerable strain on my conscience. She attended the fashionable Presbyterian church in town. Now, any self-respecting Fundamentalist knows that the Presbyterians are liberal. Obviously, any religious group that openly allows their young people to engage in dancing has to be liberal. The term "liberal" lacks a precise definition. It generally refers to a person who not only tolerates all sorts of worldly activity, not the least of which is dancing, but is also ignorant of the fundamentals of the Christian faith. And many pious people will refer to someone with whom they disagree as a liberal, which is about as close as some people come to calling anyone a dirty name.

Had I asked Jo Lynn, for example, if she knew Jesus Christ as her personal savior, no doubt her response might have been, "Jesus Christ as what?" And that says it all. As we know, anyone who does not know Jesus Christ as his personal savior is going to hell. Dancing is not going to do him any good either, not to mention all those things it leads to.

Or let us suppose I had asked her if she were "born again," another special phrase used by the members of our church. It was totally out of vogue until Watergate conspirator Charles Colson wrote a book by that title and Jimmy Carter popularized it in the 1976 election. I could imagine Jo Lynn responding, "I got born once and my mother said that was quite enough." Now there you go again, that just proves that a liberal is not a true Christian. The Church fathers are quite straightforward on this point. Indeed, even as a boy I had read Christ's words on this topic when he shocked that unsuspecting religious leader by telling him he had to be born again in order to go to heaven. But I was too shy to use such shock treatment on the most wonderful person I had ever met.

However, it soon became obvious that my romance with Jo Lynn was made somewhere other than heaven. We both began to have some misgivings about it. After all, just how much enjoyment can a beautiful, intelligent girl get out of a relationship with a guilt-ridden Fundamentalist who was stumbling over her feet on the dance floor. By mid-year, Jo Lynn sent two of her friends to inform me that while she respected my religious convictions, she was more interested in sensible and safe dancing than in having a relationship with me. I knew she was right. In a sense, it relieved me of a burden that I found difficult to reconcile—namely, that I had to engage in a certain amount of deception to keep my dancing activity from my family.

I did some more dancing that year, occasionally, until my mother discovered it, which caused a certain amount of debris to get slung up against the fan. Fortunately for me, peer approval was not totally limited to one's ability on the dance floor. And though the romance with Jo Lynn was over, our feelings of respect for each other continued to develop.

Our high school–cum–junior high had a newly refinished gym floor that was the pride of Mr. Ketchum, our PE instructor and football coach. Mr. Ketchum took seriously his duty to ensure that no person would ever so much as place one street-shoe-clad foot on the out-of-bounds line. The offender was guaranteed to receive the Ketchum cuff.

The Ketchum cuff, developed by him and adopted by no one, was a unique slap that he perfected over a number of years and applied to the back of the victim's head. It was accomplished by cupping the hand in a head-shaped curvature so that the impact was delivered evenly over a hand-sized area at the back of the head. Being an athletic coach, Ketchum favored the boys, and limited all cuffing to us. Though I never received one, I assumed that the sting from a moderately priced cuff lasted about ten seconds.

David Ashford, in our all-boys spelling class, probably received the distinction of getting the most Ketchum cuffs. We sat in those antique desks in which the writing surface extends from the back of the seat in front and all the desks are attached by two strips of wood running the length of the row. Each desktop contained an obsolete ink well and the etchings of our predecessors, now in high school and college, informing us of the romances of bygone days, "John + Sue = love"— that sort of thing. The underside of these desktops contained the remaining unused portions of John's or Sue's gum, which gave me things to wonder about in class: How are they doing? Did they graduate from college? Did they get married? Do they now put their gum on the underside of their kitchen table?

Such mind-wandering, in addition to goofing off, were just about the only things of interest to do in this all-boys class that was really phys ed converted to spelling once a week. So Mr. Ketchum would patrol the aisles. Up and down he would walk. There we sat, everyone of us possessing a vulnerable target right there at just the proper height for the Ketchum cuff. And Mr. Ketchum was an ambidextrous cuffer. He could cuff a student on either side of the aisle. We had a special problem when he made his way from the back of the room; there was no time to anticipate.

Obviously my hometown, comfortable as it was becoming,

was not free of disciplinary problems. It was disciplinary difficulties that had perfected the Ketchum cuff in the first place.

I don't think I ever knew anyone who disliked Mr. Ketchum. Even David Ashford did not dislike Mr. Ketchum. So keen was Ashford's insight into human behavior that he even seemed at times to feel he had earned the Ketchum cuff, that it was the proper response to his behavior. I have wondered ever since if Ashford ever went to college and, if he did, did he take psychology. Maybe they straightened out his boyhood intuition about his behavior.

I was chatting with Jo Lynn and her friends one day when I noticed that one of her notebooks was covered with small, intricately written words. Looking closer I could see that it was my name, neatly written in rows and columns covering the entire notebook. Even if the romance was dead, the feelings hadn't yet been buried. What a warm feeling it was for a person so unsure of himself to have my admiration returned from such a fine person. I thought I should look for the opportunity to tell her that the feeling was mutual.

In the spring, the entire eighth grade took a day off from school to plant trees for the forestry department. On this occasion they lined the boys up in one line and the girls in a second line and paired us off together. Each boy wielded a pick to dig the hole and his partner held the seedlings and planted them. Jo Lynn and her two friends saw to it that they were positioned in the right place in line so that she and I could spend the day together planting trees.

We later meandered through a local carnival together. It wasn't much of a carnival in a small town like Reedsport, and we didn't do much, didn't say much, just enjoyed being together.

That summer my buddy Andy and I bicycled through town across the bridge over the Umpqua River onto an island where Jo Lynn lived. We would just stand and talk over the yard fence to her and her younger sister. We'd enjoy the warm, clean, Oregon air and sunshine, wish that summer would never end, and create some of those good ol' days.

And good ol' days is what we did for the next four years. We began in August by knocking our heads together on the football field, and every spring we were anxious to move the seniors out and improve our standing by a level.

Sophomore year was the year we got to take typing. The phrase "got to" did not mean that the opportunity was available. It meant that the alternatives were nonexistent. Roger Travis won distinction for getting the most keys jammed at the same time. He had every key in the typewriter depressed and stuck. Our junior varsity football team was having its second good season even without Jimmy Brandow, who had been bumped up to varsity. In the last game of our season, the varsity coach let Jimmy join the rest of us sophomores and freshmen for a game against a poor, unsuspecting, visiting school. We scored fifty or sixty points that game and Jimmy ran for a touchdown just about whenever he wanted.

Refraining from dancing was not necessarily construed as a social disease. Actually, there was a whole host of religious denominations which abstained from such worldly practices, thereby keeping their youth pure and unstained. And one fellow student was in fact the daughter of a preacher of a nondancing church. We became involved in a variety of activities together both in school and in church. After we began to date, a serious romance started to develop. The mutual respect I shared with Jo Lynn notwithstanding, it would appear that this romance was made in heaven itself. So it came as somewhat of a surprise when I heard that her mother had said, "There's no way my daughter's going to marry a Baptist."

This was difficult for me to understand. Certainly there were prohibitions against marrying a pagan. We even agreed with the Catholics on that one, though to marry a Catholic would be almost as bad (no doubt the feeling was quite mutual). But this was different because we were both non-dancing Protestants. The mystery was compounded by the fact that our family was neither Baptist nor even attended a Baptist church.

The small-town grapevine being what it is, maybe this statement should be ignored, I thought. There must be a logical explanation for it, and I racked my brain trying to figure out what it could be. I went to my pastor for advice. He was a ruddy outdoorsman, an athletic individual, just the type one might expect to find pastoring in a small, rural, logging community.

"Generally speaking," he told me, "the Protestant church could be fairly divided into the Calvinists and the Arminians."

"I suppose it is safe to assume that her church is in one of these camps and ours is in the other," I said, knowing that Dad had attended a Calvinist school.

"You've got it figured out," he said.

"Are the differences really that great?" I asked.

"Calvinists and Arminians do not have a history of peaceful co-existence," he told me. "They are sort of like ranchers and farmers, crabs and lobsters, Hatfields and McCoys."

"You're kidding!"

"No, I'm not. Several centuries ago, if they didn't agree with you they might just burn you at the stake. It wasn't a bright hour in Church history."

"What ever happened to that 'be ye kind one to another,' Sunday school stuff?" I asked.

"You have to remember that the great reformers never went to Sunday school. They were all raised in the Catholic church," he joked. I knew he wasn't degrading Catholics, he simply couldn't pass up the opportunity to poke some fun.

"Didn't they know about the two greatest commandments?"

"Theology, my boy, theology," he said. "What's the use of keeping the great commandments if your theology is all messed up?" He was still joking. The whole thing sounded like a joke.

In an old bookcase in the upstairs of the $75-a-month duplex we rented, I found an old set of the great classics. It was located in a back corner of the hall where no one ever went. I sat in the corner and began reading Calvin on determinism and free will.

Distinctions between these two groups was a fast-paced bore. Failure to make the distinction properly, however, had severe consequences: For example, the obscure theologian Servitus; he discovered just how short-lived the career of an aspiring theologian might be. After being sentenced by the Catholics to be burned at the stake, he somehow escaped and, finding himself threatened by Protestant zealots, eventually took refuge in Calvin's city, Geneva, the city of God. To his dismay, the most tolerant, reformed Christians of the then-known world queried him about his personal theology and discovering him to be ignorant of the correct answers, tried him, found him guilty, and burned him at the stake.

While one would like to be remembered with some last words of notoriety, the line, "Is it hot in here or is it just me," might not get a lot of recognition in Church history. It only slightly beat out the previous booby prize, "Do I smell smoke or is Attila just burning the rolls again?" reportedly quoted by a Calvinist caught in Arminian territory with his theological pants down.

These quotes never actually made the history books but were the result of a reading between the lines by a boy with an imagination and a pastor with a sense of humor. One thing was certain: Servitus no doubt lacked appreciation for John Calvin's sense of humor.

It all made me wonder if God takes his theology as seriously as does the average theologian.

So, when my girlfriend's mother said, "There is no way my daughter's going to marry a Baptist," what she really meant was that Calvinists walk sideways and Arminians walk straight and we won't let you take her for your mate. Presumably, she reasoned that, if her daughter were to marry a pagan, at least there would be some chance that the heathen could be converted, while a Calvinist might be beyond.hope.

So one romantic relationship broke down over a severe difference of opinion in regard to dancing and a second broke down over theological issues discussed by many a theologian but understood by only a few.

Still, there were other girls who didn't dance or involve themselves in "worldly" activities who were less ideologically demanding. I knew two such girls whose "commitment to God" kept them from so many types of socializing that there was very little left for them to do but go out, park, neck, etc. No one accused these girls of being boring dates, but the logic was fascinating. Based on their religious convictions, they refused to engage in the worldly activity of dancing because it led to more involved physical contact that could, if my ninth-grade biology teacher was honest, lead to unwanted pregnancies and shotgun marriages.

Given the religious conviction, the actual behavior was even more enigmatic. While all the pagans were out there engaging in the wicked activity of dancing and thereby exposing themselves to the possible temptation to get it on in parked cars, these righteous girls were heading straight for the parked cars. I knew a lot of guys who would have been happy converts to their religion. They could save the time and money necessary to get a date warmed up on the dance floor.

So there were all sorts of different reasons for being religious. It was amazing where theological inquiry could take a person. I started out thinking that dancing was wrong because it could lead to premarital sex. When I leave this town and go off to college, I thought to myself, I'll find some high-powered theologian and ask him to prove to me that premarital sex is wrong. I could anticipate him saying, "Well, among some of our young people, it has actually led to dancing."

Junior year opened a new phase for me. I thought that I had long since recovered from my brother's death, but now our home had really emptied. Joe and Joanna had gone to college leaving just my third-grade brother, James, and me. It was a constant reminder to me that Danny was gone and raised again the religious questions attached. Our culture only allows a certain amount of time to recover from the loss of a loved one. Grief beyond that period is not considered normal. After all, life must go on.

The issue was then compounded by our leader on the athletic field, Jimmy Brandow. In addition to his excellent play in football, basketball, and baseball, Jimmy was an outgoing lover of life.

I didn't have any classes with him, but his unique belly laugh could be heard many classrooms away. We would meet in the hall between classes and find out what his teacher had said that was so funny. There was never any doubt about who that laugh belonged to. His teacher could actually get a laugh from all the surrounding classes since the rest of us were laughing at Jimmy laughing. His vivacious spirit was contagious on the football field as well.

Jimmy's high-powered personality finally got the better of him. When he was up, which as far as we knew seemed to be all the time, he was really up. But when he was down, he found it too much. One afternoon, shortly after football season in our junior year, Jimmy left school in deep depression over a personal problem, went home, called his parents, told them he loved them, took his gun into his room, and ended his life.

Our class went into shock. A little like the shock we had experienced the year before when President Kennedy was assassinated; only this was different, much different. It didn't happen in a far away place around an unknown person. This time the center of the tragedy was right here; the object of the tragedy was us.

Again I found myself faced with the heavier issues. The customary few days that one gets to put these tragedies behind him were simply not enough. When I saw Jimmy walk into my brother's funeral service three years earlier, how could I have imagined that I would soon attend his? And then there were those questions. Where did Jimmy come from? Where is he going? Who are we all anyway? And the real question, too real to be audibly verbalized: Where is Jimmy right now?

The answers that comforted me in grief over Danny did not work now. Jimmy was one of those who never heard of "Jesus Christ personal savior." Fundamentalist theology puts these people in hell. Was my friend Jimmy Brandow, therefore, in hell? And to further complicate matters, there was a crystal clear part of this thinking that put the blame for not having informed Jimmy of the truth squarely on my shoulders.

My friend was in hell and I was to blame. This would definitely take more than a few days for recovery. It just didn't seem fair. How would I like being sent to hell because of something Jimmy had neglected to tell me? The unfairness of it alone was reason enough to believe it to be untrue.

My emotional stability was severely threatened on three fronts. First, the grief over the loss of a super guy. Second, the idea that a friend could be in hell because of my neglect. Third, the only relief from the unbearable second would demand a denial of my faith in God.

At Jimmy's funeral, the preacher spoke about his life having ended due to an illness of the mind. If anyone was mentally ill, I thought, it's this preacher. Jimmy got more out of his sixteen years than most people do in a whole lifetime. No one loved life more than he. He wasn't nuts. He was in pain and he relieved it in the only way he knew. Until I got my questions answered, I wouldn't know if Jimmy might not be having the last laugh on all of us, though I wasn't about to follow his example to find out. If the Church fathers are correct, it would be risky to run off to meet one's maker without precise preparation. Truth must be out there waiting to be discovered. My sanity would depend on finding it.

No doubt many other students were asking questions similar to mine, though never out loud. Recovering from a major tragedy like this means that one is finally able to return to normal, meaningless small talk, pure drivel by comparison to the realities of life and death.

One month later I came into physics, for my first afternoon class, and was greeted by Marty, "Hi, Mark, how ya doin'?"

"All right, Marty, how you doin'?" I was lying, but what am I supposed to say—"Well, I'm wondering where Jimmy is and how he's doin'?" That would stop all conversation and put everyone on notice to keep their distance. The time limit to get yourself together was up and getting yourself together meant forgetting your lost friend and the attending questions about the meaning of life and getting on with the pressing trivialities at hand.

As time passed my classmates were able to return to the status quo; I was apparently alone in my struggle. It must have been during this period that my roots in Reedsport began to deepen. I now knew two people in the cemetery. The listening trees behind my home grew closer. What I really needed was to make an effort to get more from my friendships, especially now that I knew how temporary they were. Instead, I fell in love with solitude.

The fall of our senior year should have been our big year to do something in football. But no one could carry the ball like Jimmy, and our big year was a big disappointment.

Our choir and band often traveled to contests and festivals. One Saturday afternoon the choir, of which I was a member, found itself in the gymnasium of a neighboring town listening to the choirs from other schools; the competition that our director had come to expect us to beat. They were singing a familiar poem:

Give me your tired, your poor,
Your huddled masses yearning to breathe free,
The wretched refuse of your teeming shore,
Send these, the homeless, tempest-tossed to me,
I lift my lamp beside the golden door.

The subject matter was too heavy for us at that young age. The picture of shorelines teeming with wretched refuse was more of a joke to us. But we listened—we were required to. There really wasn't enough lyric in the poem to make much of a song. So after singing it in unison, which wasn't too exciting, they broke into four-part harmony, singing the same words again.

The words seemed to take on new meaning in harmonies, as if they extended a land of opportunity. The basses moving smoothly off the tonic and dominant to the color tones gave a thick, rich quality of sound that reminded me of huddled masses that I knew *did* yearn to breathe free. The alto and tenor lines wove an increasingly complex harmonic structure that built intensity in spite of the soft volume level. My eyes watered as I contemplated the drama of it. And then with a key change and a dynamic increase in tempo and volume, the chorus sang it a third time. It was as if they themselves were extending their own personal emotion-filled invitation to the world to "Send these, the homeless, tempest-tossed to me"— then building the excitement of that line to the powerful climax led by the soprano section on the fortissimo high note, "I lift my lamp beside the golden door."

The tranquillity of the idyllic Oregon coast made it impossible to appreciate the full impact of that piece. But I knew. And I put my forehead down on my hands to hide the tears I could not stop.

In the spring, the choir was engaged in an exchange program with a large school in Portland. This school had things our school could not have experienced: a significant group of mentally handicapped and a number of black and

Jewish students. The term "jew" had no racial significance in my hometown. It was a verb used synonymously with "bargain" or, more commonly, "cheat," often in connection with describing some unfair grade or some disliked administrative practice.

A few months earlier I had made the mistake of describing to my mother how someone had "jewed" me out of something. For some reason she felt that it was more important to discuss my linguistic habits than to hear about the unfair treatment I had received. I explained, of course, that no one at school had anything against the Jewish people. We were all just as indignant about the Holocaust as anyone. So when one understands what the true meaning of words is, that concept which exists in the mind of the speaker, one will realize that nobody at Reedsport had any anti-Semitic thoughts when they used a phrase like "I got jewed."

Some time later, when the Portland choir was scheduled to visit our school, our choir director approached me privately. "The choir students from Portland will be staying in individual homes just as we did when we went there. Since there are some black students in the choir, I anticipate a potential problem."

I knew what he was coming to. He was hoping that our family would be willing to entertain these black singers in our home. Racism? Here in my little town? Theory had labeled this a big-city problem even though it was rumored that an old law existed on the books in Reedsport making it illegal for a black person to spend the night here.

But really there were no racial distinctions in my hometown. There might be some people of lower class, or an antiquated law on the books, or a harmless misuse of the term "jew," or maybe even a slight nervousness about an occasional overnight visitor. Every community is entitled to a little hypocrisy, I supposed; especially of this tolerable sort. Who would even recognize it?

Naturally racism in the mid-sixties was a major classroom

topic, but always applied to the country and the world, never too close to home. Since Jo Lynn and I took a variety of advanced courses together, it was common for us to become involved in these discussions and our mutual respect continued.

Creative writing involved a daily challenge to do something different. Like the day Mr. Knudsen asked us to write a piece proving that two plus two does not equal four.

I used some sophisticated mathematical proof, relying mostly on confusion. Jo Lynn would take a more sensitive approach to these problems. She wrote a piece in which she appealed to rabbits for support. How can you expect, she wrote, for Flopsy, Mopsy, Peter Cottontail, and his gorgeous girlfriend to ever hold their total down to just four.

We had a vigorous class discussion of morality going one day when Mr. Knudsen quoted Jim Case, the retired preacher from John Steinbeck's *The Grapes of Wrath*, "There's no such thing as good and bad, just things people do." Interesting, I thought, and we all seemed to feel the same way. We liked Steinbeck.

But I recalled the Ketchum cuff and doubted if he would have agreed with Steinbeck's character. And I recalled my mother rescuing that little old lady next door from the trajectory of my deadly dirt clods. Maybe my mother and Ketchum hadn't read Steinbeck. I doubted that Ketchum's cuff and Mom's stick were used because the offenders were "just doing things." They seemed to mete out punishment because they were convinced that the things these people were doing were actually *bad* things. I thought I could make an interesting argument that Steinbeck's ex-preacher was wrong.

I raised my hand to make a point along this line, but then asked myself if I really wanted to tell the dirt-clod-throwing story. Did I want to become the living proof of the concept and have everyone saying "shame, shame" while pointing the left index finger and stroking it with the right. And then, it would be just like Jo Lynn to suggest that we were both right, some people fall into the preacher's category while others did actually do bad things. And if I had already proved that people do bad things by telling the dirt-clod-throwing story, this would leave me stuck—and in the wrong category.

I put my hand down. Maybe it's only natural that an out of the way, small town junior high school football coach like Ketchum and a housewife like my mother would be unfamiliar with such theories.

On our senior sneak I insisted that Jo Lynn ride the big roller coaster with me since she was afraid.

"Look at that thing, Mark. Tell me, just how secure does that look to you?"

"You're too smart for your own good, lady. C'mon, we're gonna get on this thing and sit right in the front."

She agreed reluctantly. "All right, but if anything goes wrong. . . ."

"Don't worry. If anything goes wrong, we won't be around to take the heat for it."

A few days later she read her valedictory speech and we were all off to meet the world, to make something of ourselves, to surprise those who predicted we wouldn't. Most of us got summer jobs in the lumber industry around Reedsport. I worked in the paper mill.

About a month after graduation, with all the good-byes having been said and the class having scattered toward their separate careers, we got the news. I came home from a day in the mill yard to hear my mother tell me what was, by now, all over town. Jo Lynn had been involved in an accident in a residential area only a few blocks from where we used to live. She was thrown from the vehicle and it overturned, ending her life.

I walked slowly up to my room to be alone and absorb it all. I stared at the wood grain in the simple plywood walls and ceiling and begun to ask again all the questions that I'd asked a year and a half earlier when we lost Jimmy Brandow. As important as the critical matters of my life—football, baseball, social acceptance, academics—were, the weightier matters of reality kept jamming their ugly faces at me. Not being alone enough, I climbed the hill behind the house to find solitude under the cover of the dense Oregon forest, my buffer from the world. Did this mean that Jo Lynn, who didn't know the meaning of the phrase "Jesus Christ personal savior," was in hell? If we Fundamentalists were right, it certainly did. And, of course, there was always the question of my guilt: Could I have prevented this fate?

The forest was so impersonal, so unsympathetic. It listened, but gave precious little in return.

Our class headed back to the cemetery. Jimmy was here when we lowered Danny's casket. Jo Lynn was here when we lowered Jimmy's. Now we met here again.

How could this possibly happen? we were all asking ourselves. And to such an incredibly nice person.

Again I was required to "readjust" to the trivialities of life in less time than I needed. Even faster now in the real world. Most of us had taken a few hours off from work to attend the funeral, then right back at it. If I couldn't find better answers to my pressing questions, I might as well start shooting everyone who says, "Hi. How are ya?" "Oh, I'm fine. How are you?" "Not bad." "Nice day today, isn't it?" "See ya later." "Yeah, see ya."

Blam! Let's see if that'll shut you up. Who gives a shit how nice a day it is? I never used foul language, I knew it was wrong, but I wondered if it would be wrong to relieve some of the tension by *thinking* a football-field word (four-letter limit) once in a while.

Some time after Jo Lynn's tragedy our high school guidance counselor decided that she'd had enough and took her own life. If conservative Christianity was right, my hometown was going to hell in a handbasket. And what was even more disconcerting was that it seemed as if there was a rush on.

Common sense demanded that I build myself a platform at the entrance to our local cemetery where my brother and two friends were already located and warn the balance of my hometown, who seemed to be hurrying toward the place, of the dangers of hellfire. Not that anyone would have paid any attention, but at least they would have been fairly warned.

Life wasn't going to stop and wait for me to get my answers together and I could hardly continue to ignore them. Reality itself could keep this matter alive, either by the memory of those friends who had died or by someone who would indiscreetly do so.

The sounds of Kabul in the afternoon were still drifting through the concrete-framed window, pressing the feeling of boyhood upon me. Mom was stirring a little as if she were about to wake. The last time I heard these sounds, I depended on her and I didn't have a care in the world. Now I'm back in this romantic land and the roles are reversed. If God is in the business of using circumstances to get people's attention, it's obvious that I haven't been paying enough attention.

I sat there listening to the sounds, watching Mom, and remembering back a dozen years when she had given me the news about Jo Lynn. After visiting Mom, our British hosts took Nancy, Dani, and me to the home of an American family of eight, where we would spend the next three weeks.

Joanna arrived later that afternoon on a flight through Rome and Karachi. She stayed with Mom the next day when we buried Dad in a private cemetery in the heart of Kabul. This was where he wanted his body interred—a quiet compound, surrounded by high mud walls in the center of a country whose people he loved.

The service was simple, attended by members of the foreign community. Many who wanted to come were prohibited from attending by severe religious taboos, which do not allow a Muslim to be associated with anything of another faith. (Conversion to another faith is considered the highest of sins and justifies the murder of the convert.) It was a peaceful compound, watched over by towering trees that provided badly needed respite from the intense Asian sun, a sharp contrast to the surrounding city. Dad's body was placed in a simple wooden box. James, Joe, and I, assisted by a few of Dad's friends, carried the box from a van in the street, through the gate that opened into the compound, and along a row of trees that led to the gravesite. Nancy and Dani followed along behind. We used ropes to lower it into the ground.

Some Afghans snuck in anyway, and a few came openly, snubbing the taboo and risking trouble. A blind man came up to me afterward and told me that he had become a Christian and how much my father meant to him. He had been imprisoned and tortured for his faith. The Sunni Muslims who dominate Afghanistan are less violent than the Shiites of Iran. The Sunnis know that God has a special place in his heart for the disadvantaged. Out of fear and respect for God, they could not bring themselves to kill a blind man. So they saw him as an annoying, "protected," gadfly. The confidence of this blind man made them nervous.

Over the next few weeks, when we weren't tending Mom's recovery, we visited old childhood locations and remembered the good ol' days. She got stronger by the day and within three weeks was well enough to attend a memorial service for Dad. We planned to bring her back to the States as soon as she could travel.

There was, however, one major job that needed to be completed prior to our departure. In the remote territory of Herat, where our parents had lived, were all their personal possessions. Someone had to make the long trip out there and either dispose of them or bring them back to Kabul.

The journey from Kabul to Herat was a two-day trip through some of the most desolate desert in the world. It required a drive from Kabul southwest to Kandahar and then north to Herat, a journey twice as far by highway as by air. The normal routine was to spend one day traveling from

Kabul to Kandahar, spend the night there, and finish the trip the next day, since traveling at night is dangerous.

The four of us got our heads together to decide who should go. James *had* to go because he still had a good command of the language, gained from his visit here a few years earlier. Nancy and Dani were out of the question. Joe preferred to stay in Kabul with Mom, and I wanted to join James. Joanna, knowing that James and I could never handle a domestic job with any amount of grace, decided to come along.

CHAPTER 4

Going to Herat Blues

It is always a bit of a risk for a foreigner to travel alone in remote areas of Afghanistan. And the risk is compounded after dark. The only highway to Herat was a joint U.S.-Soviet effort—in a display of foreign aid, the U.S. had built from Kabul, the Soviets from Herat, until they met each other in the southwest corner of the desert at Kandahar.

There is hardly an automobile built that is considered reliable enough to be secure while traveling out across the desert. Our new friends, close friends of our parents, offered us the use of an old Travelall. No vehicle maintained in Afghanistan over a period of years can possibly have the reliability expected in the West and this vehicle was no exception. We thought that if we started early enough from Kabul, sometime just before dawn, and made good time, we could possibly make the entire trip to Herat before nightfall.

The sun was just showing its first rays of light over the jagged mountain ranges surrounding Kabul as we pulled away from the last vestige, however primitive, of civilization we would see for a week. James jabbed the horn to help a local shepherd move his sheep off the road. We heard nothing.

"Unbelievable! Unbe-sucking-lieveable!"

"What's wrong?" I asked.

"We've got no horn!"

"Are you serious? We're gonna drive across Afghanistan in this bucket of bolts with no horn?"

The shepherd gave us a curious look as if to say, "How'm I supposed to know you're there if you don't honk?" We knew what he was thinking. "These Americans are even dumber than local rumor has it." We just shrugged, smiled, and gave him back as curious a look as we could.

"We are doomed!" I said, shaking my head in disbelief. "There is no way! Every goat between here and Herat will be standing in front of us waiting for us to honk the horn." In Afghanistan, the horn on a vehicle is used the same way brakes are used in the Western world. Indeed, you might even get by without brakes if you just had a louder horn.

"Hey, forget the goats, I can dodge them," James said, wiggling the steering wheel around as if preparing for action. "It's the Afghans I'm worried about."

As the day began to dawn and the traffic increased, we wondered if this would be an insurmountable difficulty. After about an hour of having people give us looks that said, "You're really dumb even for a foreigner," we decided we might never get to Herat without a horn. We found some loose wire in the back of the vehicle (actually there was loose wire all over the thing), ran it from a hot lead on the battery to the horn, and ran a second wire from the ground through the fire wall and up to the steering wheel. James stripped the end, tapped it to the choke knob and bingo, the horn sounded.

"Hey, we're ready now!" I called out.

"Look out you nomads. We'll never slow down again!" With that, James, Joanna, and I set out across the lonely, desolate desert of southern Afghanistan. We soon discovered that our horn could be used for more things than chasing off sheep, goats, and bystanders. On the long desolate stretches where not a soul or a goat would try to exist, James honked out the rhythm of a song by tapping the bare wire to the choke knob. "All right," he asked, "tell me what tune I'm playing?"

I wish I could say that Joanna appreciated the game as much as James and I did. When it was my turn behind the wheel

James would get out his guitar and mess around a bit with the blues. His primary creation on this trip was a composition called "I Got 'em Goin' to Herat Blues."

Not more than a hundred miles outside of Kabul, plenty far away from anywhere, the machine sputtered and died.

"Okay, what'd ya do?" James asked.

"Nothin'! I think we're outta gas," I said.

"You're dreamin'! We got plenty a gas."

"Well, we're not using it right now," I said as I guided the vehicle slowly off the ragged pavement and onto the sandy shoulder. We both knew we had plenty of gas, we just didn't know which tank we were running on, so our gas was in the wrong tank and the switching valve was apparently defective.

We found an old juice bottle, siphoned some gas out of the full tank, carried it around, and dumped it into the empty tank. I held my finger over the siphoning tube while James took the jar around the Travelall, emptied the gas into the other tank, and brought it back for a refill. We shuttled a number of jars full of gas that way, took the air filter off, primed the engine, and were back on our way again. Each such little incident gave James another stanza for his "I Got 'em Goin' to Herat Blues."

Joanna never did develop an appreciation for the blues, at least not James's style anyway. It was no secret to Joanna that I had strongly opposed her coming on this trip. The military control of the Afghan countryside was in question. And while the situation was not nearly as treacherous as it would later become, there was a significant Soviet presence in the country at the time and the tension, which would later throw the country into total war, was currently in place. I was concerned enough about my own ability to elude a dangerous situation, but taking along a sister who was five months pregnant could severely complicate the situation should a problem arise. I had argued against the idea to anyone who would listen. I hoped I wouldn't find myself running out across the Afghan desert looking back over my shoulder only to have the view of my pursuers blocked by a pregnant sister struggling to keep up.

It was too late to turn back now. So on we went, tapping our ground wire against the choke knob, making a horrible racket playing Name That Tune, singing crazy songs about traveling to Herat, and generally making our poor sister's fifth month of pregnancy even more difficult to bear. I had always wondered why many of my relatives had expressed considerable pity over Joanna's lot in life—four tasteless brothers and no sister. What after all could be nicer than to travel across the barren deserts of Asia with a couple of warm, loving, mature younger brothers, honking the horn constantly and singing songs while having serious doubts about their ability to keep the vehicle moving?

There were times when James's vocal cords grew tired and he needed to rest before his next turn behind the wheel. Then the desert grew quiet, the engine droned on, and an occasional nomad in the way made a nice break from the monotony. Sometimes they would look right at you, and I wondered what they were thinking. Were they having a lousy day? Or didn't they think of days as good or lousy? I had to wonder how on earth they could sustain their lives out here in this wasteland. I remembered how the obvious inequities had bothered me as a boy. We had so much. They had so little.

What would it ever take to make this country productive and wealthy like the West? Should we just be more generous? There certainly were many people who, like Dad, had come here at great expense to help the Afghans.

One such person tried to get the Afghans to plant Tamarisk trees, a tree that takes in moisture through its leaves instead of roots. He knew that the plant could bring great productivity to Afghanistan, but he couldn't get the people to cooperate in planting them. He finally asked an American English teacher who understood the language and culture to see if he could figure out why the Afghans were so opposed to the use of this tree. The teacher was told, "We believe that evil spirits roost in the branches of the Tamarisk tree, so we won't plant them anywhere except in cemeteries." Try as he might, it was impossible for the agriculturalist to get these devoutly religious people to plant trees that would have done so much good for their country.

But it wasn't just an occasional superstition that hurt these people. It was the entire moral fabric on which their culture was based. I recalled hearing Dad tell me once when we were riding through the countryside, "These people need the Lord." I didn't fully understand what he meant. It appeared to me that they needed money.

But he had closer contact with the culture. Cheating was pervasive, by student and teacher alike. To prevent the common practice of teachers selling tests to students in advance, the Ministry of Education required that all teachers submit a large quantity of questions for any test. The ministry then selected a few that it presented to the students at the time of testing.

On one occasion, a teacher arrived at the testing session and was given the five questions that had been selected from the twenty he submitted. Realizing that the students would not have time to compute and solve all five questions, he eliminated the fifth, reducing the test to only four questions. One student, however, not only got all four answers perfect, but also gave the correct answer to the fifth question, which had not even been asked. The Ministry of Education, it turned out, had sold him the answers to the five questions they selected. It appeared that they were collecting the questions to ensure that they had a monopoly on the ability to cheat.

Occasional indiscretions like cheating shouldn't be surprising, however. Shiite Muslims state that it is all right to lie about money, women, or war. A liar could get a lot of topics into those categories.

In the distance on the left, maybe 1,000 yards away, was a group of nomad tents. It was hard for me to imagine that their lives would really be better if they "knew the Lord," as Dad had suggested. Still, I had to wonder how a culture that is based on cheating can ever get its economy off the ground.

Dr. Christy Wilson was an American English teacher at Habibia. One day, as he was leaving for school, the landlord's representative arrived to collect the rent. Dr. Wilson counted it out quickly, asked an Afghan friend to check it, and left. When the two Afghans recounted it, they discovered there was an extra bill. The landlord's representative suggested they split it between them, saying, "We'll get *sawawb* for cheating Dr. Wilson." *Sawawb* is virtuous merit that Allah accredits to his followers, based in this instance on *jihad*—evil inflicted against a non-Muslim. The Afghan friend, trusting his own conscience more than his religion, refused, and returned the bill to Dr. Wilson. These devout religious convictions not only provide a means of spiritual merit, they are also profitable. They do little, however, to stimulate international commerce.

We arrived in Kandahar in excellent time and spent a half hour in the bazaar buying our favorite Afghan dish: kebabs and nan. Nan is a large flat bread, about two feet long by a foot wide and a half inch thick. It is made with freshly ground whole wheat flour and very little yeast. From pre-dawn the Afghans bake it continuously in open ovens.

The bazaar vendor pulled a half dozen skewers off the coals and emptied the kebabs onto the middle of the fresh hot nan, handed it to us, and asked for fifty afs, about $1.30. I sunk my teeth into a kebab wrapped in nan. "Mmm! The Afghan form of the hot dog."

"Only this is a whole lot tastier," James answered.

"You're not kiddin'. And a lot more nutritious, too."

"How about some Cokes?" he asked. "I bet you never thought you'd see these way out here."

"Nope." We bought a few Cokes, which never taste the same as back home, but in the heat of the desert are wonderful. "You ready to hit the road, toad?"

It had been seventeen years since I'd stuffed myself with this delicious combination of lean charbroiled lamb and fresh hot bread. We stuffed ourselves again this day, took some for the second leg of our journey, filled up with gas, and were headed north to see if we could make it to Herat before nightfall.

The highway from Kandahar to Herat is a sparkling example of creative Soviet construction. It is made from large concrete slabs connected together, each slab probably thirty to fifty feet in length. As the tires of the vehicle hit the seams between the slabs, it gave our ride an interesting rhythm, sort of a metronome to which we could play our Name That Tune songs with our horn blasts. We wondered, as we drove along, if the Russian engineers had a different leveling method than that used by the Americans. Some of the beats got quite loud. And if we were annoyed by this strange highway, we had no idea what our unborn niece was going through in the backseat. This style of highway construction is in itself enough to make anyone a capitalist. If the Afghans had dental problems before, they had nothing to worry about now, because anyone who rode this highway had no teeth left. (The simple truth is that the highway was constructed of steel reinforced concrete that enabled it to carry vehicles many times heavier than any used for commercial freight.)

A few hours down the road, with the strains of "I Got 'em Goin' to Herat Blues" dying out, I climbed into the back of the vehicle for some rest. A couple of propped up suitcases isolated me from the front seats, gave some shelter from the sun, and left me alone to be lulled to sleep by the rhythmic bumping of the highway.

Tragedy is not as difficult to take when there are people around. There are things to keep you busy; conversations that need to get done. It all helps the time to pass without forcing you to face the issue. But when you're alone with your thoughts, with a mind that will not go to sleep, the ultimate questions refuse to be ignored. Danny, Jimmy, Jo Lynn, and now Dad—all gone—somewhere, and all too soon forgotten. The air from the open windows in the front circulated back my way. It was dry and warm. And with my head buried comfortably in a pillow, I remembered them; all of them.

It was no wonder that twelve years ago I passed up going to university in the fall, thinking that a small, three-year Bible school would be more likely to have the answers I was looking for. It might even know the questions, too.

I met a guy in class the first week, Mike Shaw, a football and baseball player, and beginning with the first chapter of Genesis we started in with the questions. Mike started us off by asking how long that first day of creation was.

"It's a day just like our day, an evening and a morning, a twenty-four-hour revolution of the earth," our prof answered.

"I don't understand how this day could be anything at all like our day," my friend inquired. "How could you measure twenty-four hours if there was no sun or earth until the fourth day?" It seemed like an excellent question that deserved a competent response.

"It was a twenty-four-hour period," was the answer again.

"Well, how do you know?" he innocently asked; such a question strikes fear into the heart of anyone for whom certitude is critical.

"Because it uses the word 'day,' and we know that a day is a twenty-four-hour period."

"If there wasn't an earth and a sun, I wouldn't know how long a day was." There are times when further inquiry works a real hardship on one's grade and the length of the days of creation was not a critical point to me anyway. I had other questions that were more basic.

"How do we know the things in the Bible are true any-way?" I asked a professor when we got an opportunity for a one-on-one dialogue.

"Well, if the Bible is the word of God, then it has to be accurate."

"Yes, that's for sure," I agreed, "but it brings up the most basic question: How do we even know there is a God at all?"

"No one can prove God to you," the professor told me. "Some things you have to take on faith."

"And what happens if you don't have any faith?" I asked.

"You can pray and ask God to give you the faith to believe in him."

"How's he going to do that if he's not there?" I asked.

"If he's not there, you won't have to worry about it," he told me.

"In fact, I'll have a lot more to worry about if he's not there because then there will be no answers at all to the funny riddle of life, where we came from and all," I said. "In that case, the answer is that there are no answers and it's every man for himself."

It seemed to me that a concept as basic as the existence of God ought to be based on something more significant than the almost indefinable word "faith." I supposed it impolite to ask, "Who told *you*?"

The overwhelming impression is that somewhere along the line God himself had told him. Of course, most people are a little too shy to come straight out and say so. But why *shouldn't* God have told them? If he can hand out faith, he ought to be able to talk to anyone he wants.

"Actually, there are arguments," my prof told me. "There's no end to the long list of arguments to support the existence of God and the truth of Christianity. But no one will ever see the validity of the arguments without faith."

I spent my first year out of high school examining the arguments. But it is difficult to place a lot of stock in an argument that one knows will not be sufficient anyway and will still require faith. And why would anyone even attempt to put forward a convincing argument if he thought that no argument could prove his point conclusively?

Even if the arguments sometimes had weaknesses, there were so many more to be appealed to that by the time one added all the arguments together with that elusive and mystical quality, faith, it did give Christianity some credibility.

But I still had a problem. The more carefully each argument was scrutinized for flaws, the more the proponent tended to rely on the fact that there were many other arguments, and that it took faith to believe anyway. So a long list of unconvincing arguments still left me more confused and less convinced.

What this inquiry lacked in persuasiveness, it made up for in conviction. There was little doubt about one thing: If one doesn't know Jesus Christ as his personal savior, he is going to hell.

"But what about those who have no idea what 'Jesus Christ personal savior' means," I objected in a debate that raged in a late night dormitory bull session. "They've never even heard the word 'Jesus.' Don't you guys find it revolting to your sense of justice to think that a loving God would send people to hell based totally on their ignorance?"

"It's not really a question of whether it's revolting or not," one classmate said. "It's a matter of what Christ said. And he said that he was the only way and no one could get to the father except his way."

"And none of you guys find that just a little bit narrow," I asked, "a little closed-minded, a little unfair?"

"If it's true, it's not a question of narrow or closed-minded, it's a point of fact," one classmate answered. "And that is after all what Jesus said, he is the only way."

"The question of fairness is unimportant, is it?" I asked. "This isn't just theory, you know. We're talking about real people with real feelings and real loved ones, people just like us who are going to spend eternity in the torment of hell and all because they happen to be uninformed. Is there any fairness in that at all?"

Another student quoted scripture, " 'Who are you, O man, to answer back to God?' the Bible says."

"If it's not an issue of fairness," I asked, "then you are saying that you are willing to believe in a God that is unfair?"

"Of course not. God isn't unfair. Who says God's unfair?"

"If Jesus said something that we can show to be unfair, then we have to conclude that he *is* unfair," I said.

"Impossible!" a few responded simultaneously. "If Jesus said it, it can't be unfair."

"All right guys," I said, going on the offensive, "if they're all on the way to hell, why aren't you guys out there on the streets warning everyone of their impending doom?"

"Don't be ridiculous," they replied. "That would just turn people off."

"C'mon!" I said, "the truth is a big turn off, is it? What about that favorite illustration of ours, you know, the burning house and our obligation to warn everyone of the imminent danger unless they repent. If it's true, and the danger is so imminent, it would only be reasonable to be in the street, stopping and warning people."

"That would do more harm than good. People would think you're nuts."

"So now you guys want to trick people into becoming Christians. They're going to find out that you're nuts sooner or later anyway. So if they're all headed to hell, why aren't you out in the streets instead of in here arguing with a heretic like me?" I recalled my girlfriend's mother who wanted to protect her from marrying a Calvinist. This discussion was helping me see the wisdom of her prejudice.

One guy finally said, "If you had lived a few centuries back, you'd have been sizzled in the flames for your views." There was no question about the disappointment in his voice. One thing is for sure, I later told myself, if there is a creator of this universe who sends his creatures to hell because their friends don't inform them of the finer points of theology, I have no interest in dealing with a deity of that sort. If God is unfair, we'll all get the shaft anyway. If he is fair, he could hardly be a party to the damnation of the ignorant.

I concluded, therefore, that God was not a Fundamentalist and transferred to Portland State University. Actually, it made my year worthwhile to be able to come to that conclusion. A lot of people spend a lot more time studying God and learn less about him than that.

I spent a hundred dollars on a used Yamaha and moved into the basement of a mortuary, where I worked on weekends in exchange for a room and twenty-five dollars a month. For twenty-five cents worth of gas I could commute to Portland State and back for a week.

Each noon, a few friends and I would go for lunch to North's All-You-Can-Eat Chuck Wagon, where we did just that for a dollar. We ate as if we hadn't eaten since the noon before (which we hadn't) and wouldn't eat again until the next noon (which we wouldn't). The Chuck Wagon ran an ad in the local TV guide that read, "Bring this ad for a 50¢ discount."

Each week we bought seven TV guides for fifteen cents each and tore out the ad each day. For fifty cents a day we ate like kings.

I ran into Sue, an old high school friend whom I knew pretty well. She and I used to have vicious debates over the Vietnam war. Now she invited me to visit her at her apartment anytime. As attractive a girl as she was, even a non-Fundamentalist might have had certain moral misgivings. Just because God wasn't a Fundamentalist didn't mean that he might not have some standards of conduct that were expected, not to mention, of course, other technicalities like V.D., unwanted pregnancies, paternity suits, etc.

I had not yet given up my childhood faith by any means. Christianity was based on a firm trust in God, and by now it was obvious that I needed that. A God could answer so many questions. Even if there wasn't one, I needed one. And if there was one, what would he be like, what would he require? I had already concluded that he wasn't a Fundamentalist, but would he call himself a Christian? Or a Muslim? Or a Jew? Some serious questions, I thought.

Serious questions had a way of being interrupted by more immediate ones; like where the fifty cents for the next noon feast would come from. Then the Chuck Wagon stopped the ad and I was totally on my own. I soon developed a diet that consisted of one nineteen-cent meat pie with potato every other day and simply potatoes on the odd days. This was augmented with bread, peanut butter, and powdered milk.

Even at only a few dollars a week, there was no guarantee that the money would not run out, which it did from time to time. On one occasion, I ate the remaining peanut butter for the first two days and went hungry the next day. I then started looking for spiritual answers to my physical problem. I remembered from Sunday school the promise that "My God shall supply all your needs." Without checking to see if there are any special conditions attached to the promise, I prayed to God, informing him of my intention to hold him to his word. After all, I prayed, this matter of food does seem like a basic need to me.

I searched the little fridge again, though I had no idea why, and discovered a bag hidden behind the vegetable drawer. In it was an old potato that had some time earlier begun to grow.

When the potato was baked, I said a genuine prayer of thanks; a more reverent prayer than the first, which had originally led me to the fridge. The next day I got a note from Dad that had two dollar bills inside; just enough to replenish my potatoes and powdered milk and buy a meat pie.

The serious questions continued in History of Western Civilization with one of the most scintillating professors it has ever been my privilege to study under. He had a special curiosity about the religions of all the civilizations he lectured on. He even joked about it at one point, saying that he would lecture for five minutes about a culture's economics, five minutes about its political structure, five minutes about its social structure, and the next two class periods about its religious beliefs. During the same term I studied Platonic philosophy, the political history of America, and sociology.

I heard my well-respected history authority say, "If anyone asked me what one single individual had the most profound effect on history, I would say without hesitation, 'St. Paul.'"

"What was so significant about St. Paul?" I inquired.

"St. Paul was the single most effective disseminator of the Christian faith. So much so that it has taken over and dominated the influence of Western civilization." Now this was a twist: an honest recognition of the influence of Christianity by an irreligious, liberal, anti-Vietnam war history prof. This old man would have danced with all the coeds he could have got his hands on, yet he was claiming that Christianity had dominated the influence of our civilization.

In Persuasive Speech class I got a really crazy idea—especially for a skeptic like myself. I chose to attempt to persuade my class that Jesus Christ's resurrection was a historic fact. Why not go for all the marbles, I said to myself. Anyone who can prove the resurrection would certainly have to score some points. My fellow students were intrigued by my willingness to take on such a challenge. No less intrigued was the diehard-atheist professor. And who knows, I thought, I might even convince myself.

I was as surprised as anyone when I stumped my class with the question, What happened to the body? "If, after all," I said to a skeptical, prove-it-to-us class, "Christ's body had been in the grave where it was supposed to be, then certainly his enemies would have dragged it out and used it as the one surefire piece of evidence that would put down the Jewish uprising that was claiming him to be the Messiah.

"The only real plausible explanation was the one originally made by his enemies: that the followers of Christ had stolen the body and conspired the resurrection myth."

My frustrated professor, anxious to get in on the question-and-answer period, said, "Why do you keep asking what happened to the body? Who knows what happened to the body? And who cares? They could have done anything they wanted with it. For all we know they chopped it up into a thousand pieces and fed it to the fish in the Sea of Galilee."

I wondered if he really thought that a group of people who loved their leader enough to endure a lifetime of torture in order to prove his greatness to the world would actually take his body and chop it into a thousand pieces. Just the thought itself was gruesome enough, especially coming from an atheist so concerned about all the evil in the world.

He was a good guy though, this prof. We both actively opposed the war so we discussed both our areas of agreement and disagreement.

"I'm an atheist," he said to me in the more relaxed setting of his office. "I'm prejudiced against God."

I laughed. This was a new one on me. "You're kidding," I said. "How can an atheist be prejudiced against God?" It was the first exposure I had to an atheist whose choice was based on his emotions.

"I don't like God," he said. "Look at the state of the world, innocent victims, starving people, the general mess we're in. How can God possibly be likeable?"

"Wait a minute, I thought the discussion centered around whether or not there was one at all, not how likeable he was. How can you dislike someone who's not there?"

"It's easy. Just look at the screwed up mess he's got us in," he said.

"You must be the one who wrote that clever poem:

As I was going up the stair,
I met a man who wasn't there.
He wasn't there again today,
How I wish he'd stay away.

Remember that poem?" My grade-school teacher never did care much for the poems I chose to memorize. "Do you think maybe God will go away if we dislike him enough?"

"Well, if I disliked you enough, you would go away." He was kidding of course. Maybe.

"Yes, I would, for the sake of my grade at least. But I wouldn't pass out of existence." I supposed he found my point interesting because he ignored it.

"Now abides these three," he joked, "the tooth fairy, the Easter bunny, and Santa Claus, but the greatest of these is God." Nothing is quite as inconsistent as an atheist with a sense of humor.

"I had no idea God shared such company. What does he have in common with them?"

"You can't see any of 'em," he said. A pretty good point on the surface.

"But there are lots of things that can't be seen and people don't equate them with the Easter bunny. I never met anyone who didn't believe in the reality of love and hate. The fact that one can't see either of those hardly dissuades one from believing in their existence. Obviously it is the effects that any unseen thing produces that give it credibility."

"Then you must believe in the tooth fairy."

"As long as my sneaky mom kept coughing up the dough. As soon as the effects stopped, the doubts started."

It wasn't difficult for me, even as a high school biology student, to see the magnificent effects of a creator whose wisdom must be infinite. And people were always in a hurry to appeal to some deity-creator to support their actions. Even our Declaration of Independence appealed to a creator to justify the cry for freedom.

I concluded by this time that atheism was a worldview quite devoid of any scholarly merit. It was simply impossible to conceive of the existence of a complex universe such as ours without admitting the existence of some deity-creator of some sort. The question remaining is whether he is in fact worthy of the prejudice and disdain my professor claims for him.

With a little self-analysis, I might have discovered some prejudice of my own against God. I could hardly say that I was thrilled with some of the things that had happened to me. But neither could I conclude that my displeasure would affect the existence of a deity.

If I was prejudiced against anything, it was Fundamentalists. So a few weeks later, when Dad came through for a visit, I questioned him. It was gratifying to see that a few years out of the house seemed to give me the respect necessary to ask more difficult questions. I had never questioned my father's intellectual ability, only his intellectual honesty. After listening to an atheist, I was more disposed to give Dad another listen.

"You're going to be surprised," he said as we drove around Portland visiting old family friends, "at the number of people on both sides of the theistic question whose minds are made up, and no amount of honest inquiry would make any difference. I'll give you an example. Everyone accepts the idea that anything which shows intelligent design must have been the creation of an intelligent mind, right?"

"I'll admit that," I said.

"Okay. Now, do you remember that science fair project you did in eighth grade?"

"There better be a real good reason for bringing that up. It easily had to be the worst exhibit there."

"All right, let's just assume that it was the worst science fair project in the history of Reedsport Junior High. As bad as it was, do you remember anyone suggesting that your science fair project was a creation that materialized out of nowhere by luck?"

"No one suggested it, but maybe they should've."

"Well, if you hadn't gone and put your name on it, they might have. The point is that even a bad science fair project is assumed to have a student behind it. And the better the project, the more work and intelligence required to produce it. But when it comes to the world, which is a science fair project to beat all, people will simply say that it materialized from nothing, with no intelligence behind it. Now a person really has to be a dedicated disbeliever to think that. If a scientist could produce even one single cell of life, much less a whole tree, he would receive the Nobel prize for science. How would he feel if we just laughed and said, 'Aw that's nothing, there's lots of living cells, even complex plants and animals, billions of them and everyone knows that they were all created by pure luck. So you don't deserve a Nobel prize, you just got lucky.' You have to admit a scientist would feel very put out by that sort of attitude." We were driving north over the massive I-5 bridge, which spans the magnificent Columbia River. On my right I could see for miles up the river's gorge, a view that put intensity into his illustration. And I had little doubt that the bridge needed a creator.

"You've got to be a pretty dedicated disbeliever to think that the universe got here by luck. It's difficult to imagine that some people aren't just prejudiced against the idea of God." Hmm, prejudiced against God. I had heard that before somewhere.

I wasn't really prejudiced against God. And even if I was prejudiced against Fundamentalism for the life-style it had imposed on me, I had to agree that its approach to the origin of the universe made more sense.

It was a curious phenomenon, this attitude of the atheists. Jean-Paul Sartre had left a strong impression on us when he turned down his Nobel prize cash. In his autobiography he wrote about his search for God in his youth. He wrote that his was a story of a missed vocation. He had been raised very much like myself, in a strict religious environment. He was greatly troubled by the hypocrisy around him. And God seemed powerless to stop it.

"I need God," he wrote. "He was given to me, I received him without realizing that I was seeking him." Sartre even contemplated a life in the clergy, but God failed to "take root in my heart." "He vegetated in me for a while, then he died." Our similar backgrounds made it easy for me to identify with his struggle. It was a "misunderstanding" that caused something to come between him and God. It seems that as a young boy he had done something wrong (he was playing with matches and burned a rug) and while attempting to conceal the evidence, his conscience irritated him.

This was the same sort of thing I had gone through as a boy, I thought, that irritating conscience. "I felt his gaze inside my head," he wrote, "and on my hands. I whirled about in the bathroom, horribly visible, a live target." He flew into a rage at such a crude indiscretion by God and cursed him repeatedly. How could God be so crude, Sartre thought, as to invade the private mind of a small child? This "misunderstanding," as he called it, caused God to vegetate and die.

For myself, I could not possibly have been more puzzled. I certainly shared his feeling that the hypocrisy of the so-called godly made Christianity look false and God powerless. But now God was "gazing on *his* hands," irritating *him* for *his* hypocrisy, and it made him angry. He had experienced God for himself as he said, "inside my head," and he liked the idea even less.

Well, which is it, I asked myself? Are we going to disbelieve because of the hypocrisy we see in others or because God won't allow that same hypocrisy in us? It reminded me of the statement of that other famous atheist, Nietzsche, when he wrote, "If you could prove God to me, I would believe in him all the less." It almost seemed as if the closer these great thinkers came to the idea of God, the less clarity of thought they expressed. While I was impressed—in fact, amazed—at their honesty, I began to lose respect for the objectivity with which they searched for truth.

And Sartre's "misunderstanding" continued. At the age of thirty this "invisible one," whom he referred to as the "Holy Ghost," kept troubling his every effort to justify himself. It was about this time, after writing his book *Nausea*, that he began to "think systematically against myself, to the extent of measuring the obvious truth of an idea by the displeasure it caused me."

I was amazed. After thinking for years that God-fearing elders had closed their minds to the facts, I found myself reading an atheist who stated outright that displeasure could be used to measure truth; the greater displeasure an idea caused, the more untrue it must be. And this idea of God is a real pain. He writes, "I collared the Holy Ghost in the cellar and threw him out; atheism is a cruel and long-range affair; I think I have carried it through. I see clearly, I have lost my illusions, I know what my real jobs are, I surely deserve a prize for good citizenship."

What you deserve, I thought as I read it, is a prize for honesty. Never before had I heard such a forthright admission of the emotional considerations involved in the theistic debate. I was disinterested in knowing how attractive the idea of a God might be. I just wanted the cold fact. Is there anything there?

I applied Sartre's test for truth to my situation, asking myself if my Christian beliefs gave me pain or pleasure. In the case of Danny's death, the belief that he was in heaven was a great source of comfort, so I could conclude it to be true on that basis. In the case of Jimmy's death and my personal failure to inform him of the hellfire to come, it gave me quite the opposite feeling, so I could conclude it to be false.

To say that there must not be a God because the idea of him gave me a pain and I couldn't stand him bothering me when I was trying to do something questionable was, to my searching mind, the last straw. I was getting a charley horse between my ears just thinking about it.

In the face of the existence of the universe and no sound answer as to how it got here, I was forced to accept that there was someone who started it, some "creator." But the mere acceptance of a creator was a far cry from the Christian teachings in which I had been raised. It called for the acceptance of the claim that the carpenter-preacher from Nazareth was in fact that very creator.

This problem of Christ was a separate issue. And the phrase

"Jesus Christ personal savior" required even more explanation. Sitting in History of Civ I heard my well-known history prof say, "Muhammad came back from the mountain with a long message from God. At least he said he talked to God. And who's to say that he didn't?" The prof even good-naturedly chided two nuns who were in his class. They just smirked and nodded in admission that he had a point.

"Why," I asked my prof in the privacy of his office, "would so much of the world, even Muslim, Hindu, and other faiths, call this man, Jesus, 'good' when they know he claimed to be God? He made the claim so boldly and so brazenly that they murdered him for it. And he made totally illogical statements like, 'Eat my flesh and drink my blood,' and generally made a total pest of himself to the religious establishment. How on earth can the majority opinion of the Western world call this man good?"

"Well," he said, "you have to admit his positive effect on history. There's no way to deny that the Christian religion has brought progress." He was admitting that I had a strong point. It did seem as if the majority view on Christ made no sense at all, and we both agreed that we couldn't imagine any intelligent man telling his followers to eat his flesh and drink his blood. Either the Western world had in its religious fervor and ignorance chased after a total lunatic, or we had to face a god in human form.

I'd been resting for a good hour when James laid on the horn up front and startled me awake. We were passing a herd of sheep and goats and I noticed that the sun was setting fast on our left. "Any idea how much farther we got to go?" I hollered up to the front.

"It's hard to tell," James called back. "I don't think we can put a lot of faith in this odometer."

By now we had figured out how to make the valve work to switch from one gas tank to the other, but we were never sure which gas tank we were using, or which one the gas gauge was using, or whether the gas gauge was even functioning at all. By the best of our calculations, we were out of gas ten miles before we reached the outskirts of Herat. But since the Travelall was still running, we weren't about to stop; especially since it was now dark and we knew it was unsafe to travel after dark. That would have been true even if the headlights had worked, and we just now discovered they didn't.

The roadway for the last few miles into Herat was lined by trees that were silhouetted against the sky, which enabled us to aim our machine roughly in the middle of the road while assuming that no one would be foolish enough to be leaving Herat at this time of night, headed to Kandahar in the same lightless condition. With the number of thieves known to be on this highway, we would have kept driving if we had been blindfolded.

It was late at night by the time we situated ourselves in our parents' home. The city of Herat turns off all electricity at 10:00 P.M., which left us groping around the house for any available bed or couch. I must have been the first to find one, because I don't remember anything else.

CHAPTER 5

Thou Shalt Not Enjoy

When the rooster and the mullah announced the new day, I had no idea where I was. I'd awakened to this duet so many times before, each time wondering what sort of games my brothers, classmates, and I might play at school, that it took a few moments to remember that I wasn't in the fifth grade anymore.

And it wasn't just the sound of the mullah. The air had a certain feel to it. Maybe it was a combination of the 6,000-foot elevation, the dryness, the temperature, and the purity of the air that told me in that first waking breath that I wasn't in Chicago. Still, the atmosphere was so peaceful that I didn't mind those few moments of confusion, and I lay there for a long time enjoying it.

After dozing off a few times, I got up, found James, and nosed around the house, which we hadn't seen the night before. I had slept in a room the Afghans call an *auwadown*, an all-glass room for growing plants. It joined both the main living room area and a small dining room. There was another door off the living room, which was shut. I presumed it to be a bedroom that Joanna had found and claimed.

"Let's see what's in the kitchen," I whispered to James, thinking we might as well let Joanna sleep. We were still in our clothes from the previous day's trip.

"Why are we whispering," James said out loud. "Joanna

101

will never sleep the way that mullah's goin'." A bell in the yard began to clang. It was a man who already heard we had arrived and came to take us to visit the hospital.

As we were leaving we were met outside the gate by a man who told us he had worked with our father and wondered if he could talk to us. We exchanged the common greetings, told him that he could, but just now we were leaving.

At the construction site we were introduced to the people Dad had worked with. Humble as it was, it would be the nicest medical structure in this section of the country and would make a major contribution to the prevention of blindness, a widespread problem in Afghanistan.

In the afternoon, James and I began our carpet shopping in earnest. We meandered through the bazaar, found a number of interesting carpet shops, and were finally led to the main carpet dealer's market by someone who realized we wanted to do some serious buying.

We entered an open area about the size of a tennis court that was surrounded by shops on two levels, a basement level and an upper level, twenty or thirty shops in all. Each shop lined its floors and walls with the world's most colorful carpets. They produced that special aroma of dyed virgin wool, tightly knotted by young boys with small fingers, then cut short to preserve the crisp definition between the colors. We meandered from one to the next looking for the perfect carpet, the one that would catch our eye and could be acquired at a good price.

There are many ways to assist the poor: One of the best is to purchase their products, assuming that they are producing items of value. The purchase of valueless products only creates dependency.

The carpet bazaar is like any bazaar in Afghanistan; everything is negotiable. When they see an American coming, they mentally multiply all their prices by a factor of about three. This makes negotiating a fascinating challenge, which James and I wouldn't think of passing up. Sitting on short little stools, we bent over and inspected the colors, shearing, and knot density of one carpet after another spread over the floor. The merchants quickly discovered that we were not going to pay ridiculously inflated prices. The Afghans respect a good, hard-nosed negotiator.

I admit that a buyer doesn't appear very generous when he is trying every trick he knows to whittle away at a seller's profit margin, while at the same time the seller tries to extract every last af from the buyer's pocket. But it would hardly be appropriate to say to someone, "I'm paying you double what it's worth because I pity your decrepit economic condition," though you'd be hard-pressed to find a seller offended by the insult. Charity in this case is disruptive; it would lead the producer to conclude that his product is worth more than it really is—a conclusion that can be fatal, and a trap that I would soon fall into.

Some years later, a partner and I capitalized two young college students who had grown up in this part of the world. They were going to provide a market for these carpet weavers by buying their goods and selling them in the States. The students had been influenced by the prevailing attitude of the day, that the wealth of the West was gained at the expense of the poor, that these economies suffered because the West took advantage of them.

Thus they felt perfectly free to pay a handsome premium for the product at the local level. The increased profit margin meant that the carpet weavers did not have to keep such tight control over their costs and, therefore, increased their production. At the same time, more had to be charged in the States, which made it difficult for us to be competitive at the retail level.

It was impossible for the young entrepreneurs to hide their consternation when, after the loss of a third of a million dollars, we had to shut down the operation. "Does everything always have to be a profit with you guys?" they asked. What these students didn't realize was that the people who were hurt the most were the poor carpet weavers. For two years they had been selling their carpets at the unrealistic prices we paid them. When we no longer bought their carpets their production crumbled; they were unable to compete with those who had been "oppressed" into producing at the lower, but fairer, prices. We had set out to help but ended up doing more harm than good.

Moving from shop to shop we were shadowed by a little Afghan boy. It's common for Afghan children to accompany and usually annoy foreigners. They can sometimes be quite pleasant; however, because they have been taught that there is money to be gained, they are usually bothersome, either by begging or by seeking some special favor. This little boy was the exception. We didn't know exactly what it was about him, but something made him very pleasant to be around. He followed us from shop to shop watching and listening to us negotiate. He was even invited into some of the shops by the merchants who normally chased children away. We were told that his father was one of the carpet merchants, and the boy's job was to move us toward his father's shop.

By the second day the merchants learned that we were negotiators and lowered their prices. We were quite surprised at how low the prices actually came—a sign of the lack of commerce and oversupply of carpets that had already been caused by the military unrest. These carpet merchants were some of the wealthiest people in the area and they were hurting. We visited each merchant's shop two or three times before finally settling on the merchandise we wished to purchase. Being the only buyers in town at the time, we had a unique negotiating position.

I finally realized what was different about the boy; he was especially gifted at nonverbal communication. He made some sounds occasionally, when he wanted to get our attention, but generally he would just touch or grab our hands and was unusually quiet.

Turning to James, I said, "I think our little friend is mute."

We clowned around with him a little bit more, and it became obvious he couldn't hear or communicate back. We spent some time discussing his problem with his father in the courtyard. A number of the other carpet merchants gathered around as we sat and talked. Once the father took his son on the long journey to Kabul to see what could be done to help him but with no success. It appeared to us that his eyesight was also affected, possibly by cataracts. The vision in one eye was completely gone.

I wondered to myself what kind of creator would allow a nice little boy like this to be deaf and dumb and now possibly go blind. Was it God's intention to use people like my father to solve the evils of his world, which, for some mysterious reason, he had neglected? Dad considered it a privilege to be a worker in the creator's world and I could appreciate his viewpoint after meeting this lovable little kid. Maybe this was after all the highest calling, to give one's life in the service of the humblest of God's creatures. But why the problem in the first place? Is it just to keep people like my father busy?

Leaving the bazaar after purchasing our carpets, we were surrounded by a crowd of children yelling, "Baksheesh! Baksheesh!" When these children realized that we were not going to hand out money and reward them for begging, as so many well-meaning tourists foolishly do, they appealed to our humanitarian interest by asking for a baksheesh for the little handicapped boy who had endeared himself to us.

"That boy has wealth that our money could not buy," James told them in Farsi. In fact, I wondered if other Afghan children might be as nice as this little boy if they couldn't hear or speak. Maybe his deafness and dumbness was, for him, an advantage.

When we returned to the compound we were met on the street outside the gate by the same man who had been there that first morning asking to talk with us. Now he wondered how long we would be staying. He said he was an acquaintance of our parents and wanted to meet us and invite us to his house for a meal. Such approaches on the street are properly viewed with suspicion as there are a variety of ways that foreigners can allow themselves to be drawn into vulnerable situations. James thanked him for his kind invitation but said that we were uncertain what our friends had planned for us or when we would be leaving. James's putting the man off made me feel bad, but caution demanded that we know more about him before accepting his invitation.

We stacked our rolls of carpet in the living room and I collapsed on the bed in the *auwadown*. I was staring at the plants around the room and still thinking about the mute boy, wondering how all the minor details of humanity were going to fit together. Minor details with major consequences. A camel, a bus, and an auto converge on a highway. A cute little boy who's already deaf develops cataracts. Could it all make sense or was Sartre right? Maybe we are nonentities existing in a universe of nothingness? This was such a peaceful climate in which to recall Sartre. The warm afternoon weather almost made me think I was suspended in nothing.

I missed Nancy. Was she all right back in Kabul? Years ago it had required a host of convoluted circumstances to bring us together.

I recalled a decade earlier when, walking from my prof's office at Portland State toward my Yamaha, I ran into Sue, my debating opponent from high school. I wasn't a very sociable person, and thoroughly enjoyed living alone, but it was wonderful to see a familiar face from the past and she walked along with me. It gave me an "at home" feeling; a feeling distinctly different from Sartre's nothingness.

"You've just got to come over to my apartment to visit me sometime," she told me again when we arrived at my bike, and she stuck her phone number into my hand. She had a cute face, but mainly she had the kind of figure that I found attractive; all the curves were in just the right places. What was to stop me from having a most enjoyable, unencumbered relationship with this girl from my past?

I knew Sue well enough to know that there were a lot of fun things she could have taught me. What good, sound, earthly reason could there possibly be to deny myself the discovery of this great pleasure. Naturally I still had that little voice that bugged me occasionally, but this might be just the indoctrination of my childhood: the old puritan taboo that sex ought to be reserved for marriage alone. Maybe this taboo should be discarded the same as I had already discarded the other taboos: drinking, movies, dancing, and so on.

The general prohibitions that the Church seemed to monopolize appeared to have the single goal of the displacement of fun. "If you're having too much fun, tell us what you're doing and we'll make a rule against it," I imagined to be the Church's philosophy. This is no doubt how they got started—all those taboos against dancing and the things to which it led, which looked like such fun. In fact, it seemed that anything provocative was considered evil: hems that were too high; tops that were too low, too tight, or in any way too revealing—all of which appeared plenty attractive to me. I couldn't imagine a skirt that could be too short or a top too revealing. Quality girls don't dress in such a manner and it's the quality girls who you would want to take home to introduce to mother, especially if you had my mother. But there still remained a serious question whether these quality females ever had any fun. Of one thing I was certain, I said to myself as I straddled my bike and watched Sue move gracefully down the street and turn the corner, we could definitely have fun together. Nothing serious, no relationship, just good, old-fashioned sexual pleasure. Why not?

The double standard is a generally accepted fact of life on a college campus. A guy dates one type of girl for fun and another type for marriage. It did seem strange that a generation which would burn down its campuses in protest over the

Vietnam war and the hypocrisy of its materialistic parents would be so willing to tolerate such an openly hypocritical double standard.

To resolve the confusion for us, along came the most controversial movie to be released in years, *The Graduate*. It seemed obvious that Mrs. Robinson had a morality by which she would measure a prospective son-in-law, though it might not even occur to her to measure herself. 'Tis indeed a rare day on earth when moral indignation turns introspective. If I really expected to marry a girl who hadn't been to bed with all my friends, consistency demanded that I behave in a similar way.

Good theory, Mark, I told myself while I kick-started my bike and hit first gear. And you're just going to pass up all those curves. You're a fool, you know that?

It was a good theory though, and I knew I wasn't being a fool. Still, I put Sue's phone number in my pocket just in case I changed my mind.

From the day Sue gave me her phone number, I got a regular urge to call her. I usually came to my senses and faced the facts: Active as my glands may be, I didn't want the negative fallout from their use to control the rest of my life.

I did not, however, always come to my senses. On one occasion I faced the facts, thought about it, and decided to ignore them. There could be no consequences bad enough to offset the ecstatic physical pleasure I was foolishly denying myself. I grabbed the phone, yanked her phone number out of my pocket, and dialed it. No answer.

Later I returned to my senses, wondering if there was somebody somehow looking out for me. It was a stupid thing to have done—but I kept the phone number just the same.

A month later the same thing happened. I am willing to endure any consequences, I told myself, if only once I could have the pleasure of a great sexual experience. I dialed desperately. Again, no answer. This story occurred with some regularity.

I cried on the day, being in my most rational state of mind, I flushed Sue's phone number down the toilet. Rational or not, over the next few months I wasted hours of good mental energy trying to remember it.

The next year, Gary, a friend from Bible school, and I transferred to a school in the Chicago area where my brother Joe was enrolled. I took a job in a church as a choir director to help meet expenses.

I saw her for the first time at my first Wednesday night rehearsal. I looked up from my music to bring in the soprano section and found my concentration thoroughly distracted. My eyes fell on what was to me the most attractive woman I'd ever seen. I lost my place in the music, lost the beat of the tempo, and the whole thing fell apart about two bars later.

"Uh, I just wanted to stop here for a moment to, uh, review that problem in the tenor section a few measures back," I told them. "Okay, let's see, where were we? Uh, top of two, please, third bar." Once back into the music at a regular pace, I sneaked a peek into the soprano section to see if what I had noticed was really there or if I had been dreaming. Sure enough, there she was: a gorgeous face framed with dark brunette, almost black, hair and the warmest eyes. I didn't know that churches as conservative as this one had such beautiful women members. Wasn't this against some spiritual code? We met later and I discovered that there was a refreshing, quiet shyness about her that was just as attractive as her beauty. Her smile was so sincere that she used it only for good cause, giving it even greater value. To make her smile would become my challenge.

But the real problem: What does a destitute college student without a dollar to his name do to entertain a gorgeous woman? I was now in the big city and could only assume that the women here, certainly those women of extraordinary beauty, would have rich tastes. Indeed, this generally tended to be the case. Nancy, however, turned out to be a miraculous surprise.

Nancy's mother was of Bohemian extraction. Apparently, Bohemians have a reputation for frugality. I was oblivious to such cultural distinctions. Nancy had been raised by parents who had a great appreciation for the value of a quarter. Many girls I had dated felt that a boy's interest in them was demonstrated by the quantity of dollars he spent on a date. Until now, I could never convince these girls that I was interested in them. So Nancy must have been sent from heaven itself. I had no idea that there were girls who were genuinely serious about things that mattered, not impressed with money, and beautiful, too.

On our first date we spent the entire time discussing the Vietnam war. The last beautiful girl who I have been serious with could not bear to discuss anything more significant than the latest Hollywood gossip tabloid.

There was a colorful arboretum not too far away where two people could spend a lot of hours enjoying not only each other's company but some very exceptional outdoor scenery, especially exceptional in the Midwest.

Entrance to the arboretum was free. For some reason, the vast majority of our time together was spent there. I suppose if I'd had enough money to do more entertaining things like going to the movies, we might not have known each other as well as we did.

Nancy was the kind of girl I could take home to meet Mom. But I soon discovered that, to be somebody on campus, I had to show that I could date a girl who had been labeled "somebody" by the "in" crowd, a kind of good housekeeping seal of approval that applied to dates. It let a guy know who's hot and who's not; it might even arrange them in descending order, best to worst. To really be "in," a guy needed to date someone who was held in high esteem, and Nancy did not go to my school or even live very close to campus.

So when the opportunity presented itself to date girls with campus status, I took it. As beautiful, sweet, and sensitive as Nancy was, these girls generally had the ability to garner more status points for me. The romance with Nancy gradually faded.

To pay for school I took a job as a jail guard working the night shift. It presented a whole range of challenges to my integrity. Lying to your superior officers was not only commonplace, it was anticipated. In some cases it was the only way to get along with fellow officers.

A year or two passed and I hadn't graduated from college on schedule, so I lost my draft deferment. My number was 81 and the draft board was at 76 when the draft bill ran out. Since Congress took so long to pass another one, I slipped through the crack and whispered a prayer of thanksgiving. I could now finish college at my own pace. Maybe it wouldn't be all that necessary to finish anyway.

A fellow student joined me at the jail and we moved into an apartment at 2424 N. Lincoln in Chicago. Located just north of the six-way intersection of Fullerton, Lincoln, and Halsted, the apartment was situated above a small grocery store next to the famous Biograph Theatre. Alongside the door to the grocery was a door that led upstairs to our spacious seven rooms. At $125 a month, it looked like quite a bargain. It was. For the landlord. Controlling the roaches was a physical impossibility. There would have been more of them, but the rest were working the grocery store down below.

The floors were so uneven that walking was a constant threat to safety. Since I had a waterbed, I laid claim to the room with the most level floor. By the time I got the water at the west end of the bed to the correct level, it had not yet reached the east end. Hardly a light bulb in the place worked. When we got them replaced, we found out why no one had bothered; as soon as we turned half of them on, the fuse blew. Then we ran downstairs to the store to get into the fuse box. Low amp fuses were no doubt the only thing that had kept the antique wiring from burning the place down. The building was already condemned, which probably worked to the landlord's favor. Anyway, if he had made the improvements necessary, we wouldn't have been able to afford the place. Difficult as it is to imagine, slum landlords provide a better service to the poor than condo converters.

These were transitional years; the years when a person doesn't know for sure what he wants to do: Go to graduate school and ask more questions? Or mark time in the work-force? Though I'd finally come to terms with God on a somewhat personal level, I still had some unanswered questions. It wasn't an encounter with God the way some people talk about it, it was more an encounter with myself. And now it was time to put the philosophizing of the academic world behind me and get serious about a productive life.

Thinking about what I wanted out of life reminded me of Nancy. I called her at the college she was attending in New York to see if we could get together when she came home to Chicago for a visit. Her interest was considerably lower that I had hoped, but a few months later we did get together and renew our old friendship. I even had to ask her to forgive me for being such a self-centered boyfriend. Apologizing to a former girlfriend, I thought? Am I nuts? Cautiously we began to pick up our romance where it left off.

While Nancy was home on her break from college, she received a call that was to have a long-term effect on her career and our relationship. Christian people like to attribute "coincidences" to the work of God and deny that luck could ever affect the affairs of human beings. They deny the existence of luck as vigorously as the gambler on a hot streak relies on it. So when the director of a large, prestigious, Christian organization, looking through a school annual, saw Nancy's graduation picture and expressed an interest in having her work for his organization, it was only natural that any normal, God-respecting person would consider such a coincidence to be the providential working of God himself.

Soon after Nancy began working for the organization, she discovered that it was considered a virtue in these circles to remain disinterested in all members of the opposite sex. "Give these best years of your life to God," her widely respected leader told them. That certainly didn't serve as a major encouragement to our relationship, which was at the time making a nice recovery.

As Nancy and I began to discuss marriage, it became clear that it would be impossible for her to continue her career with this organization if she were married. It came as a shock to me.

"Getting married to me is not a sin," I told her, surprising myself at the words that were coming out of my mouth. I had always assumed that if a sweetheart refused to marry me, it would be for a better reason than that.

"It would be if God didn't want me to," she answered.

"True," I said, "and who says he doesn't?"

The argument raged for months. Nancy came away from her job with a line of arguments. I spent hours explaining why they were illogical. There were other things about this prestigious leader's teachings that I felt were wrong, and Nancy and I debated these as well. Our dates were lessons in theological haggling. We were at least learning how to quarrel. He was always so "godly" and I "just didn't understand."

Spiritual leaders are not required to adhere as closely to the rules of logic as the rest of us. They seem to have the ability occasionally to declare for themselves a special dispensation, suspending normal rules of deduction. As one once said to me, "When you are as spiritual as I am, you will know I'm right." I never had figured out a way to debate that line. Maybe I should have asked him, "Do you know everything?" I can almost see his spiritual little head nodding up and down. (I'm quite sure that "little" is the correct word here.)

I strongly felt that Nancy was confusing the wishes of God with the wishes of the head of this particular ministry. But even to think that they were not synonymous was to challenge his spiritual authority.

Nancy's boss arranged for a few staff members to travel with him out of town for a week. With a complete change of scenery and out of my influence, he counseled and prayed with her (in private situations), told her how indispensable she was to the work, and about the great opportunities that lay ahead for her to serve in his organization if she could "lay aside every weight" and commit herself completely to God. Naturally I was the weight that had to go.

Nancy couldn't sleep that week. She knew that we were meant for each other, but there could be no higher calling than to be directly involved in the service of the king of the universe. How could anyone refuse that? All her boss was trying to get her to do was to see that she would be happiest if she followed God and did the right thing. Nancy went back to her motel room to be alone and cry. She knew what she had to do. The conflict of the week could only be resolved by a commitment to end the romance. Admitting it to herself produced a new wave of tears.

After she returned, I stopped by her house. We drove a few blocks from her home to the Jack-in-the-Box on the corner of Seventeenth and Thirty-first streets.

I don't know why I didn't fall apart. I should have. Instead I said, "Okay. I would be the last one to keep you from serving God. If that's what you really think is best, then we'll call it quits, all right?"

"That's all?" She was surprised by my ready acceptance. "Okay? It's over? Just like that? Is that all you think of our relationship? Doesn't this bother you?"

"Of course it bothers me. But I don't know what you want me to do about it. You're wrong if you believe you must choose between God and me. I haven't been able to convince you of that, so what can I do? Maybe God can get through to you some day. When he does, I'm sure there will be plenty of nice men out there just waiting for you."

That line was below the belt and I knew it. But I figured that anything goes in this game. If I lost this woman, at least I could say I had given it my best, if not lowest, shot. The other guy wasn't playing fair either, taking my girl off to another state, away from me, privately counseling her, and using his high-pressure persuasion to manipulate her thinking.

I continued. "You seem to think that the highest calling for Eve would have been to snub Adam, go off into some corner of Eden, and sit there in solitude worshiping God."

"Hmm, I never thought about it that way. That's interesting. I wonder what 'he' will say about that." She thought for a moment. "But I'd have to quit if we got married."

I took home an emotionally distraught and confused girl that night. It was only slightly better than getting dumped. This situation called for some prayer, and I did have some obscure inner confidence that God was on my side.

Then it happened. The break I waited for. One day in the staff Bible study, one of Nancy's friends speculated about the meaning of a particular Bible verse. This was, by coincidence, the same topic on which Nancy had heard authorities speak, so she knew that her friend was mistaken, simply unfamiliar with the setting in which the author had written. "An easy misunderstanding," Nancy thought, and was just about to make her contribution to correct the direction of the discussion when the leader of the organization began to speak.

"Well, he'll set the record straight," she thought to herself. But to Nancy's shock he agreed with her misinformed friend. He showed no awareness of the cultural setting and made some fascinating spiritual points that Nancy knew the original author never intended.

"Mark is right!" she realized in utter amazement. The light suddenly dawned. This man, as saintly as he is, does not have all the answers. Now that she knew he was wrong on this point, insignificant though it was, she was even more horrified to realize that she felt no freedom at all to express her difference of opinion. They are straight out wrong, she thought, and there is nothing I can do about it. Fear ran through her body as she realized how long she had been in this situation yet completely blind to it. "This is what a cult is like," she thought, "all truth coming from one man and his faithful followers unable to question him."

She tried to convince herself that her revered teacher did, in fact, receive counsel from his top assistants so that it wasn't just a one-man-worshiping organization. But when Nancy went to a staff party, one of the top men in the organization, confided in her, "It is such an honor to work for this person. I have never been around anyone so God-like." The fear she felt before turned to quiet panic. She felt a cold chill down her spine. The top man was surrounded by yes-men who worshiped him.

Nancy had to admit that all truth was not interpreted by this one particular individual in spite of his high standing. She decided to continue her career with the organization and to resolve our personal conflict by committing to marry me at some time in the future. I had no idea how long this might be, but at least I had achieved something: commitment to a future marriage. Though I knew that if we were to actually go through with a wedding, she would lose her job—a job at which she was quite good, too.

Thanksgiving weekend was approaching and, with four days off, we planned to go to Colorado where my parents were living and surprise them with the announcement. Nancy informed her boss of her personal commitment to me and our decision to delay wedding plans indefinitely so that she could serve his organization. He agreed, saying it would be fine. The following day her employment was terminated.

"It's out of my hands," her boss explained. (His relative handled all the firing.) She went to lunch, where the holiday spirit had taken over and a party was in progress. With her career just destroyed, and her emotions turned inside out and upside down, how could she possibly tell all her friends that she was fired and would never see them again? She remembered other girls who had suddenly left without saying good-bye. They were said to have lost "the vision of the work," were not "spiritual" enough to be truly committed. Nancy knew that she would be spoken of this way tomorrow. Now she knew why others had left without saying anything. How could she say to her friends, "Our Christ-like leader has decided that I am unfit to continue in the work." The discussion that would ensue would only cause her to break down emotionally. "The only thing I can do," she thought, "is leave and try to put myself back together."

"What in the world am I going to tell people?" Nancy thought as she drove home. "And what about Mark's parents? Who will believe that I've been terminated for deciding to marry?"

Nestled among the pines at the foot of the towering Cheyenne Mountain was a little cabin where my parents lived; the ideal place to shock them with a romantic announcement. We all enjoyed a wonderful few days together.

"Well, when do you have to be back at work, Nancy?" my dad asked as we were returning to the cabin from lunch. There was a pause while Nancy's heart sank a foot. This was it. They would find out. What on earth could she say?

"She doesn't have a specific time to be back," I answered for her. Dad knows only too well about my ability to answer a question while leaving out all the pertinent details. So an answer like that to a straightforward, innocent question, from a person who wasn't asked, following an awkward pause, assured him that he wasn't getting the whole story. The fact that he didn't say anything certainly didn't mean that we had skirted the issue. He knows that he can communicate more with silence anyway—a silence that says, well, you can tell me what you're not telling me or you can just let me use my imagination and think something up.

There had been times when anything he could imagine would be better than the truth, so I would just let him imagine. But Nancy had nothing to be ashamed of unless it was her taste in men. (And she would soon become accustomed to being questioned on that score.) Over the next few days, Nancy and I explained all that we had been through in our struggle to resolve our future. Knowing that my parents held her employer in the highest regard, Nancy had no idea how much of her story was taken seriously. A close family friend also found our story hard to believe. She eventually wrote the organization asking for an explanation and was surprised to hear that we had represented the facts quite accurately.

The following week I had a discussion with her former boss over the situation. Reasoning with a religious man whose mind is already made up is a fascinating exercise. I now have a lot more respect for the atheist who said, "Christians are so closed-minded they can't think straight."

I have often wondered if such behavior on the part of God's children reflects poorly on God himself. I can almost imagine God saying, "Hey, don't blame me for that guy's behavior. I'm doing the best I can with the bumbling saints I've got. You're the ones who put him up on a pedestal where he doesn't belong." Indeed, it seems that anything put on a pedestal tends to become a god.

There were countless thousands of people around the world who viewed this man's opinion as plain, old, eternal truth. I was thankful that God gave me a mind that could decide for itself, and I determined to increase my respect for God and exercise great restraint in my respect for the highly respected. It was during this period that I began to realize that I wasn't a religious person after all. I just liked God.

The hurt that Nancy endured at the hands of her well-meaning religious leader was minute when compared to that suffered by her friends who stayed on with the organization. Over the next few years scandalous stories of immorality within this particular group bore out the wisdom of Nancy's decision. It confirmed again that the powerful, the well respected, and the educated have no unique corner on truth.

Engagement: that period of time when two people are

committed to one another for life and the Church won't let them prove it. It is the ultimate in the paying of one's dues. Save the sex act for the wedding night? What for! If I'm going to buck the religious establishment, I thought, I might as well get something really good out of it. But I was engaged to a "good" girl.

Actually, I knew that the puritanical ideas about the marriage bed held higher status than the taboos to which I had been subjected. They came straight from the scriptures—something about purity, chastity, fornication, and monogamy. Keeping these rules was by no means fun, and those who scoffed at our rules were having a blast—interrupted only by an occasional fit of fury at an unfaithful spouse.

An engagement period characterized by self-control and restraint lays a groundwork of mutual trust and respect that pays immeasurable dividends down the road. It was a little like a strenuous wrestling workout. It produced some reward in the long run, but for the present there is precious little pleasure to be had.

Serious thought about our wedding night stirred again the ghosts from my past that haunted me. All those things that dancing led to, which seemed as if they'd be so much fun, were in fact labeled sinful. Would the marriage license magically remove that label and suddenly enable one to call beautiful what was once shameful? And what about those tight tops and short skirts that had been such an attraction? Nancy would never wear those. It was somehow difficult for me to imagine the Almighty guiding me to marry a provocatively clad female.

As the Church and the wicked increasingly shunned each other, both saw fun and morality as being mutually exclusive. A most desirable time could be deliciously wicked. For anything to be delectable, it must have some element of wickedness. And the Church made no effort to counter the claim, indeed seemed to acquiesce to it. Could marriage to a woman as conservative as Nancy fulfill all those "deliciously wicked" desires for which I had starved for so long? Maybe to be moral, I'd have to give up some of these finer things.

Our wedding, honeymoon, and subsequent marriage did a number on this myth. Whoever thought up this whole idea of sex as a means of procreation had an unbelievable imagination and a keen interest in my personal pleasure. Yet the myth was destroyed by more than just sexual pleasure. A whole range of emotions assisted in its destruction. Modern-day thinking was finding that the marriage contract inhibited a good romantic relationship. Hollywood was showing romantic relationships everywhere except within marriage. In fact, it seemed that the marriage contract would be the kiss of death to a good romance. After all, where is the love if you are obliged by a contract to stay? Where is the passion if you remain with a partner because the monetary cost of leaving is too high? The marriage obligation seemed to stifle love.

Lucky for us, things aren't always as they seem. Obviously we aren't nearly as well-informed on these matters as all those Hollywood writers and contributors of intellectual articles to *Playboy*. But we found just the opposite to be the case. We found that the marriage commitment was the highest expression of love.

Modern love seems to need the freedom to leave, otherwise it was confining and restricting. The freedom to leave absolutely precluded security of any sort. It means that separation is an option that could be employed on any problem— emotional, financial, sexual, anything. I wondered how I would feel about Nancy if she insisted that she keep open her option to leave me? What if she said, "Mark, I just can't love you unless you give me freedom to stop loving you and start loving someone else." I compared that to the marriage commitment: "Mark, I love you so much that there is nothing, absolutely nothing that will ever be able to separate us. I seal my love with this vow: I will never, for any reason, leave you." The comparison made me laugh. It's a small wonder there is so much insecurity in these modern, enlightened relationships. What we had was a statement of real love. It was out of the power of that committed love that we found the deepest emotional security.

It was an ironic twist of events. I had for years held in highest esteem, almost worshiped, the pursuit of education, knowledge, wisdom, modern thought, the intelligentsia. All that notwithstanding, Nancy and I, because of our upbringing, followed some old-fashioned, puritanical, antiquated, obsolete, scriptural rules. Now we found ourselves indescribably happier for having done so.

For a number of years I had been exploding a variety of myths that plagued me from my earliest childhood—God and Santa Claus are figments of human imagination; miracles like the resurrection are a joke to any scientific mind—that sort of thing. These were academic questions that sent me constantly toward the library. But this current myth, the myth that Christianity is no fun, was in some ways the most interesting of all. It takes a myriad of forms: Church is for women and children, God is for sissies, Church is a bore, Christians are bores, sex between husband and wife is a bore, God is a bore, good sex is reserved for the wicked, if we're having too much fun we must be doing something wrong, and so on. The exposure of myths takes much study and often great emotional strain. I only wish every myth could be exploded as neatly as the last one, which was accomplished in an ecstatic encounter that would get even better over the years. For me, this was the most important myth of all to explode. It was, after all, truly where the theory of religion met the real world. There is no question that I was always curious about whether the claims of Christianity were true, but even more important, once having determined them to be true, was the issue of whether they were really useful. As a friend once so nicely put it to me, "Just because it's all true doesn't mean it's necessarily for me." In my years of academic study, I had learned countless theories that were doubtless true. But I was hard pressed to find anyone who cared about them one way or the other. Useless truth is in the end just that—useless.

But I was experiencing real usefulness, finding myself happily experiencing more pure physical pleasure than I ever anticipated getting by breaking the rules. This was indeed a mysterious relationship I had developed with the Almighty. Was he playing some sort of game with me? With one hand, he forced me to give up my craving for the shapelier sex; with the other hand, he handed out pleasure.

This is a strange faith. I couldn't help wondering how many more of my desires might be fulfilled by simply giving them up.

That settles it, I thought, from this moment I'm taking the abject vow of poverty. Would it be too presumptive now to just take a peek up toward the sky to see if there was any cash falling?

Anyway, it was a very good year. I graduated from college in the spring, seven years after my high school graduation, got married the next day, and began to live happily ever after. If it took material things to make one happy then we were the most miserable people in the world. We lived in a $65-a-month house that was, even at that price, no real bargain. It consisted of four rooms: kitchen, living room, bedroom, and bathroom with no interior doors. It was infested with rats who could not be persuaded to live elsewhere, and I still defy any human being to drink the water and remain healthy. It would, in later years, be known as our scenic cottage by the river; the Chicago sanitary canal, that is. Nancy developed a variety of other names for the place. After a year of engaging in theological bickering in order to get the woman of my dreams, I was the happiest man in the world and rats, foul water, and sanitary canals were not going to affect me any.

Three months later, my new bride and I settled into a humble one-bedroom apartment on the north side of Chicago where we could be closer to our schools. My vow of abject poverty was paying off in a big way. The price of gasoline doubled that year, leaving precious little money left for tuition, books, and food. Fortunately, we had a good size stack of wedding presents still in their boxes, which we could return whenever we had a short-fall of cash.

"We need thirty dollars, dear. Which one of these presents do you think we ought to return this month?" I would ask the bride.

"That nice set of towels in the box on the top," she called back from the kitchen. "I sure hoped we wouldn't have to return those. Remember who gave us those?"

"Yeah, what a shame." That's about the way it went that year. We started the year poor and ended it destitute.

CHAPTER 6

Hypocrisy

I woke up to the sound of the bell clanging in the yard. It was dark. "Hey, you awake in there?" It was James calling from the kitchen. "That's probably our dinner guests."

"Yeah, I'm awake," I called back. I sat up, rubbed my eyes, and stretched. The plants around me and the sound of that bell reminded me where I was. My napping pattern made me feel as if I had perpetual jet-lag. "Well, are we going to let those people in or not?" I asked, still half asleep and half joking.

"James is out there letting them in," Joanna answered from the kitchen, where she busily tried to put some sort of meal together. "I have no idea who these people are. Do you? Sometimes I'm glad James is the only one who knows this language. He can do all the talking."

"Joanna," I said slumped over the dining room table. "This guy's got a master's degree and is fluent in a lot of languages, including yours."

"Well, why don't you see if you can wake up, sit there, and behave yourself. And keep the conversation going." She was half joking, too—at least I was pretty sure she was.

James brought the guests into the house and introduced them. The man was dressed in Western-style clothes, his wife in very modern Afghan attire (no veil), and his three-year-old was wearing a fancy child's outfit. A man of his education is extremely rare in this part of the country and would be a threat to any political entity that wanted control. After dinner, James and I agreed to give them a ride back to his home.

When we got into our vehicle and out of earshot of anyone who could have overheard us, he asked me if there would be a missionary coming who would replace my father. This question took me by surprise, because there are not now nor have there ever been missionaries in Afghanistan.

"My father was not a missionary," I said to him, "and he'll be replaced by an engineer, not a missionary. It seems most strange for you to be making this kind of inquiry."

"Your father has been teaching me from the Bible," he told us.

"Not unless you asked him to," I replied. It was strictly forbidden for any foreigner in Afghanistan to do anything to "Christianize" an Afghan. He told me how, as a student of Western civilization, he had read about the Reformation and the arguments put forward by Erasmus and Luther on the issue of justification by faith in Jesus Christ—not by the Church's system of works.

"When I read it," he said, "I knew that this was the true way. Doing good works is one of the main tenets of Islam; without good works a person could never get to heaven. But anyone who has really tried to be good knows himself well enough to know he could never be good enough. So I became a believer in Jesus Christ. And I asked your father to help me understand more about it."

I had to admit, this was a new one on me. I had never before heard of anyone being converted to Christianity by reading a history textbook. Just wait till the publishers hear about this, I thought, while our Travelall bounced through the narrow side streets of Herat. I could just see the headlines: MUSLIM READS HISTORY BOOK—CONVERTS—DIPLOMATIC SCANDAL BREWS. This could make a textbook writer's head roll.

Once again I found myself surprised. The remote carpenter

126

from Galilee had written his signature so powerfully across history that I found a Muslim in the farthest corner of the globe who came to the same conclusion about him as I had. It had taken me years of study to become convinced that the carpenter was God. Meanwhile, this man, raised in a Muslim home, saw it after one chapter in a Western Civ textbook.

On reflection, I wondered why I should be so surprised. Isn't this what anyone might expect to find if the itinerant preacher from Nazareth was as he claimed to be, the creator of the universe? "The engineer who finishes the construction on the hospital may know something about the Bible," I told him, "but exactly how much I can't say."

"He won't know as much as your father."

"That's probably true," I said. "Do you have a Bible?"

"Yes," he told us. "I read it all the time."

"You can learn God's way by reading the scriptures, quite apart from having someone teach you formally," I told him as we arrived at his home.

By the time James and I got back to the compound, the electricity had been turned off and Joanna was already asleep. James konked out as well, but I'd had a long nap and was wide awake. I sat in the simple surroundings of the *audadown* reading late into the night by the light of a candle. I read with fascination a collection of stories people told about their near-death experiences and subsequent impressions of immortality.

The narratives confirmed for me the intuition of immortality and encouraged me that I would see my father again. No doubt Dad sat right in this very spot in this *audadown*. Now he was having a grand time getting reaquainted with Danny. Danny would be teasing him about getting there first. Dad always predicted he would. My thoughts also drifted back again to my two lost friends, Jimmy and Jo Lynn.

But I couldn't forget our dinner guest: an Afghan man stuck off in a faraway corner of the globe. He had concluded that Christianity was true, and it was hardly a piece of guesswork, so often confused for a leap of faith. Having grown up with it, why had it taken me so long to see the light? What happened to me was more like an event, an encounter with myself. It bore some resemblance to the story of our dinner guest, but maybe a little more like Sartre's encounter. It certainly wasn't anything substantially out of the ordinary. Nothing like the gloriously transforming religious experiences the saints had.

But then I wasn't a saint. Neither was Sartre for that matter.

Almost a decade earlier I was deeply engrossed in philosophy and Biblical studies—not with a call to preach, but with a mind still full of questions needing answers. I worked the midnight shift at the Cook County House of Correction. Each morning at 8:00 A.M. when I got off duty, I headed to campus to study philosophy of religion. And I got answers all right. I got answers to questions I never knew existed. But what I really needed was an encounter. It happened during that period when I lived over the grocery store, next to the historic Biograph.

I stood one day in the check-out line, purchasing a few of the simple meat pies and potatoes that were my regular diet. The store was tiny, about three aisles, and not very clean; there were just enough people milling around to keep the cockroaches from coming out of hiding—sometimes. I wiped a layer of dust off the carton of cheap margarine I held while waiting for an overweight, poorly dressed woman to pay for her groceries. She was surrounded by dirty, unruly children who begged and whined for the candy and gum that is always strategically located at check-out counters. She tried to ignore them but was unsuccessful. I felt sorry for her as she told them to shut up and wondered what sort of image she might have of herself. What contribution could this sloppy woman with her undisciplined children be making to society? I felt depressed for her, but the overwhelming attitude I had was one of thankfulness that I was not her.

While I would not doubt for a moment that an attitude of superiority is wrong, I must admit that the feeling actually gave me a little pleasure. I wondered, just for a second, how much energy had I, for my whole life, exerted toward the goal of thinking myself better than the next person. In actual fact, I thought, it would give me immeasurable pain to think that I could be considered on the same level of these folks around me, not to mention lower.

I stood there thinking about my small town high school days. High school society was a classic example of a pecking order: who was most popular this week, who was going with whom, who was down and out, who was dirty and disrespectful, who was a nerd and just didn't fit in. It was easy for me to see those caste struggles appearing around me because I had seen them on a macro scale all around the world—castes based on money, power, sexual attractiveness, or any other standard available.

No one ever had the courage to put it into words, but we all knew how the pecking order worked. My classic encounter with it flashed again before my eyes—an incident on the eighth-grade gym floor.

The eighth grade lined up to practice the graduation walk using an imaginary aisle formed on Mr. Ketchum's shiny new gym floor—in stockinged feet of course. A buzz of excitement and anticipation filled the gym. It was a big time for all of us, the culmination of eight years of schoolwork and entrance to a new era in our lives: high school. They lined us up in two lines, a boys' line and a girls' line, and assigned each of us a partner to walk the graduation aisle. My partner was a girl named Sally who was to us a social outcast, a genuine misfit. What she was really like, no one was actually interested enough to discover. I didn't know exactly where she lived, but I supposed it to be in those dilapidated houseboats along the slew that ran through the center of town. It was obvious that her parents were unable to buy her the kind of clothes necessary for acceptance by a middle-class student body.

For some reason, a last-minute change was made in the order of seating and aisle-walking partners. A friend of mine, in a jovial mood, as we all were that day, came clowning up to me and said, "Boy, you sure are lucky they changed this thing around. Otherwise you would have had to walk the aisle and sit the whole graduation alongside that ugly ol'—" He was stopped when he realized our conversation was being over-heard by its victim, standing only a few feet away. "Oh gees," he whispered, "there she is." And he was off to continue his merrymaking elsewhere as I glanced her way only to have our eyes meet.

Just for a moment, less than a moment, a quick fraction of a second, then I looked away. We're only children, I thought. While these sorts of things may be commonplace, there was certainly no doubt that I knew the difference between right and wrong in this situation. I had spent four long years rubbing shoulders with people who could make this girl look wealthy by comparison. I didn't need to be a scholar in human iniquities to recognize the obvious. My life was a workshop in the fundamental value of every human being. It was intu-itively obvious to me that a person had value that existed in a dimension into which the yardstick of the dollar could not reach, much less measure. Yet in that instant when our eyes met I saw a person who was measured by it anyway and knew it. I saw personal injuries that went far deeper than what any amount of money could heal. I saw desperate eyes filled with fear; her personal value in question. She questioned it only because we questioned it. Boldly, shamelessly, cruelly, we questioned it.

Is this normal, innocent childhood behavior? I asked my-self. I suppose it is, but no less contemptible.

Well, go on over and say something to her then, I answered myself.

Oh sure, guy! Like what?

A nice word of any sort at this point would be invaluable, I said, continuing my conversation with myself.

130

Who made you the protector of everyone's feelings, I answered. You don't know what to say anyway.

It wouldn't even require a "nice" word. A simple "Hi, how are ya?" couldn't be too outrageous. It might be the kindest piece of meaningless small talk ever uttered.

Thusly, I engaged myself in a struggle. Would I go and give even one little kind word? That would be threatening. Risky. It would be so much easier just to ignore the situation, and let time make it go away. All these thoughts occurred in the two seconds following my encounter with her eyes.

I did nothing that day to heal the incredible offense. About one thing I was certainly wrong: Time did not make it go away. I remembered it forever. And if I remembered, how much more would she?

It wasn't my fault, though. I had made a conscious effort to avoid the hypocritical games that my peers played with each other. It was always so much easier just to go along, not make waves, just let status quo sort of run its course. There may have been a few victims along the way to be sure, but no one really noticed.

In point of fact, as I reflected back while waiting for this tacky woman of little apparent worth to get her groceries stacked up with her cigarettes and beer, I had little doubt that my refusal to join in the pecking order gave me a sense of accomplishment of which I was proud. I never verbalized it, but no doubt I was a little thankful that I was better than my peers for refusing to stoop to such a level.

Everyone knew that the most loathsome trait a person could possess was to think himself in some way better than others. We even had a name for it: We called it "stuck-up." It was the dirtiest label you could pin on a person. There was nothing worse. What an irony, I thought, for people who operate on a pecking order system to condemn one another for being stuck-up. The goal in life is to be ahead of the next guy, but just let anyone catch you thinking that you are, and you'll be labeled stuck-up, which puts you on the bottom of the heap.

Thinking of myself at the bottom of a heap that included these people around me was simply unbearable. Was it evil to consider myself just slightly better than these folks?

And what about my hometown friends? After all my efforts to avoid the pecking order mentality, did I consider myself better than they? I sure hope *they* didn't think so. But their perception of me was not what scared me right now. It was that intimate critter inside myself that had me disturbed. To avoid being too personal, I asked myself about him:

Does he in reality consider himself better than other people?

The answer was self-evident, startling. It wasn't just that they engaged in the woeful art of dancing, they would be by now participating in all the evils to which it led: pregnancies, drunkenness, debauchery, and the like. Good night, if I couldn't be better than they, I was in trouble.

It was as if God himself was saying, "You are guilty of the very thing that even the 'unregenerate' dancing 'sinners' know by simple human intuition to be evil." I certainly couldn't stand anyone who thought himself better than me. Yet here I was, guilty of the very thing I despised in them; thinking myself superior, which made me the lowest of people. I was in a pecking order in which the first rule was that you had to go to the bottom every time you tried to pass someone.

My poor mother; for years she had painstakingly cultivated for me a strong self-image that was now taking a turn for the worse—a crash. While my friend had rudely snubbed a low-class girl in eighth grade, I had, while knowing it was wrong to snub her, not only thought of myself as better than she, but also as better than my friend for having known it was wrong.

Hypocrisy had never escaped my watchful eye. I'd seen it everywhere, even in my little hometown with its simple value system. And I knew that the hypocrite was himself the last to notice it. Finally the light was beginning to dawn. I wondered if there could be a person as proud as myself.

I was ripped apart by this dilemma. I purported to be a follower of God himself. That *had* to make me morally superior to my eighth-grade sweetheart, who for all her admirable qualities was concerned with more temporal matters.

How many people, I wondered, considered me to be holier than thou? If I was going to be a child of God, and I could think of no more moral goal in life, then my job would require me to be holier than they. I should thank God that I was holier than they and proceed to figure out a way to avoid communicating the attitude to others.

Ha! The hypocrisy of it all clobbered me. I would secretly possess the knowledge that I was superior, while communicating to others an attitude of humility. When they saw my humility, then they could confirm the accuracy of my hidden opinion that I was superior.

Maybe the answer was to strike a compromise and think of myself as equal to everyone. That might work. The fat lady in front of me was now paying cash for her cigarettes and beer after using food stamps on the groceries.

My healthy self-image shuddered. "I'm going to think myself equal to this!" I thought with such conviction that I checked to make sure I hadn't said it out loud. Impossible! Unthinkable!

I took my few groceries and shuffled the five steps from the grocery store to the door leading up to my apartment. It was obvious that I would not philosophize my way out of this predicament. A glance to my right and I saw the large telephone pole where John Dillinger died. I wondered if he ever threw dirt clods at his next-door neighbor. Plodding my way up the stairs into my apartment, I dropped my stuff on the already cluttered kitchen table and sat down in the corner of my room to cry.

How many people would put it in the simple terms of my hometown crowd and say that I was a stuck-up jerk? I wasn't, of course; I was just shy.

The peers of my small town whose moral judgments I had zero respect for turned out to be 100 percent right. The attitude of being stuck-up was the most despicable a human being could possess. The way I thought about that woman in the grocery store downstairs was nothing short of absolutely wicked. I, Mr. Cool, Mr. Holier-than-thou, Mr. Talented, was flat out wicked. The shock of it all inundated me. The more I analyzed it, the worse it became.

It wasn't just the realization that I genuinely thought myself better than others, but it was the fact that my goal in life was to improve myself to the point that it would in fact be true; so I could with honesty face myself in the mirror and say that I was good, better, maybe even best—all relative terms that can only be defined in relation to other people. Even then, some objective measurement must be employed; quantity of money, power, influence, sexual attractiveness. Incongruous as it seemed, my life goal was to become stuck on myself, the very thing everyone agreed to be the worst of qualities.

My memory did a life-scanning review. From the most recent, the lying that I did to my superior officer, to the most ancient, the dirt-clod throwing at the little old lady, all were really nothing more than symptoms of this real matter of pride. Bad as all these memories were, they were merely by-products of the self-centeredness that I was now encountering head on.

What a horrible thing, this memory of mine. It was bringing my whole ambitious life to its knees. All these memories paled by comparison to the realization that I thought myself better than other human beings. I was by now crouched in the corner of my room staring at my crooked waterbed as it sloped away from me. It was as if someone had opened a little door on me and given me a peek inside—a peek at that part of me that I had kept so successfully hidden, hidden even from myself. And I was absolutely horrified at the sight. Could I be seeing myself for the first time as God sees me? There's no way I could continue to live with this character.

I tried to pull myself together and ask myself what the big deal was. Maybe God was trying to get at me the way he had tried to get at Sartre when he felt guilt over concealing his misbehavior. Weren't these things after all minor infractions, a prideful and selfish thought, a cover-up of a mistake? I was truely making something out of nothing.

I'm not Hitler, after all, I reassured myself. And it *was* reassuring, at this low point, to know that I was at least better than someone. But I couldn't convince myself. I knew history too well. Wasn't it Hitler's conviction of his racial superiority that caused him to do what he did? He was just like me except that he had the power to deal with the "undesirables." I was, in fact, a Hitler who was merely out of power.

Come on! I've gone nuts. I'm no Hitler! But even if I were better than Hitler, the issue would not go away. Hitler wasn't the sole source of all the problems in the world. Indeed, there was many a preacher who was himself a source of many a problem, and I knew lots of them. One who rebuked me publicly for going to the movies was himself involved in sexual perversion. I didn't mention it right there in the middle of the conversation. (But if I had, I'm sure his wife would have lost interest in winning the argument about my movie-going.) Technically, he was practicing what he preached because he said that we were all sinners. We just hadn't expected him to prove it personally.

Now I was proving it personally to myself. I lay crouched in the corner shaking my head and knowing that I was not going to get out of this.

Sartre had his encounter with God, now it was my turn. And I wanted to respond the same way. Let God vegetate and die just like Sartre had. It would be easier. Then I could think about people however I wanted.

It was my moment of truth, my moment of decision. That's

why it did make a difference what I would do right now, even in the privacy of my own bedroom. It could make all the difference in the world and I knew it.

I had always seen my faults as minor shortcomings of a basically good guy who needed some rough edges smoothed off. Now I had caught a glimpse of the real Mark Ritchie and discovered that the rough edges were symptoms of a rotten core that needed a total alteration.

Where was all that religious upbringing now that I really needed it, all those slick and easy answers I had learned at Bible school? In that moment, I rejected everything I had ever been taught. I didn't need theology. I didn't need doctrine, legalism, dogma, rules of behavior, guilt trips, or fancy soteriological words ending in t-i-o-n. It all seemed so useless right now. I needed nothing but relief for my weary, guilt-ridden soul.

"Dear God," I said almost out loud through tears of remorse at this sudden self-analysis. "I am truly the lowest of your creatures, the scum of the earth. If I ever had to meet someone like me, I would hate him! I think I am meeting me and I do hate me! I'm sorry! Please help me! What will become of me?" Crouching in the corner of my room, I quivered from the shock that I was such a far, far cry from the person I thought, from the image I had so laboriously, and quite successfully, shown to others. I wondered what percent of my life I had spent trying to convince myself and others that I was something that I'm not. "God, I'm at the bottom. If you don't help me, I'm screwed!"

I breathed a big sigh at having admitted it to myself. Just admitting it helped me to relax. Admitting that I was the problem, I was the scum, I was the lowest, seemed to remove all the conflict. After all, I was giving up my superiority.

But then something strange happened. Describing it is sort of like a dull person trying to communicate a hilarious situation. Finding himself unable to recapture the humor of that moment, he says, "I guess you just had to be there."

That's the way this was. I could never have understood it without having gone through it. In the trauma of this moment I was overwhelmed by a feeling of peace. It was as if someone was saying, "Don't sweat it. It's all right." Almost as if God liked me this way—the dirty, rotten, proud, stuck-up, arrogant person that I was—he actually seemed to want to overlook it. Nothing mysterious or inexplicable happened, like hearing voices. Just a simple, indescribable sense of well-being came over me.

Could this be what it means to come to repentance, I wondered? "Repent"—the word that strikes terror in the heart of any self-respecting person. Was I actually calling myself a sinner? Maybe this is what forgiveness feels like? Could this be what that humble man meant when he said, "God be merciful to me, a sinner"? I remembered that old favorite hymn of my father's:

> *When I survey the wondrous cross,*
> *On which the prince of glory died,*
> *My richest gain I count but loss,*
> *And pour contempt on all my pride.*

Like the words of most hymns, these never made a lot of sense. My dad and this hymn writer must have had an experience similar to this. I certainly had dumped contempt all over my pride.

Is this all God required of me: the massive consumption of humble pie? It all seemed too easy. And I had to admit, my self-image, which crashed to bottom a moment ago, was now existing in a completely new dimension.

It was as if I had sunk so low that when I admitted my awful moral problem to God, I fell right out of the bottom into a completely different world. A world where my view of myself was no longer based on what others thought of me. How could it be? I had just admitted being a total jerk. It was based on the fact that the creator of the universe was willing to overlook my jerkiness and accept me as I was, albeit with a few changes in mind. Instead of impressing myself and others with my all-around coolness, a better idea occurred to me. Why shouldn't I attempt to become the very kind of person that the creator had intended for me to be in the first place? The concept was exhilarating, like being connected in a meaningful way to the universe. It was like starting a new existence, a new lease on life—like being born again. Could this be what they meant by "born again"?

The thought that the Fundamentalists might actually have some cognitive meaning to that hackneyed phrase sent a shock wave to the core of my brain. Nevertheless, I had to admit this was like a new beginning, a fresh start, a new direction, a whole new birth of a new life.

I wondered, could this be what it means to know "Jesus Christ as a personal savior"? After all, I had just been saved from myself. My poor mind had not yet recovered from the first blow when this one dropped its load. I was more interested in enjoying my new peace of mind than in solving Fundamentalist theology. It was as easy as they had always said. Confession is good for the soul, all right, and I did it with bitter tears.

It was puzzling, this matter of God just forgiving and forgetting. I assumed it to be wrapped up in that central symbol of Christianity—the cross. I recalled the words of the sacrament, "This is my body, broken for you." Did it all end right here, in this mind-blowing, liberating experience? Could all that dead, meaningless theology really make me free from my own load of guilt? Jesus had said, "If the Son will make you free, you will be free indeed." And I truly felt free, free indeed.

No wonder I hadn't understood all that strange atonement talk that was so irrelevant. It *was* irrelevant to me because I had never really seen myself. Now I saw, and I needed nothing so much as a moral messiah.

It was all so simple, so easy, maybe too easy; just admitting to being a rogue, consuming some moral humble pie and being free from guilt. I suddenly remembered my parents. Of all the people I had known, they had been the most regular recipients of my less than saintly life-style. It seemed only reasonable, now that I saw myself as I really was, that I should call them and seek their forgiveness. I reflected for a moment on what this might entail. I had never before sought the forgiveness of a Fundamentalist—God's, but not a Fundamentalist's.

Well, maybe I had spoken a little hastily when I said that stuff about how easy all this was. I looked at the phone on the floor not too far from where I sat in the corner of the room. I definitely had spoken in haste all right.

After all, what if everyone who had ever done anything wrong to his parents were to call them up on the phone to apologize. It would heal some family relationships no doubt, but Ma Bell could never handle all that business. The telephone lines would be so overloaded that kids would get hooked up with the wrong set of parents. Those in New York would be telling someone else's parents in Tallahassee how sorry they were for having done things those people's children probably never did, though they might have if they'd had the money. Anyway, there's no chance in the world that kids everywhere would start doing this. The fact that the thought occurred to me caused me to wonder if I could be suffering a mental deterioration. The fact that I was reaching for the phone was even more frightful evidence of it.

Go ahead, big boy. Just grab that phone, call them up, and tell 'em just how sorry you are for having been such a turkey all these years. Go ahead, clown, this is easy, too easy. Come on, you shot your mouth off about a minute ago. I always have been just a little too quick with the tongue. Now it was getting on my nerves.

So this is what it means to stop trying to get ahead of the next guy and start being a child of God himself: I get to call people and grovel at their feet in utter humility. A wimp, I get to become a wimp. I'll never be proud of myself again. I'll never feel good about myself again. I'll never feel better than anyone again.

I picked up the phone. I knew the number. Would I really admit after all these years of disagreement and disrespect that I was the one who was wrong? I couldn't remember the last time I was wrong about anything. I couldn't have been wrong about everything. Certainly they had earned some of the inconsideration and disrespect I had shown. How much, I wondered? Ten percent maybe? Thirty percent? Who knows, maybe even 90 percent. Maybe *they* were really the problem. Actually, I knew that it really didn't matter how much of a problem they had caused, the only way to deal with my guilt was to focus on and ask forgiveness for the problems I had caused. My father must have told me at least a thousand times, "Mark, why are you always so concerned with the other guy? You are only responsible for correcting your own behavior." What a poor communicator he must have been. He spent all those years teaching me that principle and never was able to get me to understand it.

I saw it clearly now. All the rebellion I had felt and shown was no one's problem but my own. I knew full well that the only way to free myself from this guilt was basically to say the same thing to my parents that I had said to God a few moments earlier.

I dialed the area code. Certainly I had a screw loosening somewhere. I had been taught by my parents that Christianity was a matter of accepting certain facts about God. Knowing God was not something that involved any good work, surely not any hard work. I had just experienced great relief from personal guilt by confessing my shortcomings to God. It was ego-shattering to be sure, but no work at all, easy in fact, just like I had always been told. But this was something else again.

If you're going to call someone, I said to myself, and tell them you're a rogue, after a lifetime of trying to prove otherwise, you should expect the struggle of your life. And I was in it. The choice was quite simple. I could continue to live with my guilt, or I could continue dialing the phone and do what I knew to be the right thing. I clenched my teeth, closed my eyes, forced myself to dial the number while every bone in me scolded my hand for doing it—and prayed that no one would be home. God can be very picky sometimes about the prayers he hears.

Dad answered and I asked if Mom were around because I wanted to talk with both of them. She came to the phone. I actually got a few words out before I started bawling. No doubt they thought I was on something. Through my tears I told them how sorry I was for the kind of person I had been. Now they were positive I was on something. My dad even apologized to me for his own failures as a father. This was a surprise. Never before has a Fundamentalist sought my forgiveness. Confession and forgiveness are concepts that apply to the "unsaved," not to the elect. Yet here was a righteous man seeking forgiveness from, of all people, his own son. Could I have unfairly stereotyped these people? Maybe they're just plain ol' sinners like all the rest of us and I was just prejudiced against them because of their failure to admit it. Not that they have any shortage of company on that score.

The talk was short and we hung up. If I could only bottle my present state of emotions, I could make a fortune selling it. God knows I could use the money. There are people out there paying big bucks for a lot less peace of mind than I was experiencing right now in this slum apartment in the corner of my crooked room with a sloping floor. Whoever said "confession is good for the soul" must have gone through something like this. What a liberating experience. If everyone could feel it, the spirit of love and brotherhood, felt only for a fleeting moment at Christmas, might be the order of the day all year long.

Aw, Mark, there you go again with that arrogant stuff, I thought, supposing the world would be better if everyone were like you. You're a totally unrealistic dreamer anyway. What a fool! People are never going to do anything this dumb.

But Dad's words kept coming back to me. "Of course, Mark," he usually started out with the words "of course." "Of course, Mark, not all people will strive for peace with God and their fellow man. But that doesn't mean you shouldn't." Now really, no one ever needed to tell me the first part. Anyone knows that there is no priority placed on God and fellow man. It was the second part that struck me with a strange force. "But that doesn't mean you shouldn't." It was a strange force because I had heard it so many times, I had stopped hearing it. But I heard it now and it seemed like the most profound thing I had ever remembered. If something were in my best interest, it would seem only reasonable to follow it, regardless of what course others may take. Elementary. That means that the idyllic world I just dreamt about could at least be experienced by me. That phone call to my parents was performing sheer magic on my emotional state. In a short moment I had come from the lowest, guilt-ridden depression to the height of spiritual freedom. If this is what the carpenter meant when he said, "If the Son shall make you free, you shall be free indeed," then it is no wonder so many have followed him. It must have been this inner peace he had in mind when he said, "Come unto me all ye who labor and are heavy laden, and I will give you rest." The trite phrases were taking on new meaning.

He claimed to be the bread of life. He claimed to be able to hand out living water that could keep people from ever being thirsty. This poor, hungry, thirsty soul of mine sure felt like it had been filled with something quite beyond explanation. The Jewish prophet had said, "Taste and see that the Lord is good." No doubt this was the origin of his famous line, "Man does not live by bread alone, but by every word that comes from the mouth of God." I had tasted. I had seen. And he sure knew how to deliver on a promise. I felt so liberated from my guilt that I could truly say that I felt united with the creator of the universe.

Crazy as it seems, it was a bit reminiscent of the time when as a three-year-old I had prayed and asked Jesus to "come into my heart." Somehow this seemed to be an adult affirmation of that childhood prayer. Anyway, it sure made me feel like a helpless little kid again. And still more phrases were taking on new meaning—the faith of a little child, our "Father" who art in heaven. Could all these concepts, which never seemed to escape beyond Sunday morning, have meaning in the real world? So many people had claimed that they were real. Now, indeed, they had done something for me, and my relationship with Mom and Dad.

There were other relationships that needed some fence-mending. That's how the whole thing got started all over again with Nancy. Apologizing to a former girlfriend is real serious humble pie consumption.

CHAPTER 7

Risk

I picked up the book from my lap and looked at the story my recollections had interrupted. My candle was half gone and only bright enough to throw shadows through the plants that surrounded me. I read another few paragraphs but couldn't stop thinking about all the events that had landed me in this special setting. So while the candle flickered, my mind kept wandering back to those early years with Nancy.

After we married, I entered seminary. Unlike my classmates, I had no "call" to the ministry, just a personal call to know that what I thought I believed had real validity. I was enrolled in an M-Div. program with an emphasis in philosophy of religion.

Each morning at 8:00, I handed the keys to the day-shift guard and headed to classes. By 1975, almost ten years after graduating from high school, I had finally put some things together. My studies in atheism coupled with research on the resurrection and other topics of interest gave me confidence at last in the academic credibility of the faith. An exquisite marriage was alone enough to demonstrate that my faith was working toward my best interest.

Only one negative: My vow of poverty hadn't made me any money and was about to be renounced.

Dad and Mom, now with an empty nest, returned to Afghanistan to construct an eye hospital. They boarded a city bus and were approached by a man who said, "I know you. You're the father of Danny, the neighbor boy we used to trade pigeons with." Dad told him the rest of Danny's story.

My brother Joe returned to Chicago from Los Angeles, where he was working for a silver dealer. He had come to do a preliminary investigation into opportunities in the silver markets of Chicago and New York. Joe called when he got to town, "How about visiting the Chicago Board of Trade with me? I want to speak to a few officials about the possibilities of doing business there." He was also interested in knowing if I had a suit he could borrow.

Like most people, we knew a little about commodities trading. If we had only known how little. We even knew where the board of trade was located.

Joe and I had a mutual friend who had done some investing in commodities. A phone call from a legitimate brokerage firm had encouraged him to invest in silver, and within a few months he had doubled his $2,000 investment. It was the most sensational thing any of us had ever seen, outperforming by far anything he had done in the stock market. The guy was soon making a bundle and I was the daily recipient of his good news. Then the time came when he had owned too much silver and the market began to drop, eventually going further than even the most careful of experts could have predicted. All his profits and all his original money were wiped out. In addition, he wound up owing money.

When Joe arrived, I loaned him my best suit, a pinstripe I had purchased for $60 from a clothing wholesaler in Portland, and I wore the bad one it had replaced. (He agreed to do the talking so I was glad to let him have the "good" suit.)

We arrived at the Chicago Board of Trade (CBT) and inquired in the president's office on behalf of Joe's Los Angeles–based firm about memberships and trading privileges. Upon seeing us come through the door, one of the exchange officials allowed a slight smirk to sneak its way onto his face. "You boys," he said, "have got to be in the wrong place."

How does one respond to a comment like that? I could only be thankful for the bargain I had struck that Joe would do the talking. He asked about the requirements for membership and the advantages of becoming a "clearing" member. Any membership required significant wealth, but a clearing member was required to financially guarantee all the trades of every member associated with it and thus demanded a very large amount of capital.

"Do you have any idea what it costs to be a clearing member?" he asked. His face told us he knew the answer very well. At least he didn't refer to us as boys this time, though the sustained smirk made it evident that he might have liked to.

"We were hoping you could answer that for us," Joe said, wondering if there would be a gracious way out of this conversation. Maybe we should have agreed with him up front, we were in the wrong place.

Making our way to the visitors gallery, which overlooks the trading floor, we were not really overwhelmed with the hectic nature of the activity. "It doesn't look all that crazy to me," I said. We had anticipated wild pandemonium. As we were chatting about the scene, we heard a loud heavy clang and the trading floor suddenly erupted into an earsplitting roar. The pit immediately in front of the gallery was packed with people who created waves of bodies moving up one side of the pit, back down across the center, and up the other side; everyone had both hands in the air, cards in one hand, pencils in the other, attempting to trade, record trades, yell at the top of their lungs, and keep their balance all at the same time.

We were stunned, utterly spellbound. Is it possible that there could be such a place as this in the real world? Was this a live Monopoly game played with real money? From that point there was no doubt in our minds that this was the place for us.

It wasn't long before his firm moved Joe to Chicago to start an operation arbitraging silver between New York and Chicago. I continued working the night shift as a jail guard at the county house of correction and attending seminary during the day. The schedule was beginning to work a hardship on my relationship with Nancy, so when Joe's arbitrage team needed a phone clerk, I jumped at the opportunity before I fully realized what I was getting into.

Getting acclimated to commodities involved spending hours with a variety of interesting people. Joe and I sat with a talented silver broker over coffee listening to his war stories. "I must have been yelling for half an hour," he told us, "and no one would come down to my price."

"You mean that if their price is too high," I responded, "you'll stand there all day trying to jew 'em down?" Like many of the people in the financial industry, he was Jewish. I realized what I said as I said it. "I'm sorry," I said in amazement at myself while he laughed it off. He seemed to be willing to see me as a person with a bad habit instead of as an anti-Semite.

"It's no problem," he assured me. "I'm used to it." He appeared sincere. It wasn't his problem. But it certainly was mine. So now what do I say? Maybe, "I'm not a racist, I'm just thoughtless, inconsiderate, and rude." I told him again that I was sorry, but I was a lot sorrier than I was able to say. I remembered my mother's words.

I stood with a phone in my ear and flashed quotes from the New York silver market to Joe in the silver pit at the board of trade. When the New York market ticked up half a cent, he would try to buy Chicago silver and flash me the sign to sell New York. I would tell the New York phone clerk who would pass the message into the pit to sell. Naturally, all the other arbitragers were doing the same thing at the same time so it turned into a race.

We soon discovered that commodities trading is unlike Monopoly in a few key ways. First, there is much more money involved and it changes hands faster than in any Monopoly game we had ever played. Second, there is a stunning lack of sportsmanship in the way this game is played. Indeed, it could hardly be called a game at all. Not that it wasn't fun at times. No question about it, when the money is flowing your way, there is a sense of sheer delight. What a shame that it has to be a two-way street.

I advanced nicely with the firm and when Joe left on vacation, they gave me the opportunity to trade in his place. That meant that I was given the responsibility to make, buy, and sell decisions using another member, a trusted order-filler who Joe had used before he became a member himself. This is where the real money is in commodities. If one can make, buy, and sell decisions and generate profit, he can be assured a lucrative career in the field. If he can't, the best he can hope for is a good salary.

No sooner was Joe out of town than I discovered that the trusted broker who was filling our orders in the pit had taken for himself certain profitable trades that belonged to my employer. A dispute arose over these trades between me, a lowly phone clerk, and this member of the CBT.

By the next day when I arrived on the trading floor, word had already spread that I had had a problem with my broker the previous day and Dick, an acquaintance, introduced me to a most colorful character. He was a small man who seemed to be showing twice his years on his face; he reminded me of a puppy dog who had been separated for two foodless days from his lifelong owner. He stood quietly listening as I was told all about him. He was down on his luck and desperately needed work. Dick assured me that this person would do a super job for me in the pit as a broker. He took me aside to fill me in on his story.

It seems that this well-worn, tough little man who wouldn't have looked out of place in a skid row mission, had been a successful trader only a short time before. He used to enter a bar shouting, "Drinks for everybody!" That was during the big grain market of '73 when prices were headed in only one direction, giving even the least confident of investors more money than they ever thought existed. This particular broker, a generous though somewhat naive fellow, found himself the lucky victim of the biggest bull market in the history of grain markets. No one in his right mind was short and there seemed to be no end in sight. A 100,000-bushel position in beans would net a speculator $1,000 each time the price increased by one cent. And the price was increasing by dollars. Many of the big names in the business today made their initial fortunes in the '73 grain market. It is hard to find any losers when all you have to do is buy and wait for the market to go up. So when a broker walks into a bar and shouts, "Drinks for everyone" on a day when the market is locked limit-up, it isn't too difficult to determine just what such a broker's position is: He is long and ecstatic. What a great time for the emotions to short circuit the brain, which they *always* do.

The great bull market of '73 was a year no grain trader will forget, ever. The uninitiated always wonders just where all this easy money comes from. How could a place where money grows on trees and can be made without work exist? One can also be assured that this question has occurred to many a farmer. Far too many investors have come into the market without a full understanding of the answer. This is a fatal mistake as anyone except the unusually lucky will attest.

The only sad part about the commodities market is that what goes up also comes down. As one observed, "In a bear market [prices falling], money returns to its rightful owners." And profits made and spent have a way of getting the attention of IRS agents.

As for this former wealthy, well-respected broker, he found himself being introduced to the lowest creature in the industry, a phone clerk. With the drawn, starving look of a beggar, he must have been saying, "If this phone clerk doesn't have mercy on me, I'm history." The IRS was after him and he was on the brink of ruin if he didn't get some type of steady work.

It was my job to monitor New York silver prices and arbitrage the Chicago silver market against it. Arbitrage—the misunderstood backbone of capitalism—simply involves buying something in one market and as quickly as possible (simultaneously if you're lucky) selling it in another. If your selling price is higher than your buying price, you will make money, maybe even a lot of money. If not, you will eventually look for another line of work.

My goal was to buy the New York silver whenever it was cheaper than Chicago silver and as quickly thereafter sell in the higher-priced Chicago market. Naturally, everyone wonders why everyone isn't doing it. It looks like a free-money game. I learned the answer to this question the first day. It seemed as if everyone was was doing it. No sooner would I buy in the cheaper New York market than the Chicago market would drop even lower, forcing me to sell at a lower price in the market that had once been higher.

It was immediately obvious: There would be ample competition in this venture. If the sell was not executed quickly enough, the opportunity would disappear as the competing arbitragers would "pick off" the good sale. The success of the team was therefore highly dependent on the ability of the order-fillers on each end.

It seemed strange to me that a member of the prestigious Chicago Board of Trade could be a smashing success one year and begging for work the next. That was only because I had not yet seen the way in which this industry moves money from one hand to the next. A limit-down move in the market might actually move as much as a half billion dollars from the hands of the buyers into the hands of the sellers.

This particular broker worked his tail off for me for the remainder of the week. It is amazing how the real world can bring a wild speculator back to his senses. Also amazing is how the intrusion of a dollar sign into a person's mind can completely destroy the objectivity of his decision making. This I would soon learn.

I made my first effort in commodities investment in 1975. Nancy and I had received about $3,000—pension money from my years as a correctional officer. At my suggestion, we gave about $500 to assist some of the poor with whom my parents were working. Nancy concluded that she would probably never get any of the nice things she had been waiting for. How does a wife tell her husband that we need a new couch worse than the poor need a meal? I told Nancy that we could invest the remaining $2,500 in commodities and possibly double it.

It was silver spreads (purchase of one silver contract accompanied by simultaneous sale of another), the most conservative way to invest. It is conservative because the investor is not affected by market moves. Since he is long one delivery month and short another, he only makes money as these prices move in respect to each other. We bought December silver and sold February six cents higher. We did not intend to take delivery of the silver in December and hold it until February. That would have cost us six and a half cents per ounce in storage and interest charges, a half-cent loss. We predicted that the December contract would rise in relation to the February contract. Then we could buy the February contract back and sell the December contract at a five-cent differential or less, giving us a nice profit. The beauty of it was that if silver went up, we would make as much money in December as we would lose in February. And vice versa if it went down.

Good conservative investing. Ha! Was that a joke!

Though I hadn't yet seen the money, I pledged it to a broker so he could invest in some silver spreads for me. Twenty-five hundred seemed like a fortune to us when we lived in a $16,000 home in a bad section of Chicago and never had more than $200 in the bank at any one time. Our investment in the silver spread went a couple hundred dollars in our favor right away. Each time the price of December moved one tenth of a cent closer to the February price, I made

$100. It looked like we could make $2,000 to $3,000 in a relatively short period.

Before long, the ups and downs of the market were giving and taking away hundreds of dollars at a time and I was getting accustomed to making and losing money by watching numbers on a board. But on the day that the February contract closed six and a half cents higher than the December contract, $500 against me, leaving only $2,000 of the original $2,500, I began to get a little concerned. (The closing price, called the "settlement," is the number used at the end of each trading day to transfer money either to or from an account.) Still believing that the market would go the other way, however, I held the position. A few days later the spread settled another $500 against me. I had now lost $1,000 of the $2,500 that we desperately needed to pay off large school debts and the hospital bill for our new baby. Not only could I ill afford to lose the $2,500, I should never have even risked the first thousand. It is common for a speculator to fail to recognize how badly he may need the money he has risked until he has lost it. But how was I to know that bit of information, never having speculated before? My concern turned to fear a few days later when the $1,500 I had remaining was reduced to $1,200.

I was now in a real dilemma. There was no way I could possibly get out of the market at this point and say good-bye to $1,300. In any case, I sincerely believed that the position (an investment in the market is called a "market position") was a good one and should not only recover my $1,300 but make me an additional couple thousand. Sure enough, in a few days I had recovered $400 or $500. This should be the beginning of the move in my favor. The next day a major collapse took away $1,000. I had now dropped two thirds of the $2,500 and I had not yet mentioned any of the losses to Nancy.

I was really in a spot. If I let the position continue, there was a remote possibility that I could lose even more money. This possibility could only be avoided by liquidating the position, getting out of the market, walking away while I still had $800. But that would totally wipe out any possibility of recovering the $1,700, which I could hardly do without.

I pulled myself together to try to think rationally about the situation. The silver spreads had never before done what they were doing. It did seem quite unlikely that this trend would continue. So I held on to the position; assuming, hoping, and praying that it would turn around. Over the next week or so it did improve and the market started to move in our favor.

The obvious problem of a speculator is to determine whether these little moves in the marketplace are the beginnings of a long move in that direction or a temporary setback in a move of the opposite direction. The latter turned out to be the case and a few days later I had only $400 or $500 left of the $2,500 that I had originally committed. Fear had now turned to sheer panic. Sleepless nights turned to genuine desperation. "Dear God," I prayed, "I'll get out of this trade if you'll just give me half of my money back." I had no choice at this point. I *had* to hold on to this position. The $500 wasn't enough to pay off our debts much less get any of the things we needed for the baby. So there was nothing left to do but exercise patience, pray, and hope. We were both in school and trying to survive on a $12,000 salary.

What kind of fool would go throw away $2,500 in the crazy commodities market? Over the next few days I did recover about $500 and was now up to $1,000. I needed $1,500 more in order to break even and was beginning to feel so much better that I had forgotten my desperate promise to liquidate if I got half my money back. The bright spot had appeared on the horizon. The next day a dramatic move in the silver market completely wiped out the remaining $1,000. My broker informed me that I had to get out.

"I can't get out now, I have to at least stay in a little longer to try to recover some of my $2,500."

"And if the position goes against you another $100, who is going to pay that?" he asked. Brokers have a real crude way of looking at reality when push comes to shove. I was now out of options. There was no more good money to throw after bad. All I could do now was to try to think of some way to explain to Nancy where all the money had gone.

A few days later, when she spoke about something we needed, I told her that I didn't think it would be possible.

"What about the money that's left from the pension?" she asked.

"I'm afraid it's gone," I told her. She didn't say anything, just looked at me.

"There has to be something left," she said after a while, but she knew it wasn't true so I didn't say anything. "All of it?"

She decided right then and there that she would have to be content with nothing. I could thank my lucky stars that I had married a woman who was not heavily into the need for nice things. Over the next few weeks, the silver spreads recovered to the levels where I had first entered the market and then proceeded to move in the direction we had originally predicted. If I were still in the market, I could have doubled that $2,500. Talk about rubbing salt in a wound. I had been absolutely right and still lost money. It felt like the whole industry had conspired to move the market against me until they had my money and then they moved the market right back to where I knew it would go. What a brutal business! These people must have hearts of stone.

I didn't mention this to Nancy, since we were now deeper in debt than ever. Getting into commodities is one surefire way of making a bad financial picture worse.

The market action that resulted in my loss is what is commonly referred to in the business as a "shake out." The tree gets rattled and all the "weak hands," those who don't really want the commodity, get shaken out. The market is no respecter of persons; widow and wealthy alike will take the hit. It is very common for the market to return after a shake out to its original level and higher. Even though the investor's original prediction was correct, he still lost money. So he counts the money he would have made if only he had the courage to stay in the market. The "would haves," the "could haves," the "if onlys," and the "what ifs" have kept many a loser coming back for more.

The firm hired a number of young geniuses from outside the industry to ensure that we had the most creative talent available, and we expanded with innovative ideas. We believed that significant improvement could be made in some of the traditional methods. I continued to advance and was eventually placed on another exchange, trading a different commodity. This would be my first opportunity to prove that I could make trading decisions profitably.

I made an acquaintance at the CBT, Max, who had just purchased a membership, and together we pioneered this new venture. It was his first day in the pit as a broker and my first day making the decisions. For me it was a throwback to days gone by. I had felt that rush of adrenaline produced by fear when taking the football field, or staring a fastball in the face with two out and runners in scoring position. Hours of training were to be put to use in a moment. When that bell rang, I knew that I would be called upon to make decisions and perform in accordance with the confidence my firm had been encouraged (by me) to place in me.

We walked onto the floor early, thinking that everyone was watching us beginners, waiting for us to buy so they could push the market down in our faces. The anticipation grew increasingly intense until, at the peak of panic, the bell rang. In a matter of moments we were madly buying, selling, taking risk, and laying off risk as fast as we could think, count, and scream back and forth at each other. At one point the action got so heavy that Max was physically hurled, along with a few other bodies, off the top step of the pit. They all landed about ten feet away in a pile of phones, phone clerks, and other bodies.

By the time the roar had calmed, it was discovered that it

had been the heaviest volume traded in the history of this commodity. We had entered the market for the first time in the wildest trading day and made over $5,000. We were ecstatic.

Max and I traded there for about two months during which we met a whole new group of traders and began taking some lumps and learning the lessons that were indispensable to profitable trading. Then, when trading volume decreased, the company purchased a board of trade membership for me to actually trade in the pit for their account. This was the big break I had been waiting for.

I stepped into the pit for the first time feeling like a rookie his first time at bat in the majors. Every trader in the pit was independently wealthy; I was a nobody from a small town in nowheresville. Would I be accepted in this subculture? Or would they all have the opinion expressed to Joe by one trader, "You don't even belong down here." I would soon discover, to my pleasant surprise, that these people were amazingly similar to everyone else I had known. There were plenty of snobs, but no more than I had encountered else-where. There were status seekers and just plain old jerks; the exchange didn't have a corner on them as I expected it might. And, of course, there were also straight-out thieves, about the same number one might expect in any profession. But there were a fair number of people who were determined to accept a person and treat him with kindness regardless of his back-ground, social position, financial statement, or ability to trade with the big hitters.

I soon discovered that this was an industry especially suited to my personality. It was fast-paced, risky, with unlimited potential for success, and I took to it like a pig to mud. It was quite possible to make a good profit without being dishonest or lucky, though either of those factors could substantially enhance profits.

I once overheard two brokers discussing whether or not it

would be right to do a certain thing. When one broker mentioned a way that it could be done so that no one could ever uncover it, they both agreed that it would be all right.

They're not discussing what's right, I thought. They're talking about what they can get away with. It's not an issue of ethics in the marketplace, it's a simple fear of getting caught.

Of course, dishonesty pays very well, even if, in the long run, one always reaps what one sows. What, after all, would it profit a man to gain the whole world and lose his soul? I'd never known anyone to get the whole world out of his soul.

It was my third day in the pit when I discovered that we had by mistake purchased ten contracts more than we had sold. By the time we discovered the problem and sold the ten contracts, the market had rallied five cents, a $2,500 profit for making a mistake.

A veteran broker initiated me to the world of trading with an old but wise saying. "You can make a lot more money being lucky than being smart," he told me. I would think on this one for years to come.

One Friday, two months after I began trading in the pit, my boss, a brilliant new acquisition to the company, told me to give him a call over the weekend. I was unable to reach him until late Sunday night. "We've decided that your services are sort of no longer needed," he told me. "We have to terminate you as of last Friday. Would you come in tomorrow and sign your membership over to me?" No reason given.

As many good things have a way of coming to an end, so did this. One might suppose that the firm needed to make room for some of the additional talent that was being brought on board to increase profitability. That required the cutting of the fat—namely, me.

Nancy and I were both stunned. Nothing like this had ever happened to us. We'd had hard times, but never this.

The unemployment line—an experience that everyone ought to have to enjoy just once. What a dehumanizing place! Everyone in line sure did look like they belonged there. I found myself checking to see if I looked as bad as everyone else did. One day a disturbance broke out in the line and the police were called to restore order. I was almost proud of the guy making the disturbance. He was the only one of us with the courage to express the way he really felt. If he had just called out, "Anyone want to start a riot?" the cops would have had to get help from the next precinct.

Around this time a letter arrived from Afghanistan. It was Dad writing, "We have heard you lost your job and are happy for you and Nancy because we know this is the will of God for you." I read the line to Nancy and we laughed. We weren't sure why.

I took a job with a brokerage firm and was soon learning about a whole new side of the industry. Along with other new recruits, we attended a training session where they surrounded us with the brilliant success stories of the industry. Enviously, we listened to their directions on how to be successful. The key was in the way one dealt with the client. Being more experienced in commodities than any of the initiates, it fell to me to ask some of the more difficult questions that a client would need to know. After a few questions into the firm's track record on behalf of its clients, I was told in front of the group that I could "either move the product, or f--- off." For some reason I found the options a bit limiting and my fellow initiates decided not to ask a lot of questions. We were there to make money for the firm and keep our mouths shut about the client.

The rude treatment brought back a bunch of memories and misgivings I had about the industry, and I reflected on them while we were lectured on how to deal with clients. I wondered if this really was a zero-sum game (the same amount of money that is brought to the market is also taken out and no productivity is achieved). Maybe that's why we need clients, to keep the money coming into the market so there will be enough to keep us all employed. That would explain why we should not be concerned with the client's profit. I began recalling some of the horror stories of the market. I had personally known some of the victims. Now I was learning how they had been dealt with.

As I sat and listened to one experienced adviser after another tells us how to sell the company's services to the inexperienced investor, I began to question why the general public should be involved in commodities at all. I suppose I could be a glutton for punishment and ask what I should say if the prospective client tells me that only the rich make money in commodities. On the other hand, why bother, since I know what they would say. "How do you think they got rich?" In actual fact, if the small investor ever communicated with the big investor, he would discover that the wealthy person is just as vulnerable in the market and in some cases much more so. (The skeptic may verify this with famed Texas oil baron Bunker Hunt and family.)

I got the feeling that I was being trained as a socially sanctioned bookie, giving the public a legitimate avenue to invest (or gamble, depending on your perspective) in something of which they are totally ignorant. I might as well become a blackjack dealer. It would probably be more fun and a lot less risky for my clientele. But I wasn't about to ask any more questions and again be told what I could do.

So for me it was back to the unemployment line.

While I was job hunting, Nancy found work as a waitress at Tonelli's in Northbrook. I looked for work during the day and took care of Dani in the evening while Nancy kept us afloat. Each night she would bring home a pizza, courtesy of the restaurant, and we would enjoy dinner together at midnight. It was the same one-meal-a-day schedule that I had kept that summer in Portland. Saying grace for a pizza when we were really hungry reminded me of the grace I said for the potato I found in the bottom of my fridge years earlier.

I finally located a job doing night duty as a janitor at a nearby grade school. It wouldn't pay much but might allow me to get back into school part-time and finish my ministerial degree. The day before I was to start, the school district called saying that the head office had reviewed my file and decided that I was overqualified. How could they expect a person almost through graduate school, who came from a high-paying job in commodities, to be a stable, long-term janitor? They feared I would find something better and leave. They were sorry and all that, but what could they do?

Unemployed and unemployable, I decided to stop telling interviewers about my previous job.

I was finally able to put a loan together, bought an eighteen-wheeler, and started doing some trucking. It was soon obvious that one needs to be an expert in the trucking business *before* making a purchase. It's difficult to make truck payments when you're broken down on some back highway in Pennsylvania. Pennsylvania is beautiful in the fall, but one needs to be able to move around to enjoy it.

I had lots of time to call home while waiting for my truck to be repaired. Nancy was trying to find us another place to live since we could no longer afford the rent. On one call she told me of a place she had found that was half the rental of our present place.

"Nance, we can't possibly afford that. We'll never get out of debt. We need a place where we can live free." I was speaking out of frustration after the twelve hours I had just put in working on the truck.

"How do you expect me to find that?"

"I don't know? Pray for a miracle." Talking to me when I was on the road was hardly a source of encouragement to her.

During one seven-day period, I had a different breakdown every day. And Pennsylvania wasn't the only place. My truck ran well enough to get me broken down in a whole variety of states.

I left New Jersey heading to Utah with a load of wire and stopped at home for a brief visit on the way.

"What is this?" I asked at my first home-cooked meal in a week.

"It's soybeans. Try 'em. You won't believe how much nutrition there is in this fifty-five-cent bag." She held up a little bag of what looked like dried brown peas. After trading them in the pit, I suppose it was time to take a closer look. "It looks like we might be able to eat for a week off this one bag." What could I say to economy like that. She began fixing them in as many different ways as possible. The nutrients were excellent, if only they could be swallowed and kept that way. Some of her creations were really quite edible, even if they did grow old rather quickly. She found she could make almost anything out of them, even nuts, and our food bill dropped to almost nothing.

About midnight I went to pick up my trailer and discovered that it had sunk so far into the gravel that I couldn't get my fifth wheel under it. I jacked it up as high as possible, but the tractor still would not fit under. The only remaining alternative was to lower the ground on which the tractor sat. Fortunately it was gravel, so after a half hour of kicking rocks, the fifth wheel fit under the trailer and at 2:00 A.M. I was off to the west.

I soon learned that my Visa card was over the limit so, being short of cash, I found it necessary to stop repeatedly for fuel, $20 at a time; that was the amount that the station attendant did not need to call in to verify. By the middle of the following morning, halfway across Iowa and having some tire trouble, I pulled into a garage where help was available. I hopped into the sleeper while they worked on changing and repairing the tire and was almost asleep when I heard the man who was working on the tire say to his assistant, "Well, you better get the driver out here to have a look at this." I knew it was more of the same: trouble. The wheel bearings had gone and the friction had seized the axle. The hub was almost red.

The truck stop located a special mechanic who was familiar with my Transtar and knew where to locate parts. He was able to find another axle in a remote part of Iowa and got someone to bring it to us. I got on the phone to try and get the

162

money that I knew this would cost. I called the shipper for a further advance but they were unavailable, so I left a message to wire $400 to my location in Iowa. I then called Joe at the board of trade to see if he could wire $400 and sat around and waited for the part to arrive and hoped that there would be money to pay for it. Both wires came; I never had so much money on the road.

By late that night, I was back on Highway 80 heading west with a full 100 gallons of fuel and an extra couple hundred dollars. I had more trouble, mostly tires, and by the time I hit the Nebraska border, I was convinced that the retreads I was sold were nothing more than an expensive way of spreading rubber around the states.

One tow and two tires depleted my cash reserve, but I had enough fuel to reach the western half of Nebraska. I would have to stop again and have the shipper wire me the rest of the money for the load just to keep me on the road. (I soon learned that this was the best way to get paid in the trucking business; hold the shipment hostage with a broken-down truck.)

How was I to know that in the western half of Nebraska, diesel fuel was available only at 200-mile intervals. So the sun was setting on yet another day when I got out of the cab to rotate one of the fuel tanks and allow the line to make use of the last few gallons at the bottom. The hitchhiker I picked up prior to the last tire change decided he wasn't as thankful for the ride as he had orginally said and caught the next ride that stopped.

I didn't blame him a bit. I only regretted that I couldn't go with him. The cab then had to be jacked up high over the engine with a built-in hydraulic system so that the fuel could be sucked up the line. I had become quite familiar with this engine compartment where I now found myself, the massive steel of the cab suspended precariously over me. Every time I climbed up on top of that engine I wondered what would happen if the hydraulic jack holding those tons of steel gave way. Certainly I would be a short-order pancake, and they wouldn't find me for a long time. But what if I was lucky and there was just enough room between the engine and the steel underside of the cab for me to only be half squished—there was lots of time for imagination on these trips. I sucked the fuel up the line, connected it back, lowered the cab down, and miraculously was on my way again.

But it didn't bring any stations within reach, and in a few moments I was out again. Now I dumped the few gallons of oil I had with me into the tanks and again jacked up the cab. I loosened the fuel line but was unable to create any flow. I started to loosen it at another point in the line but it was in a position too awkward to reach and my hand was starting to hurt from the cramped position.

It was now dusk, almost dark; I couldn't recall the last time I had slept, was in the fourth day of a day and a half trip, and I was certain of only one thing: I would never see Salt Lake. It was a great time for an emotional breakdown. I started to sob. "Good God," I said, "what does a guy have to go through to provide for his wife and baby. Please, God, why don't you show some mercy and let the hydraulics of this cab give way and kill me. Nothin' else on this crate works. Why should the hydraulics? Being dead would be such sweet relief from this." I have never been more serious about a prayer than the one I sobbed while spread out over the top of that engine. Out of the corner of my eye I saw a Nebraska State Trooper step up alongside my cab, and I just had to know how loudly I prayed that prayer.

The officer got me the help I needed. I made Salt Lake the next day, reloaded in Idaho, and, after spreading two or three more tires all over the highway, was soon talking to Nancy from a potato warehouse in Chicago where I was dumping my load.

"I found that free apartment we needed," she told me excitedly. I was too tired to care.

"Oh yeah? What's the catch?"

"We stay in half of a duplex free in exchange for looking

after the place and a little secretarial work that I can do," she said. "And they have even offered to pay me for that."

"Hmm," I said.

"C'mon, aren't you excited?"

"Maybe. I dunno; we'll talk about it later."

"You said it's the only way we'll ever start getting out of debt."

"Maybe. I dunno; we'll talk about it later." What a thrill it must have been to have such an excitable spouse.

The line I hauled for reorganized under chapter eleven bankruptcy, so they were not obligated to pay me for my last three loads; about a thousand-dollar loss. They were in business the next day though, and expressed willingness to have me continue hauling for them.

Before I got out of Chicago on my next trip, the truck engine blew. This was the first time it had ever broken in town, but it would be the last because I could never afford the repair bill.

We had moved so many times that we were reluctant to ask friends and relatives to help us again. Instead, each day we took a load in our Volkswagen van and held a garage sale to free us of the large items. The stairs that led to our coach house circled the inner walls of a tower to a landing at the top, which had no railing. It was the only way to move large items in and out, but extremely dangerous for a one-year-old, so we permanently blocked that section of the landing with a long and grossly overweight chest. "What about this big old chest?" I asked while crossing the landing taking stuff down to the garage sale. "We gotta get rid of that ol' beast."

"You so much as move that thing and I'll kill you," Nancy answered. I knew she was still paranoid about giving Dani even the slightest chance of falling off that landing onto the steps at the bottom of the tower. Nancy and paranoia have always gone together and I stand out of their way whenever convenient.

On our last day we took a load into the city and dropped

Dani off at my sister's nearby so we could be completely free to move, clean the place up, and get our desperately needed security deposit back. Using ropes we lowered the chest and a few other large items over the landing and Nancy spent the day cleaning. Not allowed to keep our dog at the new place, we made an emotional trip out to Crystal Lake where we gave our beautiful Samoyed back to the breeder.

We now had two things of value left: Nancy's washing machine, which we bought new when she was pregnant with Dani, and the van we drove. I wiped out the washing machine when I dropped it down half a flight of stairs onto a concrete floor while moving it into our apartment basement. On our last trip, after Nancy had spent the whole day making sure that the place looked much nicer than it had when we moved in, our landlords told us that they would not be returning our security deposit. Something about work they had to have done on the septic field and a rag that was found that looked like it could have been a diaper. We were both furious.

"Y'know, I knew we shouldn't have paid them that last month's rent," I told Nancy as we drove away, helpless to do anything to defend ourselves. "But I told myself that it wouldn't be right."

"Well, we don't have much of anything left that anyone would want to cheat us out of."

It was almost midnight and raining when we picked up Dani and arrived at our new home with the last of our furniture tied to the top of the van. As exhausted as we were, we still had to get Dani into a makeshift bed and get the small amount of furniture we had left out of the rain. It was not the kind of neighborhood that would allow us to leave anything in the van either. I started taking furniture off the top while Nancy ran with Dani through the rain to the door only to find that the very old man who lived in the basement had latched the huge interior dead bolt. We could hear the phone ringing.

"Whoever's calling sure is patient," I said. "That phone never stops. I'll go around back." But the back door was also locked from inside with a dead bolt. I was too tired to care about anything. In anger I tried to take out the frustration of the day and the bolt with a kick to the middle edge of the door. I had completely underestimated the solidity of that old construction and only hurt my foot. Nancy was ready to cry and I wanted to join her.

The next day the van engine threw a rod. Now I was in the same dilemma that had caused me to laugh at other people. Should I be upset that the last thing of value we had was ruined or should I be thankful that it hadn't broken until we were all done moving? We gave it to a nearby service station for $100.

The day after was Thanksgiving. We sat in church counting our blessings, which could have been counted on one hand with all the fingers amputated. Nancy was thinking that in all our troubles, we had never lost our health. That was certainly something to be thankful for. But if God was trying to see how much we could do without, why should we remind him of anything?

I borrowed a car and drove back out to the coach house to pick up a few things we had forgotten. I put Dani down inside the door as I checked the place over. While I was looking around, Dani somehow was able to reach the doorknob and toddle out onto the landing. He saw the drop off and got down on all fours to back over it. When I opened the door, his lower body was over the edge, hands grabbing the floor, and feet desperately groping to reach the first stair, eight feet below. I dropped my stuff and dove for him, grabbing his armpits and lifting him from certain tragedy.

I recalled my dilemma and decided to be thankful.

CHAPTER 8

The Importunate Man

Nancy bought after-Thanksgiving discounted turkeys, cooked, carved, and froze them and we lived on turkey for the next few months. Shopping for Christmas took no time at all that year, though we were the recipients of a lot of nice and needed gifts from generous friends and relatives. The situation had the effect of severely mixing the emotions, especially of those inclined toward pride. So while we were blessed and moved by the generosity, there was also an absolutely irresistible temptation toward self-pity.

Then we got a surprise check in the mail; several months' back unemployment we had never collected. We used it to buy an old Chrysler. It was a nice-looking car with a massive chrome bumper surrounding the front end and those tiny deluxe lights on the top of the front fenders that light to inform the driver of the status of his headlights and turn signals. And since it had over 100,000 miles on it we got it for a good price.

About a month later, Dad and Mom let us borrow an old car they weren't using, so we sold the Chrysler for cash to live on. We were driving to a nearby currency exchange to transfer the title. The buyer, a fellow just out of the service, was driving, his father was in the backseat, and I was in the front. While making a left-hand turn at a green light, a guy on the cross street ran his red light and sandwiched his car between us and the oncoming traffic. The crash was horrendous.

"Well, that's the end of that deal," said the buyer's father in the backseat. I knew he was right and I looked over my shoulder to see a police officer right behind us. He had seen the whole thing. Thank God, I thought, at least I'll get reimbursed from that guy's insurance. Within minutes I discovered that I had given thanks too soon. "That guy" was an illegal alien with no driver's license, no insurance, no I.D., no nothing.

He went straight to jail. The man in the coming car was coming home from surgery in the hospital. They took him back. My bumper was one third of the way through the wild driver's passenger compartment covering both his front and backseat areas.

We were pacing around the accident and I was telling myself that I was sure I had hit the bottom out there in Nebraska and was regretting having thought that, because maybe someone was trying to tell me that things can always get worse when some wise guy said, "Well your car doesn't look all that bad." Who said that, I thought. Let me get my hands on the idiot. The front third of my hood was so far buried into the accident it wasn't visible. The other two vehicles were obviously totaled. When we pulled the cars apart, the crowd that gathered was stunned to find the Chrysler undamaged except for a few minor scratches on the bumper. There was no scratched paint and even the head-lights and parking lights were still whole. Even the little fender-top lights were unscratched and working. The weight of the heavy bumper had destroyed the other car while protecting ours. I guess I'd given up being thankful too soon.

The buyer changed his mind about backing out. "I'm more sold on this car now than I was before," he said. If I hadn't been so shocked myself, I would have raised the price.

I walked home to our apartment with $550 in my pocket and told Nancy the story.

"A miracle!" she exclaimed. I'm real slow and skeptical to call anything a miracle. But I did keep the money.

My brother Joe broke from the firm that had terminated me and began trading for himself. Through the kindness of a successful trader, Joe was able to put together a loan that would enable me to begin trading again.

It was the big grain market of '77 and, as they say, "Any fool can make money in a good market." Any fool can also tell you that that is an exaggeration, but for me it was the break I needed.

In 1977, the world-famous Bunker Hunt family's interests took a turn away from the oil fields of the South and into the soybean fields of the Midwest. Fueled by an estimated half-million-dollar-a-day income from oil, this group had some extra cash they could afford to lose in the high-risk business of commodity speculation. Their selection of a time to buy was fairly good, since there was a general shortage of beans from the year before and considerable concern about this year's crop. The Hunts compounded an already explosive situation by purchasing enough beans to keep their descendants alive for a few millenniums.

I began trading in the soybean oil pit for a soybean crushing team that Joe was running. We attempted to buy beans and sell their by-products (meal and oil) when the beans were underpriced, and to do the reverse when the beans were overpriced. In a quiet market, this operation is barely profitable. Nothing was very quiet in '77.

Along with our brother-in-law, Gary Ginter (he married Joanna), who got us started in the business in the first place, and another trader, Ron Bird, we formed a partnership. Since we were soybean crushers trading at the Chicago Board of Trade, we called our partnership Chicago Board Crushers and moved into a tiny office on the fifteenth floor. Everything went great until the secretary got tired of explaining to people why we couldn't crush their boards. We changed the name to Chicago Research and Trading.

About all a trader had to do that year was to buy the market and watch the Hunt family and all the other speculators who had purchased everything they could get their hands on. When they started to sell, it was time to get out and go short. It wasn't as crazy as the '73 market, but there were lucrative opportunities every day and Joe saw to it that we missed very few of them. He directed things from the meal pit with Ron in the beans and me in the oil. We bought and sold like madmen through five months of wild market action. I finally found myself in the right place at the right time.

Nancy and I were soon out of debt, I paid off the loan on the membership, and a career in commodities was born. A career where success would never be determined politically, but only by the results produced on the bottom line of the account balance sheet.

Also, this time there was no employer to take all the profits. Every penny we earned went straight into our pockets. No salaries or profit sharing to negotiate; just earn the money and keep it.

"There ought to be a law against making this much money," Joe said one day as we were leaving the floor after an unusually successful trading session.

"Did you ever think, when we were growing up in Reedsport, sharin' that little room and playing baseball, that it would all come to this?" I asked. He didn't need to answer.

When yelling and screaming in the pit, it was almost impossible to imagine that we were making monetary transactions. But when I took that first $15,000 out of the account, deposited it in my bank account, and Nancy started paying off the debts that had hung over our heads for so long, it became obvious that this was no mere game.

We sent $4,000 to Dad in Afghanistan to start a chicken farming venture. We wanted as many Afghan families as possible to have some laying chickens that would produce more protein for the household. The remainder of the money got us out of debt.

Trading for one's own account was a lot different than

trading for a firm. If you lost the firm's money, one could always look for another firm. If you lost your own money, you headed straight to the poor house. The gravity of the personal stakes involved created a subculture all its own; a cross between the devil-may-care attitude of the blackjack table and the seriousness of an ecclesiastical council. It made people behave in inexplicable ways.

In the middle of a crazy grain market, Roger, conservative and well respected for his talent as a broker, was long 500,000 bushels of beans. He was approached in the center of the pit at mid-session by a friend inquiring about the feel of the market. His friend was also long a substantial position and they both agreed that the market should go higher, the position was good, the market looked strong, and the two of them were giving each other all the typical kinds of encouragement that traders do when they share a common position. Suddenly, as they were speaking, Roger began selling his positions and in a few seconds had liquidated his full 500,000 bushels on the market.

"What on earth are you doing?" his friend yelled in surprise. "I thought we just agreed that we like our long position! The market's going up! Why are you getting out?"

Roger shrugged sheepishly. "I figure we can't both be right."

It does sound stupid and it doesn't make any sense, but in fact that is the way many traders trade. And who's to argue with a successful trader? When too many people agree on one direction in the market, many traders—whether out of superstition or for some logical reason—start getting nervous and think about getting out, maybe even reversing the trend.

The simple fact of the matter is that no one knows the future with any certainty at all. Refusal to admit that explains why so many people lose money investing in commodities.

Every day I continued to be amazed at how quickly my mind could forsake its propensity toward rational thinking when confused by dollar signs. And the more I got to know people in the business, the more I realized that I wasn't the only one with the problem. It seemed to be a human trait.

When I awoke, the Afghan night was so quiet I could hear James sleeping in the next room. A large, multifingered leaf hung just above my head as if it had grown there while I dozed off. The candle had disintegrated to a pile of wax. I blew the wick out and groped past a couple of plants toward my mattress.

In the morning we were again approached on the street by the same mysterious man. "He still wants us come to his house for a meal," James told me.

"Do we have any idea who he is?" I asked.

"Nobody seems to know him, but the people around here say he has come here every day since Dad died looking for us."

"It's just strange that no one knows him," I said. "I don't see that we have any choice but to go, even though we don't know for sure who he is. He's been here almost every day. I say we have to make some time for him." James told him we would come to his house the next day for the noon meal.

The following day, our last in Herat, he came to our compound at noon and we walked together toward his home. It was an indescribable day. The kind of weather one would not know how to create. The Herat winds were coming at us from our left. The Herat wind is actually a very light breeze, moving at a constant two miles per hour. It blows six months out of the year during which time it never stops; blowing so slowly and steadily that one actually has to stand very still just to feel it. To call it a wind is misleading because it is really a very slow, constantly moving air mass.

He led us from our compound a block and a half to the main road, where we turned to the right and walked for a distance with the wind. The temperature was precisely that of one's skin surface, producing a warmth that seemed to invade the body and tranquillize the soul. When walking at about two miles per hour with a two mph breeze at our backs, as we were at this moment, it seemed as if the air were absolutely, impeccably still and the warm, soft sunlight embraced me; it was a quiet, peaceful, serene moment.

The contentment in the atmosphere drew me into its magnetic field; the cleanest of air, the most placid of sounds, and I was overcome with the feeling that I could stay right here and live happily ever after, forever free of the stress of the West. I had stepped out of the twentieth century into a scene from Hilton's *Lost Horizon*, set in the Himalayas not far from here.

This is it, I thought, that incredible, all-encompassing warmth that some people use to describe heaven. We turned right down a narrow side roadway and again felt the moving air touching us from the right. Forty yards later, we passed through a wooden gate built into a ten-foot-high mud wall and found ourselves in a garden. This might be the warmest and kindest spot on earth, I thought.

We were led through the garden to the back of the compound, where this man lived with his wife. He showed us into his home. The walls were mud, the roof was mud, the floor was mud, and the door was an opening cut in the mud wall. Entering the room, we sat on cushions positioned against the wall on the dirt floor. I presumed this to be the only room in his home and found it exceedingly comforting to be in the humblest of homes associating with the people Dad had considered an honor to serve. The man's wife waited on us, serving tea and traditional Afghan food similar to what we had eaten in the bazaar in Kandahar.

Sitting on the floor in his home, enjoying his generous hospitality, he told us stories about his work with our father. He told us that Dad had been like a father to him and because of that, he considered us to be his brothers and sister. When he had heard of the accident, being ignorant of the details, he had taken a bus from Herat to Kabul only to hear the news of

Dad's death and learn the news that there was no way he could even see our mother.

His concern left a warm impression. For an Afghan to travel from Herat to Kabul was a bigger undertaking than for us to come here from Chicago. Certainly it was a greater financial sacrifice for him. This was indeed like meeting a long-lost relative, a loved one of our father's, and it reminded me of the words of Christ when he said that no one would give up father, mother, houses and lands, brother and sister, who would not receive back a hundredfold in this life. I was sitting in one of those hundred houses, eating the food served from one of those hundred brothers who had been earned by my father's sacrifice to God. It wasn't the fanciest house in the world, to be sure, in fact, it was the simplest I had ever been in. But I also knew full well that the gold coast of Chicago offered no luxury more comfortable than what I was enjoying. The high-class restaurants where we wined and dined our business associates could never prepare food to taste like the simple fare of a grieving, poor man, served with kindness on a dirt floor.

Our new friend, adopted brother, told us that he and his wife had no children. To be without children in Afghanistan is not only a disgrace, it is also a significant economic threat. Without children it's impossible for one to be secure in his old age. He also told us what it was like to be a Hazara, a minority race in Afghanistan severely discriminated against. Only allowed to hold manual-labor jobs, he was considered to be no more than a beast of burden. These people are identified by a very slight oriental feature to their face, thought to be the result of the invasion of the fierce oriental warrior Genghis Khan in the thirteenth century.

A man could hardly have more going against him. He was the citizen of one of the most backward countries in the world. He bore the disgrace and insecurity of being childless. And he was a member of a cruelly treated minority race. I was finding comfort in my time of grief in the most unsuspecting of places.

We stepped out of his home to be greeted by the friendly sunlight of the garden and were again surrounded by the warm Herat wind. He walked us out through the garden toward the main entrance to the compound where he would say good-bye. The serenity of the atmosphere invited me to move here and stay forever.

As we were leaving he reached his hand into his pocket. James turned to me. "He wants to know if we need any money."

His request stopped me short. Though I hadn't yet made my first million in the market, I was well on my way. I was a well-respected independent trader on the biggest commodity exchange in the world. I was Mr. High-rolling, High-shooting, High-financial hotshot. I made more money in a fifteen-second trade than this man would make in his whole lifetime. Yet here he was, reaching into his pocket and wondering if I had a need and if he could help.

I recalled the question I had asked myself when our plane touched down: Could my God prove useful at this time of great grief in a forgotten land? I knew what was going on. God was poking fun at me. It was a setup. The most imaginative writer of fiction could not construct a scenario as beautifully coincidental.

I could almost hear him chuckling, "So you think I'm powerless to comfort my grieving children, do you, you spoiled little child of puny faith?" There was no comfort like this to be found in my civilized West. God had dragged me halfway around the world and all around this country of Afghanistan in a broken down Travelall to allow me to experience the most overwhelming expression of love and kindness I would ever know.

I thought it all over while standing there in the warm stillness among the flowers, shaking my head in speechless awe while controlling my tears. That rule about money not buying happiness that I had so insisted on learning for myself; God had just handed out lesson number one. One of the most satisfying moments of my life had been single-handedly delivered to me by the most cash-poor of his creatures.

The long ride back to Kabul gave me hour upon hour to savor that moment, the climax of the events of the last three weeks. What culpability did God share in my father's tragic death? It wasn't he, after all, who caused that foolhardy bus driver to drive like a madman and run my parents off the highway. My father had been a victim of the free choice of a fool. I wondered how much human misery existed purely as a result of free choice. Could I have made this world a better place by eliminating the freedom of such individuals to inflict this pain on each other?

With the warm air of the sunny desert blowing in the window, I tried to imagine what the world would be like if I were God and I prevented every person from performing any evil act. We would become puppets, of course, but think of all the pain that would be avoided.

I recalled my professor who honestly admitted his prejudice against God. If I were God I wouldn't even allow him to think such thoughts. And that guy who got all the recognition for accusing me of murdering everybody once? I'd burn up his manuscript before it got published. I would make it impossible to say or do an unkind thing. The world would be an intricate puppet show and I the divine puppeteer. And Steinbeck's character, the retired preacher, would have the last word—there couldn't possibly be any good or evil, just things people do. I'd do away with evil no matter how much of the fabric of humanity I had to destroy to do it. I'd certainly keep irresponsible bus drivers from killing people.

While this was the attitude I had arrived with, I was now confused. The incident with the Hazar had connected me with Dad in a way that I had not known while he was alive.

When we arrived back in Kabul, Mom was well enough to attend a memorial service for Dad. And soon she was strong enough to return to the States for better medical attention.

Joe left a few days ahead of us. On another sunny and warm

day just like they had all been since we arrived, Joanna, James, Nancy, Dani, and I made our way with Mom across the bright concrete jet-way toward another old plane. We turned at the top of the stairs and waved good-bye to new friends; people who stopped what they were doing for three weeks to help us through a storm.

Dani sat between us again when the plane lifted off the runway. I looked out the window at the scene I had seen three weeks earlier, recalling my embarrassment at the hands of that Copenhagen ticket clerk. I remembered wondering if my father's moral system might fade after I got him buried and forgotten. Now I had some priceless pieces to add to that confused puzzle.

I supposed that a lot of people might have thought the same thing; from Pilot and Herod all the way down to Bertrand Russell: "This little fad will no doubt soon pass and we can get on with business as usual." That's probably what the slave traders thought when William Wilberforce first started nagging the conscience of England with his self-righteous, pompous nonsense about the immorality of the slave trade. Staring out the window of the plane, I was suddenly overcome with the feeling that putting a humble engineer into the ground in a god-forsaken country in the farthest corner of the world would have little effect on anyone's ultimate moral obligation. And he was a quiet, humble man, whose greatness was consistently overlooked—especially by me.

The plane banked and headed south, giving me a complete look at the city, with the two mountains, our old playground, sticking up in the middle.

CHAPTER 9

Cautionary Tales

Fall had come to the Midwest by the time I returned from Afghanistan and stepped back into the pits at the Chicago Board of Trade. It looked different now—this fantasy world in which a maximum amount of dollars changes hands with a minimum amount of work—described by a reporter as a place where brokers wade knee-deep in $20 bills.

It is a world of make believe, where money grows on trees, dreams become reality, a Disneyland for adults. Almost everyone I meet wants to know how they can get into the business and make a fortune. When I discourage them from doing so, they only become more convinced, thinking that I am just trying to preserve a greater portion of the pot of gold for myself. Little do they know that the gold is not held by a few as a result of their ability to keep others away. It is held by a few because the others find consistent ways to lose. And the futures industry is a most convenient place for the public to lose their money.

Though not all brokerage houses are like the one I had encountered earlier, it is impossible for a client to know what sort of house he is dealing with until it is too late. Even if an investor does tie in with a profitable brokerage house, he could wind up losing money in other ways—theft, for example.

The world of the pits is no different from any other world. It has its constant temptations to compromise. Let us say, for example, that a broker who fills orders for a group of commission houses has an out-trade with a local (an independent trader who trades only for himself) and owes him $500. The next morning the broker holds orders to sell 500 and buy 200 on the opening. So he sells 400 in the pit at $7.51 and buys 100 at $7.52. The remaining 100 he sells at $7.51 to the local to whom he owes the money and then buys 100 back from the same individual at $7.515. The customers' orders are all properly filled and the local makes $500 to satisfy the money owed to him on the out-trade. The ethics of this could be argued at length, but there is nothing improper about the way the orders were filled. Indeed, the customer's order that was filled at 51½ actually received a better fill.

Now the broker and the local meet the next morning after discovering how easy it is to make money. Now the broker holds orders to sell 500 and buy 700. He buys only 200 at $7.54 and the opening range is established at 7.52 to 7.54. (The "opening range" is the range of prices traded in the first few seconds after the opening bell. All opening orders must be filled within the opening range.) The broker still has 500 left to buy and 500 to sell. So he sells 500 to his new friend, the local trader, at $7.52 and buys 500 at $7.54. His customers' orders are all filled within the allowable price range and the local trader has started off his day with a tidy $10,000 profit.

It could be argued that the customer got what he was entitled to. But, unfortunately, sometimes he doesn't. Suppose a broker sells a large order for a customer in a falling market. He may sell 100 contracts at a number of prices. Say he sells 10 contracts at 72, 20 contracts at 70, the next tic lower, and 10 more at 68. Then he offers the market down two more tics to 64 and sells 10. He has now sold only half his order while the market has dropped 8 points—just what one would expect to happen with a big order. He may have to offer the market at 60 to sell 20 more and then sells another 10 at 56 and the remaining 20 at a price of 50. The following represents what he actually did for his customer.

SOLD	10	contracts @	72
SOLD	20	contracts @	70
SOLD	10	contracts @	68
SOLD	10	contracts @	64
SOLD	20	contracts @	60
SOLD	10	contracts @	56
SOLD	20	contracts @	50

He sold 100 contracts at an average price of 62. But the quote board shows the market trading all the way down to 50. So he sells 100 to a friend at 50 and gives that sale to the customer who never knows the difference. The 100 contracts that he sold at an average price of 62, he takes into his own personal account. Then he buys 100 from his friend at 56. They have now each made 6 points on 100 (at $10 per point, a profit of $6,000). The customer, who deserved a sale at 62 but got 50 instead, lost 12 points on a hundred, $12,000. Every dime they made came directly out of the customer's pocket since he deserved to get the prices that his broker took.

(In actual fact, there is no commodity in the industry that trades in that kind of tics or has a pricing structure in any way similar to what has been described here. However, I do expect to be contacted by the lawyers of a number of brokers from a variety of pits who will claim that my description is dangerously similar to their client's trading style.)

In some pits, and on some exchanges, the little habits have grown to fairly substantial proportions. One broker told me that he had seen $70,000 change hands on one opening. And it was nothing out of the ordinary. He said that opportunities for an order-filler to steal were so great that he finally had to stop filling orders altogether. It was the only way he could deal with the temptation. He claimed that he knew people who would fill orders for free so they could have the opportunity to steal from their customers. Sickening!

I'd been in the business a lot of years when I moved to a new exchange to try some new ventures in different pits.

While there I ran into Max, an old friend I hadn't seen since our early struggling days. We began discussing the main topic of the era: the enormous fines and suspensions that were being levied by the exchange. We had both been called as witnesses.

"How do you take this high-pressure den of thieves?" he asked me. "I figured you'd be long gone outta here after all these years."

"It's really only when I'm working over here that it's bad; the pit I usually work is full of honest traders. But you're right about the pressure. And I'll admit, I wouldn't be able to take it if I didn't know there was some ultimate meaning somewhere."

"And it ain't here," Max added to my thought. "You know that for sure."

"You've been down here a long time, Max," I said. "Tell me why you've never gotten involved in all the stealing? You've filled orders for customers."

"You really want to know? I'll tell you the truth, exactly why. Years ago you guys put the fear of God in me—that is the bottom-line truth. You and your brother Joe and all those guys you used to associate with. Really. That's it. You guys put the fear of God in me. If it weren't for that, I would be out there on that floor right now bucketing orders."

Hmm, I thought, maybe God really does have some influence on people.

Sometimes dishonesty has a way of reaping its own reward, as in the case of the trader who was going through a divorce. In order to conceal his assets from his wife and the courts, he maneuvered a significant amount of money into a fellow broker's account. The understanding was that his friend would keep the money until after the divorce settlement and then return it. The friend with the money then proceeded to make a trade with it and lost just a small amount. Naturally, he needed to recover that so he made another trade attempting to recoup the loss. One thing led to another and as anyone might be able to guess, the story had an ironic ending. By the time the shrewd fellow got rid of his wife and returned to get his money, there was not a cent left.

How does a friend defend himself in a situation like that? "You were going to lose the money to your ex-wife anyway, so what difference does it make?"

While the exchanges have yet to come up with a good way to legislate morality, they, like most legislatures in the Western world, feel they owe it to their constituency to try to do so. Therefore they make all sorts of rules that can be reduced to the simple concept of "don't lie, cheat, or steal." Then the lawyers go to work in an attempt to redefine those terms.

In all fairness to the industry as a whole, it would be completely wrong to end a discussion of dishonesty without placing things in perspective. The average commodities broker does not deserve the negative reputation that results from the behavior of a few. The entire industry works on the honor system. Every trader who steps into the pit is bound only by his honor to live up to every trade he makes. Millions of dollars change hands daily by this method. Nothing is signed; there is not even a handshake. Sometimes there is not even a verbal exchange; merely the wave of a hand or the nod of a head. Any trader can cheat any other trader any time he chooses and there is nothing that anyone can do to stop him. The amount of integrity required to carry on business as it is currently done in the commodities industry is nothing short of phenomenal.

Donald Trump tells a wonderful story of his first encounter with Walter Hoving, the owner of Tiffany. He tells how Hoving had come to a verbal agreement to sell him the air rights over Tiffany but Hoving was leaving town and wouldn't be back to sign papers for a month. Trump expressed concern that Hoving might change his mind over the next month and he needed a commitment. Hoving's reply was a classic. "Young man," he said, "I made a deal with you. That's that." And it was. Trump was impressed, and even more so when Hoving stuck by the deal in the face of pressure from others and market conditions that would have paid him handsomely to back out.

Every deal that is made in the commodity pits is made exactly the same as that deal between Trump and Hoving; on word of honor (or hand signal of honor).

Recently one exchange levied unprecedented fines and suspension penalties against some of its members. The new rule requiring the exact minute of the day to be placed on each trade has also helped. Many of us opposed this rule because it is so inconvenient, but we have endured it in the interest of increasing the level of honesty.

Naturally, each exchange states somewhere in its fine print the expectation that each member will uphold the high standards of the exchange. Lawyers have a field day with such language.

While trading at another exchange, I saw one trader of significant financial size and status buy a 100-lot order from an offering broker. A smaller trader, whose bid was made at the same time and price, had an equal right to get the trade, but the offering broker elected to sell all the contracts to the large trader. This is commonly done and saves the selling broker from having to record transactions with two different brokers. However, it is considered common courtesy for the larger trader to share some of the trade with a smaller trader. In this particular case, the smaller trader wanted 10 lots and minimal civility would demand that the 100-lot trader share 10 lots or at least something with him. On this occasion, the smaller trader did what came naturally.

"Come on, I was bidding, I'll take some of that trade, too," he said to the larger trader.

"Aw, go to hell! I don't give a shit about you!" was the response. In this particular situation it wasn't just the words used, but the way in which they were delivered, that gave one the overwhelming impression that he meant every word he said. Fortunately for me, my first pit experience hadn't included such people. I would have headed right back to Reedsport and applied for a job in the saw mill, where treating people like people is still considered a virtue.

It's a bit tricky for an exchange official to go up to a trader and say, "Look, let's try to uphold the high standards of the exchange please." The guy would just answer, "What high standard? Is there a rule that says, 'be nice'? If so, it discriminates against me."

I began to take note of what Max and his friend were telling me. In some pits brokers bucketed trades as a matter of course—the sort of thing that tended to give the whole industry a bad name. I had to give the exchange credit for trying to clean up the stealing, but the exchange has found it almost impossible to force a moral code onto an unwilling recipient.

The broker who solicited the services of an employee of one of the major exchanges to perform a sexual favor for him in the elevator could certainly be thought to have failed to uphold the standards of the exchange. But in whose opinion? The exchange does not spell out precisely what sort of sexual activity is not permitted in their elevators between consenting adults.

Warnings about unscrupulous people seldom stops the naive from entering the sexy world of high finance. Almost everyone thinks he has the ability to distinguish between the moral and the immoral. That's why the immoral have such a heyday.

Christian people, especially pastors, are uniquely susceptible to this pitfall because they think some supernatural power has delivered them from greed. They also feel that since God is on their side, and "all things work together for good," that the Almighty has a personal stake in their welfare. Anyway, since they are not at all greedy, all their proceeds will go for good causes. Of course.

One person came into the business with the highest of intentions. He had a sincere Christian faith. We worked side by side and soon became friends. He thought Jesus Christ would speak to him through the Holy Spirit about his investments. I tried to explain to my new friend that the Spirit of God truly could guide all genuine believers, but that God had given us a brain and expected us to employ that as well. My friend, however, found it to be much less of a mental strain to move around the floor of the exchange, somehow maneuvered by the Holy Spirit, while he meditated for some inner vibration as to which pit he might enter and establish a position in the market.

"Why do you think God doesn't want you to use your brain to decipher market activity just like everyone else?" I asked him. "Don't you think that this God of ours could assist you in your decision making?"

"Your brain is capable of making all sorts of mistakes," he told me, as if I really needed to be informed. "The Holy Spirit, on the other hand, never makes any mistakes."

"Did you ever think that your brain might be making a mistake right now?" I asked jokingly. (Well, sort of jokingly.) "All right, let's tap into this information source and get going. Why don't you just tell me the high and low for the bond market for tomorrow. That's all I ask, just two very simple numbers, the high and the low. I'll take it from there. I won't need any help after that. And what's more, I promise never to ask for any more information."

"Doubters, unbelievers, and scoffers will never be able to take advantage of the power of the Holy Spirit," he responded to my skepticism.

"Yeah, that's what I was afraid of. I don't mean to doubt that God could make a great trader if he chose to. After all, he did instruct his servant Joseph to buy grain at bargain prices for seven years—that has to be the speculating record of all history—but that doesn't mean he's in the business of commodity speculation today. In fact, tell me why these miracle workers with all their healing power, all their visions of the future, words of knowledge, prophecies, and so forth have not come down here to make some money? They are always telling us how much they need to feed all those poor people. Why doesn't God just send them down here to make a fortune? They could use God as their trading adviser. Just think, he could even make an appearance on Louie Flukewiser's 'Wall Street Week': 'Hello. This is Flukewiser here. I'd like to introduce to you my guest for this week, the greatest investment adviser of all time, please welcome God.' "

"This is not funny, you know." Sometimes these people don't have the keenest sense of humor.

"Maybe we should get those who claim to be tapped into some otherworldly information source to come down into these pits," I told him, "we could find out soon enough which ones were phonies—though I have a feeling they know better than to try."

My friend, however, didn't know better. He'd read one of those popular books about the signs of the times and the coming of the end of the age. It had so many tips to help the Holy Spirit lead him toward the right pit—like the obvious prediction that gold would take a quantum leap in value. His stay in the industry was so short-lived I hardly got to know him. And somebody else had to cover the Holy Spirit's debit.

When I returned from a trip abroad, our hostages had been held in Iran for a month, causing the price of gold to jump $100 to just under $500 an ounce. Feeling that this trend had to continue as long as political tensions were mounting, I decided I had better sink my teeth into a gold position. So I purchased ten contracts of gold on the International Monetary Market and the price immediately crashed the daily limit. Some bureaucrat someplace came out with an irresponsible statement about the great prospects for peace breaking out in some unknown part of the world. Naturally, all the panic-stricken longs liquidated their position in a huge sell off. Twenty grand down the toilet. And for me, $20,000 was a big hit.

But I held the position with the solid conviction that as long as the Iranians were fanning the flames of hatred, the economic stability on the globe could only remain in doubt, bureaucratic optimism notwithstanding. Sure enough, over the coming weeks, the price of gold slowly recovered, and by Christmas I had a nice present, not only my $20,000 loss back, but a profit of at least that much as the price of gold continued to make record highs around the $500 level.

Following Christmas, my wife and I reflected back on a year that had been our most successful in the market. Having theoretically committed all our material resources to God, as we knew Christians were supposed to do, we were somewhat frustrated by the fact that we found it difficult to responsibly donate these large quantities of funds. Nevertheless, some sort of offering of thanks was in order. So after Christmas that year, we wrote a check for $10,000 and put it in the offering plate at the church where we had been active for a few years. It never occurred to us that this expression of thanksgiving might give rise to a strange turn of events.

Since the grain market was quiet, I was not going to the trading floor during the holiday season, but instead met a friend early the next morning for breakfast at the Country Kitchen in Highland Park. The days being so short in Chicago this time of year, it was still dark and a thin blanket of fresh snow covered the roadway. It was coming down pretty hard as I drove the van around the cloverleaf at Central and up over the expressway. Chicago's news station WBBM was giving the financial news and the price of gold just before the hour.

As I reached the top of the cloverleaf, I heard the morning gold fix from London, up a whopping $30. I pounded on the steering wheel with excitement. No doubt another one of those bureaucrats had been talking about something. I was dumbfounded. While I was sacrificing myself by giving God $10,000, my investment in gold was netting me $30,000 over the weekend.

I had heard all those stories people told about how you can't out-give God and all that stuff, but this was ridiculous. Could this be what Jesus had in mind when he talked about any one who sacrificed anything receiving back a hundred times as much? Talk about an investment opportunity, a guy could really sink his portfolio into this one.

The price of gold continued up another $20 during the week. I had started out by sacrificing $10,000 and ended up with $50,000 stuck in my pocket.

So now I was in a quandary. A week earlier we gave a gift out of thanks for a good year; should we give something this week out of the thanks for a good week? Well, good grief, I thought, what actually did I have to lose? I was $40,000 ahead of where I started out last week. So the next Sunday we wrote out another check for $10,000, figuring we were still $30,000 ahead. The next week the price of gold jumped another $50 and I raked in another tidy $50,000 and I began thinking about the story of the goose that laid the golden egg, about keeping the goose healthy and all.

I was definitely on to something here. Maybe I should start the "Church of the Frustrated Commodities Broker." The service would amount to nothing but the passing of the plate. Maybe we'd sing the commodity traders' altered hymn, "What a Trend We Have in Jesus."

That Sunday we put another $10,000 in the same collection. We shared much in common with the leadership of this church—concepts of ministry and concern for the poor.

I don't recall exactly how much longer this little racket continued, but the price of gold soared to a high of $850. I began to wonder if this could be the quantum leap my friend had prophecied. In this business any prediction will come true given enough time.

Just as all good things must come to an end, so all market rallies have a way of drawing to a close. Blinded by the shock of incoming dollars, if not plain old-fashioned greed, many bulls in a market will take leave of their senses until long after it's too late, simply forgetting or choosing to ignore what everyone knows: that what goes up must come down.

I had taken leave of mine as well. And of all people, I should have known that God is no cosmic genie who manipulates markets. I also knew that preachers who tell people to give so that God will bless them with more always suggest that the money be given to their ministry.

The shape that a market will take when totally dominated by a group of sophisticated, yet panic-stricken investors going belly up is an amazing sight to behold. The day of reckoning occurred on a Tuesday when the market opened locked limit-down. There was really no good way to get out, although if one were not in too great a state of shock he could have sold gold in the cash market and spread his commitment off against his futures contracts. Like many others, I preferred to sit and wait, hoping against irrational hope that some miracle could stave off the landslide. It didn't.

I had lost $200,000 in one short little day.

I could not see how the sun could possibly come up tomorrow. I did not even consider myself to be a lover of money and I thought this must be the end of the world. It was a losing day to make all other losing days look like peanuts. The foolishness of the suicides that followed the stock market crash of 1929 suddenly didn't look so foolish. I felt at that moment as if I could make good use of a gun, and I wondered how the real greedy lovers of money must be feeling.

Stumbling my way in somewhat of a daze up to our little office, I thought I might ask Joe, more of a gun owner than myself, if he would lend me a bullet. I knew he wouldn't—he knew I'd never pay him back.

Was this some kind of a setup? God was playing some sort of game with me to get all that money. That settles it, I told myself, that's the last $10,000 check I'll ever write to any of his churches. Have I gone through all the grief of this industry only to be led like all the other bulls to the slaughter of a market crash?

How much better off I would have been never to have left my hometown, never to have gone away for seven years of college and another seven years of seminary. I could have just settled for a good job in the logging industry. A demotion, a layoff, even a firing would have been wonderful news by comparison to this debacle.

To make matters worse, the sun did come up the next morning. I lay there in bed groping for anything that would help relieve the pain. "What, after all, is your life," I remembered reading. "It is like a vapor which vanishes in a moment." I wished mine would vanish even if it wasn't the end of the world. I still knew there was a God even though he seemed to have taken a vacation for a day.

"Take the lilies in the field," I recalled Christ's words. "They don't work. Yet Solomon in all his glory was never outfitted like one of them. If God dresses the grass of the field which is here today and gone tomorrow, how much more will he dress you?" At least now I knew what it meant to be here today and gone tomorrow. But even with as big a loss as I had taken in one day, I still had more food and clothing than the vast majority of anyone on earth.

And there was more. "Lay not up for yourselves treasures on earth, but lay up for yourselves treasures in heaven." And, "He who shuts his ear to the cry of the poor will cry himself and not be answered."

From childhood I had heard that cry. I entered this industry to be one who would make a difference, one who would reach out with the love of God to do as Christ said, to share with him who was needy, to care for the widows and orphans, to provide assistance to the oppressed.

These were lofty ideals to which I had given lip service for years. Now I was reacting with the emotions of a greedy money-monger. If all my money were really at God's disposal to do with as he wished, why should it bother me so much if he chose to take a couple hundred thousand of it and spread it around to some other investors? What difference did that money really make? I still had my wonderful wife and beautiful boy (and now another on the way). In God's great eternal plan for history, how much difference was that $200,000 going to make?

I reflected on this for a moment. For all the most noble, the most holy, the most sanctified reasons I could think of, for all the most spiritual goals that could be found in the Good Book, I thought, I want that money back! I paused for a moment. *Now!*

I knew, though, what was really happening. It was simply one of the down periods in the ups and downs of my business, even if it did happen to be the biggest down I had ever experienced. I knew that God allowed the bad and good luck to fall on the just and unjust alike. God's children are no luckier than anyone else's children.

I was being comforted not by any mystical feelings, but by truth. Plain, old-fashioned, simple truth. I knew there was a God. I knew I was one of his creatures. I knew he cared about me. And the simple fact of the matter was that the most basic of all prayer requests that he taught us, "Give us this day our daily bread," had already been answered for me in unthinkable abundance. I was overcome not only by the innumerable blessings with which I was surrounded, but also by the depth of despair to which I had sunk while sitting right in the middle of them.

Here it was: another one of those feelings I wish I could bottle and market to the world. It was lesson number two in that Money-Can't-Buy-Happiness school of hard knocks that I had insisted on attending.

After what I'd been through with the gold, I was even more negative about encouraging anyone to try this business. I ran into a financial adviser who, after a few moments' conversation, commented, "Y'know, you're the first commodities person I've ever met who actually told people to stay away from commodities. I've been trying to keep people out of commodities for years. Maybe they'll listen to you. Would you be willing to be a guest speaker at one of my seminars? If I could just get people to stop investing in commodities, I could save my clients a fortune."

So off I flew across the country to preach a message that I knew would not gain me any points in the industry.

"Why," I said to his audience of investors, "would you want to take your hard-earned money, put it in an extremely high-risk industry where statistics are stacked horribly against you, and invest in some 'thing' somewhere about which you are almost totally ignorant?" My approach was so simple and obvious it drew laughter. "Does that sound smart? It's probably because you have complete confidence in your adviser-broker. But did you ever ask him how much of his own money he has put behind his advice?

"When he tells you he can't afford it, doesn't that make you wonder about his past recommendations?"

I explained how the complexity of the marketplace enables almost anyone, armed with a few clever tricks, to develop a trading system that looks profitable. He may even convince himself that his system is profitable. One thing is certain, though: It is simple to demonstrate a sure thing to even the most intelligent of investors. The vast array of so-called profitable systems currently for sale at astronomical prices confirms the high demand for quick money.

"I have been asking for years," I told my audience, "and am still asking: Why would anyone ever sell a profitable system? I have never heard a satisfactory answer to that question.

"Of course there is my answer, long scorned by the less scrupulous wing of the industry: It is no longer—probably never was—profitable. Naturally, any system can be demonstrated to have had a profitable track record at some time in the past. Appeal to past performance is, after all analysis is complete, a sophisticated way of saying that since there have been Lotto winners, the lottery must be a good investment.

It was not my intent to publicly indict all brokerage houses. Certainly there are some that make profits for the client. But I have little doubt that clients take the vast majority of the risk and get a small fraction of the profit. And almost no one has enough money to try all the brokerage houses until he finds a winner. This situation was best summarized by Duke of Duke and Duke in the movie *Trading Places*, when he told his brother-partner to explain to the street con artist Billy Ray how Duke and Duke make money regardless of what happens to the client. Billy Ray responded the way anyone should, "That beats anything we have on the street."

I didn't want to publicly indict all expert advisers either. The problem is that for every expert there are a hundred masquerading as experts, and it takes an experienced expert to tell the difference. I told this seminar of investors the following story:

My partner and I were approached by an expert who wanted to trade an account for us in exchange for a percent of the profits. He had the best of credentials and was a regular contributor to the industry's periodical publications. Since he was a recognized success in the field, we gave him authority over a $25,000 account that he increased to $35,000 in a few days. However, he was not trading according to the style we had agreed to, and we spoke to him about it. With an account of this size one should never be investing more than one contract on any one commodity. But how does one tell an expert who has just made $10,000 that he's wrong?

He soon lost that $10,000 and another $10,000. A week later my partner and I discovered that he had disappeared and we had four short soybean contracts we didn't know about, and the market was exploding on the upside. Not only had he lied about the way he would trade, he risked much more than he agreed to, lost it all, and disappeared without informing us of our open position. Even the most seasoned experts do strange things when they get dollars on their brains.

He later wrote me a letter of apology, stating his intention to somehow repay the money. I haven't heard from him since, though I do see his articles occasionally in *Futures* magazine. The terrible fact is that the vast majority of experts out there simply aren't. And many who are experts can't trade.

"It's time we all admitted," I said in conclusion, "that the same human emotions that entice one to sink his hard-earned money into the lottery also draw a person to commodities. The main difference being that commodities has the capability of attracting the sophisticated, educated, wealthy investor. Before he realizes what he has gotten himself into, he is throwing good money after bad, more money than he ever thought possible. His good judgment completely blinded by dollars, he makes decisions he thought only his starry-eyed son-in-law or senile father-in-law would make. (Many a starry-eyed or senile in-law has found his reputation for poor judgment usurped by the family's favorite businessman who foolishly got smeared in the futures market.)"

At the conclusion I asked if there were any questions. There were a number. "Your soapbox routine is quite convincing," the first one commented. "I'll never invest in commodities again. But you have left us quite puzzled as to why you continue to invest and how you can make money if money can't be made? I've heard it suggested by commodity advisers that some traders want us out of the market so they can keep all the money for themselves. How would you answer that?" There was an outbreak of sighs and nods that told me they all had the same question, also a general feeling that he had stated the question in such a way as to place maximum heat on the speaker.

"Well," I said, clearing my throat and looking at my watch, "I guess that's about all the time we have for questions." They were appreciative of a little humor.

"Seriously, though, a good question. Let us suppose, sir, that your expert commodity adviser persuades you to take some of my profits by entering the market and buying soybeans." He nodded in agreement. "He places an order with a broker in the pit to buy 100,000 bushels for your account. That broker shouts, 'Where can I buy it?'

"And I just happen to be in the pit and say 'At two.'

"So he buys your beans at $6.52. A moment later the gentleman sitting to your left, also having been persuaded by his expert to 'take' some of my money, enters an order to *sell* 100,000 bushels. He places that order with a broker in the pit who shouts, 'What's bid?'

"Again I just happen to be in the pit, which is no big coincidence you understand, I'm there all day, and I say, '51 bid.' Since that is the highest bid, he sells it to me at $6.51. Now, if the price of beans goes up, you make a lot of money and your associate there loses a bunch. The reverse is true if the price goes down. I, however, have no position at all because the beans I sold to you I bought back from him and I made a penny per bushel, which will add $1,000 to my account, which I will write a check for, put the cash in my pocket, and do with as I please. Now, I defy any adviser to explain to me how your decision to play commodities in any way reduced my profits. Quite the contrary!

"May I ask you, sir, since you started this, what is your profession?"

"I'm a surgeon," he answered.

"And you make good money doing surgery?" I asked.

"I have a good practice, yes."

"Look," I said to him, "I'm pretty good with my hands and I love to work with the human body; do you think I could be a surgeon?"

"Well, it's demanding work, but if you wanted to badly enough, you might be able to become a surgeon."

"That's great!" I responded. "I'd like to start this weekend.

How much money do you think I could make doing surgery this weekend? I only want to work weekends and evenings, y'know, some income to augment my regular trading." They got the point.

"I have no objection to seeing any of you come into the business," I concluded. "I welcome you. But I do object to the part-time, armchair trader who thinks he is going to outsmart the marketplace and make a fortune in his spare time. This poor fool is little more than a bankruptcy looking to happen."

Afterward a man came up to me with a genuine interest in entering the industry and asked if there was a book or course of study one could follow. I have been asked this question for years and have never had an adequate answer. But now there is a book I can recommend that will enable a person to become a successful commodities trader, if it so happens that he has the unique and totally undefinable temperament for it. If a person can fully master one third of the content of this book, he is ready to become a successful commodities trader. I do not exaggerate when I say that there is more information to help one become a commodities speculator in this one book than in all other such books I have seen combined—that's correct, combined. I have given it to a number of people telling them to come and see me when they have digested a third of its content. None have reported back and I don't expect them to for a few years at least. Most investors prefer a quicker, easier route to a fortune because they still do not understand that there is none (other than luck, of course).

The book that stands completely alone in its class is entitled _____ . (I regret to say that the title had to be censored because a friend, reading a rough draft of this manuscript that included the title, went out and purchased the book, and soon thereafter began investing his savings in commodities. He made good money for a few weeks, then lost all he made, all his savings, and a lot more that he didn't have. He was ruined. I will have no more of such on my conscience.

The author of the book, who must know more about commodities than anyone I have ever met, knows enough that he *does not trade.)*

I was comfortably settled back at home in my recliner getting caught up on family matters and watching the local news when my tranquillity was rocked by a TV commercial. The ad showed a nerd standing in front of a silly-looking contraption saying, "This is going to make me a million dollars." The contraption then fell humorously apart. This scene was followed by a man with wings and a propeller mounted on his beanie, launching himself from atop a building with the same stupid-sounding voice, "This is going to make me a million dollars." The consequences were as hilarious as the real film footage of man's repeated flying failures.

The conclusion of the commercial: "Don't be a fool. Play the Illinois State million-dollar jackpot game." And the picture showed the pot of gold and the rainbow.

I could almost feel my temperature rise as my blood began to boil. I looked for something to throw at the TV. Is there no end to what they will do to poison our children's minds? I recalled my second-grade teacher, Mrs. Lipscomb, and her famous words: "Boys and girls, let's put those thinking caps on." Was she nuts? Now my state tells us to take the thinking caps off and make our fortune playing the lottery! Is this the best we can do for leadership? I wonder if these people ever read anything after dark. Yet they mock the hard work of invention. Edison failed more than five hundred times before he discovered tungsten. Some of his failures were probably more humorous than the lottery commercial. Thankfully he didn't follow their advice.

Presumably the same elected officials who brought us the lottery make use of airplanes to facilitate their busy schedules. But now they mock the visionary work of the Wright brothers and recommend in its place the lottery. Could it be that the great personal character of these men is a thing of the past? It is a sad question to contemplate right here in Illinois, the land of Lincoln.

I had just spent a lot of my time and money trying to convince people that investing in commodities is a losing proposition and our leaders came right out in public and told us to put our money in a known loser. No wealthy or educated person wastes his time and money on the lottery. Only the ignorant, the uninformed, the naively trusting—and especially the poor, get sucked in by it. It is another form of oppression.

And the most insidious thing about it is that they really do convince people that they have a reasonable chance of winning when the cold facts say precisely the opposite. All they have to do to "prove" their point is put a rags-to-riches winner on the tube. The mathematics that demonstrate the lottery to be a rip-off are difficult to appreciate when the rewards are so luscious, so immediate, so easy. That lovely moment of hope teaches people to put their trust in luck and stop going the extra mile to improve themselves and their families.

Where will the state stop in its quest for income? If we legalized drugs and prostitution, we could get additional tax revenue. In actual fact, the lottery has so much in comon with drug pushing and prostitution. It holds out a quick and easy short-term solution to a person's problem—in exchange for cash, of course. The disadvantaged are always the easiest victims of the short-term-solution trap.

There are intelligent people who invest in the lottery as a fun way to take a long shot on a fortune. They invest money they can afford to lose, thinking that this is precisely what the commodity investor does. This common conception that the commodities trader takes big risks to make a fortune is an insidious half-truth based on a fundamental misunderstanding of what it means to bear risk. While it may be true that the commodities trader takes big risks to make a large amount of money, he does so only when the odds are sufficiently in his favor. The point is demonstrated by what I call the Law of Gambling or Investing:

1. If the odds are in favor of the risk-bearer, then he is investing.
2. If the odds are against the risk-bearer, he is gambling.

Corollary: If the risk-bearer doesn't know what the odds are, he is a gambler and a fool.

The novice commodity investor-gambler and the lottery player may convince themselves they are investing, while in fact they are gambling foolishly. In commodities, we take lots of little risks, but only with favorable odds. To do otherwise is to take risk for no logical reason, but rather for sport, for the thrill of hoping to win, or for the rewards that come from luck. Following this course has resulted in the demise of many a commodities trader. The temptation to gamble is an occupational hazard of a commodities broker.

Around the floor of the exchange we have a saying: "You can make more money being lucky than being smart." It would be true, of course, if you could only be consistently lucky. Instead, it's a joke; it's humor based on the premise that luck is a two-edged sword; it gives and it takes away. The very phrase "consistently lucky" is humorously self-contradictory. But the state has taken this joke and passed it off as true.

Taking risk when the odds are not in your favor is just foolish. There is no nicer way to put it, it is foolishness; which is in the end what the lottery is: a tax on foolishness.

So the state tries to enhance its position by assuring people that their wasted dollars go to a good cause—education. Thus many intelligent people play the lottery with the thought that they are helping someone somewhere. It's another form of the old ends-justifying-the-means argument, namely, the money that the state earns by giving people a bad deal will go for a good cause. Is there a good way to spend bad money? To

202

carry the question to its ridiculous extreme: Would giving drug money to Mother Teresa justify the sale of drugs? While their intentions are good, it is sad that many such lottery players unwittingly fund the problem.

Let us face the brute facts, the lottery is supported with the grocery money of hungry children.

The ad I saw on my TV sent me a loud and clear message from my elected officials in Springfield: "If you fools will stop trying to *earn* a million dollars, and get a pie-in-the-sky vision of winning the lottery, we kind and generous leaders will keep your welfare checks from bouncing!"

Demonstrating the lottery to be a raw deal is easy. The commodities industry is much more complex. The public knows that the lottery is a bad deal yet they waste their money there anyway. The wealthy investor might be in commodities just for the action, which he can afford—for a while anyway. Vegas action would be a lot cheaper, but it doesn't have the status.

These naive commodity speculators would never admit it, but they have a lot in common with the poor, dreaming Lotto player.

An even more interesting question is how much they both share in common with the commodity or stock speculator. The answer requires a precise definition of greed. I thought everyone knew what greed was until the news broke about the inside traders on Wall Street. Then I heard a psychiatrist on national TV try to explain why a wealthy man would engage in illegal activity to add more hundreds of millions to his already wealthy portfolio. The psychiatrist's first response was that his action had nothing to do with greed. "This man has more money than he can ever possibly spend," he commented with an air of certainty. "That demonstrates that his need for more couldn't possibly be greed." Now I was really puzzled. I had always thought that greed was the desire on the part of a person to have a great deal more than one could ever need. Now this psychiatrist, who certainly should know, says that a person who strives for more is not greedy if he can show that he has no need for it at all.

One of the inside traders demonstrated the confusion. He was well received at a prestigious business school when he said, "I think greed is healthy. You can be greedy and still feel good about yourself."

The first maxim of speculating is that no one should ever risk money that he needs. But if he doesn't need the money he is risking, he certainly doesn't need the profit which that speculation could bring. Does that mean that his aim for further profit is based on greed? Who's to say? Looking back on my first investment in commodities, I doubt if I understand what part greed had to play in my actions. It may be the most difficult of all vices for a person to recognize in himself. I'd heard people admit to having a variety of vices from time to time, but I'd never in my life heard anyone admit to being personally greedy. This motive (or vice, depending on your definition) plays a significant role in the yells and screams of the commodity pits of Chicago; more than we understand.

"He who has the most when he dies wins," was a quote attributed to one of the inside traders. I sat at our dining room table, staring out the window, and watching this news unfold.

Don't these greedy people know that their only security is in their ability to preserve their conspiracy? Yet somehow in the end they wind up being persuaded to rat on each other. It reminded me of what I called the Law of the Pressurized Conspirator; the principle that the greater pressure that is applied to a conspirator, the more likely he is to reveal the conspiracy. It was this very principle that had finally convinced me that the resurrection of Jesus from the dead was a historic event.

Watergate conspirator Charles Colson was the first to notice this principle of the pressurized conspirator. In his book *Loving God*, Colson observed that even with all the power of the presidential office to be preserved, his small band of loyal followers of the president could not contain the Watergate coverup for more than three weeks. As the enemies of the White House increased the pressure, the men of power gave in to the instinct of self-preservation. Indeed, the likelihood of exposure increased as the pressure on the individuals increased. For purposes of comparison, Colson hypothesized that the original founders of the Christian faith were a band of conspirators like those involved in Watergate; that they had, as my atheist professor suggested, disposed of their beloved leader's body in some hidden spot and proceeded to proclaim him miraculously alive. They soon found themselves the objects of the most cruel torture. And the more widely they spread their story, the more misery they had to endure. After his own experience as a conspirator, Colson observed that they could not have endured the pressure and kept their story intact had they been conspirators.

While U.S. Attorney Rudolph Giuliani told how Ivan Boesky would lead him to the other inside traders, I scribbled out a chart comparing Boesky, Colson, and the disciples. I suspected that these groups might not be as comparable as Colson had originally thought. In fact they were opposite. I drew circles around the positive motivating factors.

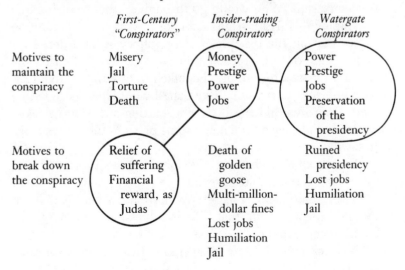

	First-Century "Conspirators"	Insider-trading Conspirators	Watergate Conspirators
Motives to maintain the conspiracy	Misery Jail Torture Death	Money Prestige Power Jobs	Power Prestige Jobs Preservation of the presidency
Motives to break down the conspiracy	Relief of suffering Financial reward, as Judas	Death of golden goose Multi-million-dollar fines Lost jobs Humiliation Jail	Ruined presidency Lost jobs Humiliation Jail

The inside traders have everything to gain, while the first century conspirators had not only no positive things to gain but were inflicting on themselves more misery than it is possible for a human being to comprehend. In addition, the exposure of the insiders would not only have removed their power and money, but would also have brought upon them great shame and possible jail terms. The opposite was the case for the disciples. Their exposure would not only have stopped their suffering, it might have produced significant financial and political reward for the individual who could have effected the exposure. Yet they maintained their story.

I sat recalling those early days of marriage when I would come home from the library and confront my new bride with some of the ideas.

"Do you realize what the disciples had to go through to pull off their hoax?" I had asked her on one occasion.

"Well, there was a lot of persecution, wasn't there?" she answered.

"Persecution! Good night, they were hunted, beaten, imprisoned, tortured, and murdered in slow, inhumane ways. Even St. Paul hunted and tortured the Christians before he was converted. Who would go through all that to maintain a conspiracy?" I read from some of my notes: " 'Tradition agrees that all the disciples except John were murdered for their faith. Andrew, for example, was crucified. During the two days it took him to die, he talked to bystanders about his faith in Jesus.' Can you believe that? I would have been telling them where we hid the body and cutting a deal to be taken down. I might have even made some profit in the process, like Judas did."

"I don't know," she said. "People have been known to die for causes that were just wrong."

"Yeah, that's right. That's why I have never been convinced by the old argument that Christianity was proven by the blood of the martyrs."

"Neither have I," she answered. "Just because someone

died for something doesn't make them any more right about their opinion than anyone else. What does it prove? Only that they are sincerely convinced, maybe misled."

"But this is different and that's just the point. The torturous death of the first-century eyewitnesses doesn't prove that they are smarter than anyone else. But it does prove beyond any doubt that their testimony was sincere. They had to have been absolutely convinced that they had seen him alive."

"Y'know, I've never thought of it like that before," she said.

"No, I hadn't either. Think about it for a minute. Can you recall any other historic event in which witnesses endured such pain while still insisting it was true?"

"No, but there have hardly been such bold claims," she said.

"And if an individual's testimony is strengthened by the amount of torture he is willing to endure without denying it, then the resurrection of Christ must be the most thoroughly established event of all time."

"Well, it would have to be," she said, "if anyone would be expected to believe it. It does seem like quite a coincidence, though, that an event so difficult to prove would also have the strongest evidence for it."

"I think it makes sense. If someone were to attempt to show his credibility for all history to observe, he would have to do it with a claim that could not be topped, one that would have the most credible support for it. A long list of tortured and martyred eyewitnesses who couldn't be forced to alter their story is pretty hard to improve upon." If Christianity were to be demonstrated false, the resurrection claim was no place to start. Yet this was the most outlandish claim of all.

I had discovered that I could not fault Christianity on its factual claims. These claims had for years appeared to lack logical support simply because I had been asked to accept them on a leap of faith; raising questions was considered unholy. I had finally had the courage to skeptically scrutinize the claims, and in the end I concluded:

That God had indeed invaded history in the form of a messiah, the carpenter from Nazareth;

That he had done the sensational things that one might expect of a god-man and left a trail of evidence that any honest mind could follow;

That he so affected people that the mere acceptance of his message totally altered lives, turning people of no account into world shakers;

That the original accounts of his life have been copied and reprinted in such great numbers and in so many languages that in all of written material there is no close second;

That the subsequent volumes of books written of him would fill whole libraries;

That as a subject of the world's greatest art he would have no equal;

That he would become the inspiration for more of the world's finest music than all other great men combined;

That his message of love would immeasurably enhance the life of any person in any century who had the humility to accept it;

That the annual celebration of his birth would re-create widespread feelings of his ancient theme of peace on earth, goodwill toward men—a theme that rings so forcefully across the centuries that it cannot be diminished even by the commercialization surrounding it;

That his death and resurrection would likewise promote annual celebrations of inexplicable proportions;

That wherever his message made inroads, societies would *always* change for the better;

That his following would grow in number (all predictions of atheists notwithstanding), now estimated at one billion, and would regularly take time from their schedules to meet and sing his praises, calling him their God;

That 2,000 years later he would give meaning, purpose, and direction to the life of a humble, mixed up person— namely, me.

Quite an accomplishment for a lynched carpenter with a net worth of zero. It made a believer out of me.

If greed is not enough to get a speculator to put his money into the market, the social status attached to a person who makes his money by wizardry is. It enables one through a variety of exciting stories to communicate that he can make money the new-fashioned way—without earning it.

But usually greed is enough. It represents the occupational hazard of the financial industry.

I was standing at the top of the bean pit one day mostly minding my own business, trying to keep my risk exposure lower than normal since opportunities for profit were down and the possibilities for losses seemed a lot higher than usual, when I noticed that a familiar face was missing from the group. "Hey, where's Tom?" I asked Jack, a fellow trader.

"Oh, he went tapo." (Tapo is short for "tapped out," which basically means that the flow of money has run out, the margin call cannot be met, and the water's been cut off at the meter—in short, you're broke. It's nicer than saying belly up, but it means the same thing.) My mouth fell open in disbelief.

"You're kidding?" I responded in sheer amazement.

"No," he said. "I've seen it coming for some time now. I could tell by the way he was trading that he'd been taking some substantial hits."

Normally the news about someone going belly up is not quite so close to home, but Jack and I knew Tom quite well. He was one of the most respected traders in the pit and one of the nicest guys anyone could want to meet. It was sort of a tragedy.

"Did he take anyone down with him, cost anyone a bundle?" I inquired. No one seemed to really know the answer to the question. In fact, even more disturbing was that no one was certain of his whereabouts. I made a number of inquiries and discovered that Tom was in a detoxification center for drug and alcohol abuse.

That Saturday morning, on the drive down to the detox center to visit Tom, I recalled the day, a few years earlier, when he and I had had lunch together. Tom had totally surprised me that day by telling me about a number of severe problems that had been bothering him, and how it had resulted in the breakup of his marriage. He was living in an apartment up the street from the board of trade and had to pass the Moody Bible Institute each day on his way to and from the pits. He told me how he had run into a small group of kids at the school who had informed him that he had to get his life straightened out with God. Like myself, Tom had been raised in a religious home, only in his case Catholic. Also, like me, he had come to realize that even with all his ability, he was systematically screwing up his life.

"I just came to the end of my rope and asked God to forgive me and help me," he had said. "I genuinely feel like I've been born again." For a person raised a Catholic to use that phrase, born again, is about as strange as for one raised a Fundamentalist to be out dancing.

"I was real nervous," he continued, "when I called my priest and told him about the Protestants I had been associating with. His response shocked me. He shouted 'Hallelujah!' " Obviously this priest was one of the new breed who was more concerned about my friend's spiritual health than he was about his formal Church affiliation.

I met Tom in the lobby of the hospital. He told me how his troubles in the pit had led him to drinking a little more after each day's market close. Troubles in trading have a way of snowballing. As a trader loses money he tries to get it back by trading bigger quantities, thus increasing the risk and making losses even bigger. Tom had been taking larger and larger positions until he was no longer able to meet the margin call. Another victim had fallen to the occupational hazard of gambling. As the gambling problem got worse the dependence on alcohol increased.

I visited Tom several times over the next few weeks as he

went through the twelve steps of AA. I attended, along with his son, an encounter group for friends and family. I recall being asked to give a one-word description of how I felt. We went around the room in a circle. "Down," I said. This was no time to be hiding my feelings. After all, not only was my buddy broke and in the hospital, but I had just dropped a quarter of a million that week myself.

On one of my visits we talked about the twelve steps to freedom. "What do you make of all this 'higher power' talk?" he asked me as we ate lunch together between sessions.

"You don't need me to tell you about the higher power," I said. "You know as well as I do that the God of Abraham, Isaac, and Jacob made this place and personally walked around here; even did some carpentry work on it."

"Yeah, that's true," he said, "but they define the higher power as 'whatever your idea of it might be.' I would think that if there is some actual power out there, one might be a little more interested in some accuracy about it, or him, or her." He laughed. "Well, who cares, y'know, whatever your idea is."

"You've got a point there," I admitted.

"Just suppose," he speculated, "that all my teachers in school had graded my tests that way. 'Well,' she says, 'whatever your idea of the answer is, it'll still be useful.' This is an odd way to approach reality."

"I wonder what they would think," I said, half joking, "if I claim that my higher power wants me to drink more so that I will abuse my children so that after a life of pain and misery they can be reincarnated as higher beings."

"That's real good, Mark. That sounds just like something you'd think of." After years in the pit together, Tom knew me pretty well.

"Seriously though," I went on, "suppose I just raise my hand at the next session and say, 'My higher power is the same one Jim Jones, Adolf Hitler, and Charley Manson had and he just makes me feel great about myself.'"

"Hey, that's great buddy. They'll ask who you're here to help and next thing I know, I'll be listed as a danger to society. It's an interesting point though. Jones, Hitler, and Manson all have a higher power. I guess for Jones and Hitler I should say 'had,' thank God. It just seems that if this higher power is as critical as they say, we might be a little more discriminating."

"It's sort of an academic discussion, don't you think, because you and I know the God who is the higher power."

"That's true. And look at all the good it's done me," he said, laughing. "I mean, being broke and drunk is not exactly the top of the world."

"Well," I asked, "are you willing to lean on your higher power to control the alcohol dependency?" The question slowed the pace of the conversation more than I had intended.

"I don't know," he hedged. "I'm not sure the answer is all that simple. I'm not convinced that a little drink now and then is that big a deal."

"Are you saying you're not convinced there is a problem that requires a higher power?" I asked point-blank.

"I guess I'm not sure," he said unconvincingly, and I could now see what Tom needed—and it wasn't some more accurate theology. He needed help with his dependency on alcohol. But how does one get help if he doesn't really know he needs it? Somehow this situation gave me a little déjà vu. Hadn't I been in this identical spot myself, unwilling to admit just how proud and arrogant I was? Just like an alcoholic, I had refused to admit I had a problem. What good did it do to know all about this higher power if one refused to admit there was a problem that required help? Oh, I knew his dilemma. I'd been here a thousand times. Blame the problem on someone else. Tell myself why I'm okay. Tell myself that no one else is any better. I'm only human after all. Make every excuse one can possibly think of. Anything to avoid having to admit that I desperately need help from someone outside myself. I knew how agonizing it was to have to eat the humble pie that God required, and I genuinely felt sorry for anyone put in that position. But I also knew that there is no solution to the human problem without the humility necessary to face one's moral need.

"Look," I said, "you say that you came to the end of your rope a few years ago and turned to God for help."

"Yeah, that's right."

"Well, this is nothing more than an opportunity to confirm that decision. Just ask yourself, 'Have I messed up? Do I need God's help?' If the answer is 'no,' then renounce your first decision and move ahead on your own. If 'yes,' then ask God's forgiveness all over again and get his help to go on."

"I don't know," he said, thinking the whole thing over. "It seems so cruel, so dehumanizing, it strips one of all his dignity."

"Well, you tell me, Tom, just how much dignity do you get after you've irresponsibly squandered your family's money in the market and used alcohol to help ignore the problem?"

He laughed. "Well, if you're going to put it that way." It was tough talk, but my friend was back to that horrible problem I had faced—a simple matter of pride. "This isn't easy y'know."

"If I knew an easier way, buddy," I said, "I'd be the first to tell you about it, because this is murder on the self-image."

Tom was able to face himself and ask God's forgiveness and not long after, by a "curious coincidence," was able to obtain a membership and get back into the pit and trade, this time under the full control of his faculties. How much sweeter it is to see relationships healed rather than terminated.

CHAPTER 10

The Love of God Compels Us

By now it was obvious that Nancy and I weren't just lucky winners in life's quest for wealth. We had been given a responsibility that masqueraded as wealth. A lot of people talked about the virtuous things they would do if only they had a million dollars. Some would even belittle the generosity of the wealthy, saying, "Well, if I had all his money, I'd be glad to give half of it away," without ever thinking to give half of what they do have.

We were ill prepared for this responsibility. I had never taken a course at seminary that taught what to do with all the money I would make while serving the Lord, though there were some who could have taught such a course. I saw them on TV, wearing a high percentage of what they earned. And if they couldn't wear it all, they would find a way to flaunt the rest, demonstrating how wealthy God wants his children to be.

But anyone who had read the gospels knew better. We also knew that to whom much is given, much will be required. And it seemed to us that the people in the greatest need usually were doing the greatest good while those with the slick fund-raising techniques often produce little of substance.

*   *   *

Joe and I entered the trading floor one day only to discover to our surprise that our position was off by a hundred beans and the market opened eight cents against us for an $8,000 loss. It was one of the biggest losses we had taken and put me in the worst frame of mind.

We liquidated all our positions because Jimmy Carter was due to address the nation that evening. When a politician speaks, there is no predicting what might happen. This was doubly true under President Carter.

When we got back to the office at the end of trading, we found that things had gotten worse. Our orders to liquidate our trades had not all been executed. Somebody had messed up and failed to get us out of our position in Japanese yen.

In a pretty sick state of mind over the bean loss and the yen exposure, I went to church that night to hear a guest speaker from England who was a friend of a friend. We met afterward and went to a small cafe. He had coffee and I had my usual chocolate shake. Throughout his talk he had never mentioned any need for funds. Knowing that unless a preacher makes his financial needs highly visible, he usually starves, I asked him about it.

"Well," he told me reluctantly while thoughtfully stirring his coffee, "I really hate to speak about financial needs. It's so easy to be misunderstood."

"Don't worry," I said. "I brought the subject up and I can always ignore it if I wish."

"I do worry, though, so many people in this country give simply because the appeal from the professional clergy is so strong. They just assume that if a, quote-unquote, man of God asks for money, it's the same as God himself asking them personally for cash."

"There's no way I could agree with you more," I said, almost excited to hear someone agreeing with me.

"So we never ask people, we only ask God," he said.

"I'll bet you don't bring in a lot of dough that way, do you?" I asked.

216

"No. Not near as much as we could, that's for sure. But you know, even though we will never have the cash that the high-profile fund-raisers have, our needs are always met. It's amazing, really. God's work doesn't need megabucks."

"I guess you're right there," I mused. "Christ did pretty well on a shoestring budget. Anyway, now that *I've* brought the subject up, what about your own financial situation?"

"All right, since you seem genuinely interested, I'll mention one item: We don't have a car."

"You don't have a car!" I reacted like a typical American, unable to imagine that life would be worth living without a car. "You've got to be kidding. Do you have anything specific in mind?"

"Yes. My family has been praying for a Volkswagen beetle that a dealer near us is holding."

"How much is it?"

"Eighteen hundred dollars." Not an extravagant request, I thought, when compared to some of the stuff I had been buying lately. I had been feeling pretty sorry for myself over the losses I'd incurred that day, which hadn't affected my standard of living one whit. So I told my new friend that we would buy the car for his wife. It made his day. Mine, too.

I finished my shake and drove him to the home where he was staying and he thanked me again, asked if he could pray for me and did so, and said good night. I should have asked him to mention those Japanese, who were very likely at that moment destroying my yen position, especially since Carter had announced plans to affect the currency to my detriment.

I felt good as I left this humble preacher, but I couldn't help wondering about my sanity as I drove home. A losing day, followed by a butchering in the yen, and I go and give away $1,800!

Joe met me the next morning in the soybean oil pit. "We're out of our yen position by now I assume?" I asked without looking at the board. Then I glanced up and saw that it had moved sharply in our favor. "Holy cow! What happened?"

"We got lucky," he answered. "No sooner had Jimmy Carter stopped talking than the Japanese started trading just the opposite of what he suggested."

"What's the matter with those guys?" I said. "Don't they have any respect for our president? So what does it look like we made on the trade?"

"On the whole thing over the last few months, you probably made $2,700, but most of that, I'd say about two thirds, was made because we were mistakenly in the market last night. And we certainly wouldn't have been if those guys in the yen pit had done their job."

Two thirds of $2,700, I thought to myself. Hmm, very close to the value of a used VW. I was learning in real tangible terms that it is more blessed to give than to receive. Of course, I always knew this to be true—in theory. Everyone knows it to be true in theory, but I felt it; a wave of emotion came over me and I caught the message, "Mark, to share with someone in need, in your whole life you'll never do better than this."

I looked out the window of the six-passenger plane to a sea of Amazon jungle that stretched as far as the eye could see. The engine was so loud I couldn't ask the pilot to prove to me he wasn't lost. So all I could do was wonder how I let myself into this mess.

Somewhere along the line I had concluded that maybe God could use the dollar more than he could the scholar. From my experience up to this point, it was difficult to say which of the two I respected more. Certainly the hippies of the sixties didn't burn and destroy the goods of the wealthy, hypocritical establishment for no reason at all (even if no one was sure what the reason was). Convinced that the wealthy could make a difference if they chose, I put my master of divinity degree on hold and continued to make money. Nancy and I had been toying with the idea of travel when a friend engaged me in a discussion of the amazing diversity of culture on our globe. He told me about a culture that demands that each time someone dies, his death must be avenged by killing someone from some other village. When that person dies, his village goes on the vengeance warpath too. It sounded like one of those conundrums that ends with the question: How many people will be left to carry on the cultural identity?

Now he was sitting behind me while we completed the last leg of a three-day trip, extended by delays to six. We were going to visit an acquaintance of his, a missionary who had, probably without thinking, invited him to "come on down and visit anytime." I had to admit to myself as we flew over mile after mile of uninhabited jungle that in my mind, there still existed some questions about the universal practicality of Christ's claims. While they have made significant inroads in the countries of the West, I wondered about the difference that the Christian message might make in an area of abject poverty, like that in which I had grown up as a boy. My studies in sociology had led me to believe that there might still be areas on the globe whose cultures were unpolluted by the obvious moral decay of the West. If so, then there should be little need for missionaries to go to these areas. After all, who needs a message of "peace on earth, goodwill toward men" if you already live in peace. Anthropologists have strongly advocated that these people should be left alone to prevent any interference from the outside. This trip would allow me to see the totally uncontacted Indian as well as the Indians who had been under the influence of Christianity.

Three hours later the roar of the engine cut back and we began descending toward the shortest strip of green grass I had ever seen. Like a small, green dash mark, it interrupted the sea of dense treetops.

"We're gonna hit that thing, are we?" I asked the pilot.

"That's what I'm here for," he told me with enough confidence in his voice to give me some. We glided in over the river and touched down gently on the soft grass.

Our plane was immediately surrounded by strange looking dark people dressed in little or no clothes with bows, arrows, machetes, and other intimidating tools of jungle survival that I didn't recognize. Stepping out of the plane, I met Mike, whose invitation got us into this. "These people around us," I asked him while trying not to motion toward them, "what's the meaning of all the weapons?"

Mike laughed. "Relax. They're the friendly ones."

"Where are we?" I asked.

"C'mon, I'll explain while we're eating. The gals have been holding dinner till your plane arrived." We approached a mud-walled house with a tin roof, met Mike's wife and sister-in-law and sat down to a delicious meal of tapir meat. "You're about a thousand miles inland by river on a tributary of the upper Orinoco River," Mike told us. I was as separated from civilization as was Herat. "This village was contacted by my parents many years ago and has for years accepted the Christian message."

After a few days of hunting and fishing, it was obvious that these were kind and friendly Indians. I queried the leader of the village as to the difference that Christianity had made there. The chief, raised a killer, had a refreshing way of speaking bluntly and to the point.

"Before we heard the message about Christ, we lived the most miserable existence imaginable. Every moment of the day our lives were consumed by fear that the people we hunted to kill might kill us. If they couldn't kill us, they would steal our wives and kill our babies. Since we've turned to Christ, we have lived in peace. Our lives have improved beyond description. When you go visit some of my people in other villages, you will see what I mean. They still live in horrible fear."

I had to admit that his was not the sort of village I had expected to find. The studies showed that these people were fierce and ruthless killers. I was therefore most curious about the debate among sociologists and anthropologists that these people should be left to live their beautiful Shangri-la–style lives in peace, unencumbered with Western ideals.

So I asked him, "You know, there are many people who believe that you ought to be left alone out here in the jungle, not interfered with at all; what would you say to them?"

"These people are ignorant," he responded quickly. "They have no idea of the amount of pain and misery that is endured by my people here. Why they would not want us to improve our lives is a complete mystery to us. They improve theirs, don't they? Do they think we are less than human, that we do not feel pain, that we do not experience grief when a relative is killed?"

"I understand that an anthropologist wanted to come to your village once and you refused him permission. Why?" I asked.

"I've been out to the big city. I've seen pictures of our naked women being sold there for profit. I know that these people write books and make money off of the misery that we live in. I know that they don't want us to change because then they couldn't take pictures and write books about our misery. These people are sick. Am I a dog that I should allow them to treat my village and my family like this?"

"You don't really sound like an uneducated Indian. You know that, don't you?"

"Almost all of what I know I have learned from the missionaries who have come to live with us," he told me.

"You know what they will say about that in my country, don't you? They'll say that you have been brainwashed by these missionaries. All you know is what they have taught you. What would you say to people who say that?"

I watched him react with impatient anger as my question was translated to him. Maybe a little discretion on my part would have been better. After all, I wasn't Mike Wallace doing a "60 Minutes" piece in the safety of someone's office. Nowhere is it written that a converted headhunter couldn't revert, even only temporarily, back to his old habits. Maybe I really did have some solid confidence in this Christian message.

221

"These people are so ignorant," he said. "They laugh at us. They mock my people. I would tell them that they weren't here to see the constant pain that I personally endured. I would tell them to come out here in the middle of the jungle, and don't bring those shotguns or any of those supplies. And no clothes. They think we are so Western for wearing clothes. Let them come out here and live out in the middle of the jungle with nothing but a bow and arrow to stay alive. We'll even help them learn how to plant manioc before we send them off to a happy life in the jungle. These people are experts at writing books, but when it comes to the real world of the jungle, they are so ignorant."

I was anxious to get off to a village where we could talk to an Indian who had never before seen the face of a white man. After another day and a half traveling up into the headwaters of one of the tributaries, I got my chance. We met a man who was the head of a small band of Indians and highly respected as a fierce warrior. He had heard rumors of the strange peaceful situation that had broken out in the village of Cosh. He had heard that it was the result of belief in a different god, and he wanted someone to come to his village and instruct his people in these new ways.

The difference between his village and Cosh was shocking. I had actually moved into a completely different culture. I inquired of his interest in this new god and why it was that he wanted a change in his way of life.

"We live in complete misery here," he said, sitting up in his hammock. "We hear that these Indians who have adopted a new god no longer kill each other, that they live in peace, that their lives are much better. We want that for ourselves."

"There are many people who say that you are only interested in the trade goods that the missionaries bring with them," I said.

"If that's what you think, then just send some Indians who have no trade goods. They can teach us about this new god."

"I'm interested in helping anyone I can," I told him, "but I must tell you that there are many people in my country who believe that you are happy here and that I should just leave you alone."

The loincloth-clad savage became animated. "Please don't listen to them. They think that because we live out here in the jungle that the bugs don't hurt us when they bite. Let them come out here and take their clothes off and see what it's like."

His favorite and oldest wife cooking a strange-smelling meal for him close by, the dense jungle surrounding us, and the simplicity of these people told me that technological progress has little to do with one's ability to reason clearly. I recalled the story of an ignorant blind man who was harassed by the religious establishment, which insisted on knowing how he had come to see. His simple reply, "All I know is that once I was blind and now I see," was similar to the attitude of these Indians who were only interested in results.

But what could I, a person caught in a different time zone, do to help? A few hassle-filled days of travel later and I had crossed back over the thousand-year barrier that prevents civilization from meeting these surprisingly insightful people. Back in the pit, with the cries of bids and offers rattling through my head, it was easy to forget. But I was certain of one thing: A person of means must bear some obligation to do something.

One of our most memorable experiences in trying to help the poor began many years earlier. It all started back in the summer of '79. The news media grabbed on to the highly visible tragedy in Southeast Asia and began using it to attract the attention of anyone with a TV. Nancy said to me, "Mark, we have to do something." Her emotional reaction was almost humorous. I knew full well that the news media used the plight of the boat people to increase ratings and sell advertising spots. I also knew that once the public tired of seeing wretched, starving people packed like sardines into little boats, the news coverage would cease and the public outcry disappear.

In the meantime, they held our attention. "We've just got to do something," she repeated.

"We're already using our money to help the poor in other parts of Asia," I responded. I knew that the massive media coverage would result in so much money and assistance pouring into Southeast Asia by every guilt-ridden do-gooder that the relief effort would turn into a three-ring circus overnight. I was also painfully aware of the incredibly low percentage of each dollar donated that actually went into the mouths of the needy in the form of real assistance. But I knew she was right, we just had to do something.

"Nancy," I said carefully, "how much do you know about some of these organizations that are making these public appeals for funds?"

"Well, they seem to have a good reputation."

"Do you have any idea," I asked, "how much ignorance the donors of these organizations share about what goes on there?"

"Well, no."

"It would strike fear into the heart of any rational person. And sudden insistence by donors of a full accounting would strike fear into the heart of most TV fund-raisers. We wouldn't buy a car without first kicking the tires. We wouldn't make an investment without first investigating the facts. So we shouldn't donate money to a nonprofit organization without having some information about what's going on there."

The number of relief organizations around the world were exploding in the wake of the free advertising available on the nightly evening news. We watched a TV fund-raiser show graphic pictures of starving, half-dead or already-dead children and appeal to our sense of humanity to give. We were overcome by how forgetful we were to be thankful, guilty for having so much. There it was again, those inequities now invading my plush family room. Nancy grabbed the phone to call the number on the screen and pledge a large donation. After she hung up they called right back to verify that it wasn't a prank.

It was a routine that was occurring all across the country. A guilt-ridden viewer grabs his checkbook and writes out a check to an organization about which he is completely uninformed, to be used by people he doesn't know, spent on behalf of people he's never seen, in a country where he's never been, using methods that he might not approve (if he could ever find out about them), to perpetuate a cause (or a bureaucracy) of which he is almost totally ignorant.

There was, however, no amount of cynicism and no amount of fund-raising abuse that could ever relieve us of our obligation as members of humanity; simply summarized by Nancy's plea, we've just got to do something. "Well, I suppose we could go there," I said one night after watching the news, "and spend some time working as volunteers in the refugee camps to get a real good feel for where the needs lie and what organizations would be the best to become financially involved with."

"We've always thought we might end up working with the poor someday," Nancy said. "Never in my wildest dreams did I ever think it would be from the standpoint of a wealthy donor."

I began calling relief organizations. "I'm Mark Ritchie," I would say, "and my wife and I are interested in volunteering our services to help work in the refugee camps of Southeast Asia." I was stunned by the lack of interest I discovered. Surely these organizations must have needed some type of help. Maybe I needed to be more aggressive in my approach. So I called them all back.

"My wife and I would like to pay our way and all our expenses while we serve your organization." Same disinterested response. It was time to try an even more aggressive third approach.

"My wife and I would like to donate to the projects in which you are involved. We would like to spend some time working as volunteers to have a more personal involvement."

The lack of interest continued to shock me. Their standard response: "The only volunteer help we are looking for right now would require a medical background. But there are a variety of projects to which you can contribute if you would like." I would try to explain that I wanted to donate to something where I had a hands-on involvement. Obviously the current consciousness in the country had greatly increased their cash flow, thereby reducing their need for people with my attitude.

But we moved ahead largely on the strength of Nancy's conviction that we were under obligation to do something. It's just that doing something was going to take a lot more courage and risk than we might have originally expected. Totally incapable of finding an organization through which we could gain some exposure to the nature of the problem at the local level, we decided to go on our own, find some refugee camps, knock on some doors, and see what could be done to help.

This approach to assistance to the poor has hardly an argument to recommend it. Nevertheless, in the face of the alternatives—to do nothing or to send a check based on ignorance—we felt it would be wiser to actually go on our own and run the risk of looking like fools. Nancy was conveniently pregnant and about to graduate so it looked as if I would have to do the job solo—making a fool of myself, that is.

With fear and trepidation I purchased a one-way ticket to Hong Kong, figuring that once I arrived there and got some feeling for the situation, I could proceed from that point. On the eve of my departure, quite by coincidence, I discovered that the president of one of the large relief agencies and his assistant were flying into Chicago. I arranged to meet them at the airport and drove them to their hotel for the evening. Nancy came with me and we invited the two gentlemen to coffee. The man shocked me when he said that the relief which went to Nicaragua in the aftermath of the earthquake so disrupted the economy that it actually created a greater disaster than the earthquake itself. My subsequent experiences would demonstrate that I was wrong to suspect him of exaggerating.

"There are a number of things that you could do on behalf of our organization while you're there, if you are willing," he told me. "When were you planning on leaving?"

"In the morning." Their mouths dropped open simultaneously as they entertained the notion that I intended to fly to Southeast Asia with no official connection. "It was really her fault," I said, gesturing to Nancy. "She kept saying, 'We've just got to do something.' What could I say? She was right."

They finally suggested that I go as a representative of their organization. I spent a day at their headquarters, then I headed west for Hong Kong for a few days and from there to Kuala Lampur, Malaysia, one of the nicest and friendliest countries in the world. Here I had to be careful to represent the Canadian branch of the relief agency that had graciously arranged my trip. The American agencies had so offended the Malays with their arrogant attitude that they had all been kicked out of the country. I was told not to mention any connection with America in order to avoid receiving any prejudicial treatment. Most of the refugees helped here were Vietnamese boat people who had escaped from Vietnam by launching from shore in badly overcrowded boats. Many of these people landed on an island controlled by the Malaysian government, a now famous and most popular filming spot.

So much of the medicine that came from Western donors was out of date that it took more time to sort it than it was actually worth. The foodstuffs as well were often so rotten and disease-ridden that it required great additional expense just to handle and dispose of it in a sanitary fashion. No doubt the donors of all this material meant well, but in their rush to do good they often compounded the problem.

My hosts were so gracious, it was shameful that anyone

could have offended them to the point of being ousted from the country. But I was not about to take the risk of asking for any details.

The Malaysian government had received bad press in the West. Reports were circulated that some of the boats that landed on the island were towed back to open sea and abandoned. Public outcry against the Malaysian government was horrendous, though I don't recall hearing of any Western governments offering to allow the Malaysians to ship those boatloads of people to their shores.

In Thailand, I worked side by side with the doctors, nurses, and maintenance personnel who had voluntarily sacrificed their own comforts and futures to help the obviously less fortunate. When I was able to get a few moments alone, I would go off by myself to spend time among the people in the camp.

Walking along the little pathway that leads between the tents, I could see up ahead the thick haze of dust and smoke that lay over the camp like a blanket of oppression. Ahead of me was an ocean of tents stretching almost as far as the eye could see, forming a quilt of faded rotten rags.

The lack of water created a dusty dryness that reminded me of the days of my boyhood in Afghanistan. It had been twenty years since I had seen at this close range the total destitution of families in hopeless conditions. The lack of any sanitary plan left an aroma that pressed down over the camp. Poverty even has its own unique smell. It brought back that feeling of total helplessness that had overwhelmed me as a youngster. Now, in my early thirties, well into an established career, it was almost impossible to remember those early days, and the youthful idealism that said, "When I get big, things will be a different." No human being could respond any differently after seeing and smelling what I had as a child. Now, it was all coming back to me—and with the same powerful impressions attached.

It was sad how little was actually being done for the poor.

Some middle-class theologians had defined Christ's words so that the "oppressed" were seen as those who are spiritually and emotionally distressed. Anyone who had walked in the shadow of economic oppression, seen it reflected in the eyes of its victims, knew that it was of these Jesus spoke when he talked of oppression.

"Everyone else is not your responsibility, Mark," I could still hear my father say while I peered into these makeshift tents into which were crowded families of ten to twenty people. Yeah, yeah, I remember.

I never intended to lose the idealism of my youth, how I would make things different when I grew up. This wasn't the same race of people, but the conditions, the smells, the looks of desperation were identical.

Translating idealism into reality, however, involved things that had little romantic appeal: hard work, sacrifice, tears, even the preservation of sanity. How do these workers maintain their mental stability in a place like this, I wondered? The answer was, some don't.

One missionary girl sat in the oppressive heat hour after hour nursing a little baby. Thirty-six hours later, when the baby died, she broke down and cried bitterly. It was Christmas day. If one could get that emotionally involved over the loss of one infant, I couldn't see how a person could keep himself together in this cradle of perpetual death.

There were signs of lost wealth here; people with solid-gold capped teeth. They are now no different than the rest of the poor of Asia, maybe even worse off. Along with the depressing smells and sights of the refugee camp were the sounds: babies crying, mothers cooking their rations for the day, children playing. Seeing the children play was especially depressing, knowing that their future held grim prospects indeed. These whom I saw were the very few who survived.

Around the dinner table that evening one of the nurses told of the early days. Truckloads of bodies had been delivered during the monsoon season. It was their responsibility to separate the dead from the living, decide who among the living were most likely to survive, and concentrate their medical efforts on them. The first job was to get the dying out of the mud and dried off. Some found themselves incapable of dealing with the situation. "Medical school never offered courses in bedside manner for these places," she said.

One morning I was awakened by a guy I had been helping with some of the construction work. "It's Sally's day off and she wants me to take her over to another refugee area ten miles south," he told me while I tried to wake up. "I'm gonna run down there with her. Would you like to come along?"

"Is it as hot down there as it is here?" I asked while thinking of a reason why I couldn't.

"It's hotter."

"Doesn't Sally know she's not gonna be able to keep up this pace if she doesn't take a day off once in a while?" I had been working for three days straight and was about to drop. The nurses got one day off out of seven. "Do all these nurses find extra work to do on their days off?"

"Well, Sally's a little different," he told me. "Anyway, no one tells her when to stop. Comin'?" I'd given up enough comfort when I left home in the first place, now I was asked to make the same sacrifice every morning? And all day long? Sally must be another of those people whom Jesus spoke of when he talked about the last being first. She certainly couldn't have commanded much status where I come from, not by my standards anyway. She reminded me of the lady I had met two weeks earlier on my way out here. I hadn't met her actually, but I knew I wouldn't be able to forget her for a long time.

On the way to the Orient, I had decided to take a two-day detour. I stopped in Portland and drove south to Corvallis to see my grandmother. She was failing fast and we didn't expect her to be with us much longer—we had held this opinion for well over a decade.

A visit to Gramma's house in the picturesque college town

of Corvallis always proves to be a trip down memory lane. Neither Gramma nor her house had changed since the days of my childhood. It was *the* gathering place for all family get-togethers.

On Sunday, Gramma took me to her church, a small country church outside Corvallis. It was the perfect size for a proud grandmother to introduce her grandson to every member, and she did just that at the pot luck after the morning worship service. While we sat on those metal folding chairs at a long table in the church basement waiting for the food to be prepared, one person after another came by to meet Mrs. Belshee's successful grandson from Chicago. Each time I thought she was about to overlook someone, she caught him, too, and I "got to" meet him. It was her day to shine and she was proud. And who was I to discourage her from proudly showing me off? I was even getting to like the level of respect that our culture bequeathes to the successful.

There was a group of women busily working to get the meal and my grandmother proudly pointed out the pastor's wife. Her husband had graduated from the same seminary as my father, a rival to the one I had attended. Her appearance brought back memories of that old stereotype: a saintly woman cares little for her appearance.

During my days at Bible school there were many such girls. They considered it "worldly" to make oneself attractive. They concentrated on inner beauty and let the "outward" appearance go where one might expect. In those days of asceticism, it would be considered an act of virtue to marry a girl who put no value on the way she looked. So, naturally, a certain amount of guilt attended those boys who were attracted to the attractive girls. It was all a part of the self-denial that made one feel as if he was pleasing God. I was thankful that God had freed me of this whole mentality, that he had truly given me all good things to enjoy, that I didn't need to feel as if I had to be some sort of misfit in order to please him.

I recalled all those things as I observed her appearance. If disregard for one's looks is a sign of inner quality, I thought, then she must have great inner quality, because she had made almost no effort at attractivenss. Not that she looked like a slob, just unkept, no makeup, the simple and tacky look. As I was making these observations, she went about her work there in the church basement, helping with the food while tending her small children. My grandmother began telling me about her.

"That girl," my grandmother said, "has been to so many doctors and they can't do anything for her. They all say that there is so much cancer spread throughout her entire body that they can't understand why she isn't dead."

Her words rolled over my thoughts like a steamroller over a child's toy. My eyes filled with tears—tears of shame and remorse. How could I possibly be more proud, more arrogant, more judgmental?

I amazed myself. I recalled that day when, seeing those sloppy people in a grocery store, I was forced to admit my great deficiencies, driving me to repentance, where I found a peaceful forgiveness from God himself. Now, here I was many years later doing the same thing I had done in that grocery store, the same thing I have always done, basing my self-worth on how I compared to others.

Sometimes these feelings irritated me; this failure to measure up to a nebulous standard of conduct that could keep me burdened with guilt. Maybe Sartre was right. Maybe it would be easier to dump this theology than to have to tolerate all the guilt it seemed to saddle me with. Though in this case, like so many others, maybe I had earned every bit of guilt I felt.

If there's anything to that statement about the last being first and the first being last, I would expect this disheveled woman to enter the kingdom of heaven way, way ahead of me.

Now here's Sally, just like the other woman. I dragged myself out of bed. I've got to find an easier way to help humanity, I thought.

When we arrived at the camp, it turned out to be a minute

settlement of lean-tos sheltering bedridden refugees. We helped set up makeshift beds and moved patients around while Sally went about the duties of tending the sick. I wondered what spurred these people to not only give up so much to be here, but also to work in such an untiring manner in this awful heat? Then I answered my own question; it was the same thing that brought me: a commitment to one's fellow man stimulated by a love of God himself. I felt ashamed, though, to think of myself as a committed person when compared to these people.

Every family that came across the Cambodian-Thai border had a survival story of movie-thriller proportions, the kind of trauma that would convert an atheist. Shortly after my departure, a massive Christian renewal took place in the camp. I was told that when the people lined up to baptized, the line stretched out of sight.

The indescribable human tragedy that I saw was the latest result of the Vietnam war. It gave me pause now to wonder how different this outcome might have been had the war been waged differently, or had the war not been waged at all. But I was in no position to judge military or political decisions with hindsight. The job that lay at my feet was to assist half a million people to make new lives for themselves. It seeemed like a staggering number until I considered all the people who, like Nancy and me, were willing to help.

I made some quick mental calculations. Those half a million refugees might represent 100,000 families. There might be 100,000 churches in America. If each church were willing to resettle just one family, all the refugee camps would be empty. And I was well aware that many Western countries were opening their borders to refugees as well. It was a unique opportunity.

For years I had heard social critics of the Western world preach against the evils of materialism and the inequities brought about by the greed of capitalism. Indeed, my own college generation had probably been the most outspoken critics of the hypocrisy of middle-class America. Now, entering our early thirties, we were becoming middle-class America and here lay before us a cause that rattled the TV of every family room in America. And it did not require one to leave family, job, and home to do something about it. All that was required was for us to open our communities to these homeless, destitute poor. It would be our big chance to make a major difference at a minimal sacrifice. Minimal, at least by comparison to the total commitment made by the nurses and doctors of the refugee camps.

I returned to the States determined to make some significant contribution to the problem. Never before had I seen a situation where the average person in civilized society could have as significant an impact as this one presented. The opportunity for cross-cultural exchange by way of taking a refugee family and resettling them in America was an opportunity of monumental proportion and there were many anxious to help.

It was, in my opinion, a job uniquely designed for the church. Wasn't it, after all, the Christian church that would be most concerned about the plight of the poor? Not only that, but the church had the organizational structure, the economic strength, and social unity to band together and assist families. And that is exactly what many churches across America and the rest of the Western world were doing. A small group of people in our own local church resettled one family, then another. Before long we had a small group of Khmer-speaking refugees among our friends. We encouraged our church to become more actively involved.

The trip to Southeast Asia got us involved on a personal level with an organization that was directly helping the people we wanted to help. But because the funding of projects in the Third World is often slow, we had no place to give the large amounts of money. So we continued giving substantially to our local church. Since Nancy and I didn't keep close track of the total, we were surprised when we were informed how large it was; well over six figures.

"Maybe we're getting just a little bit carried away on this thing," Nancy suggested. "It might be wise if we eased off a bit until we can be sure how they'll handle the money."

It wasn't long after we began to give the big dollars that we became involved in a typical controversy over the use of the funds. Nancy and I criticized the proposed budget for being too small. The church had taken in funds far in excess of its current budget and showed no faith that this trend would continue. Naturally, we hoped for a budget that would serve the needs of the poor, in this case, the homeless refugees. Others had different priorities.

Squabbles among the spiritually enlightened have always been a source of fascination. How wet should you get when you're baptized? Where did Cain get his wife? Did Adam have a naval? Is it possible to be a Catholic and a Christian at the same time? How much of the church's budget should be used to assist the poor? These are real congregation splitters. In one such debate a person said, "Doesn't it say somewhere in the Bible that God helps those who help themselves?" This is what I call the infamous, Doesn't-it-say-somewhere-in-the-Bible-that, line. The line is always finished off with anything that will support the speaker's opinion. And even though it starts off sounding like a question, it always ends like an edict. The likelihood that these hypothetical biblical quotes are accurate is usually a matter of pure luck. Though on occasion someone will actually open the Bible to find out. In the case of this popular quote, it was actually Ben Franklin, not God, who said it. I surmize that he was overhead muttering this line under his breath as he reached for the food while everyone else was patiently waiting for a long-winded preacher to finish saying grace.

An archbishopric was once offered to a gentleman of prominence in exchange for the spiritual act of donating 1,000 ducats on behalf of each of the twelve apostles. Is it any surprise that the gentleman thought that the seven days of creation would be a more holy figure from which to work? He offered 1,000 ducats for each of the days. So who could have guessed that the ten commandments might offer the most godly number of all? The archbishopric was delivered and the 10,000 ducats donated.

The actual theology behind most squabbles could bore a saint. But the emotional involvement of the key players can be quite intense—each having heard somewhere, or read some-place, or thought the Bible might have said something (which he has no precise recollection of) that proves that God agrees with him. All opinion to the contrary is anathema.

In one such quarrel I was personally told by a group of sincere Christian leaders that they had never been wrong about anything. Up to that point I thought that the only educated people who made that claim were God and the Pope—and I had some doubts about one of them. How does a person struggling to find truth engage in intellectual combat with those who claim equal infallibility with the Pope? Maybe I should have asked them for a tip on the market. To interject a sense of humor into a spiritual quarrel might be viewed as an act of pagan sacrilege. This is no laughing matter, I could hear them saying. It would cause me to develop a certain hypothesis over the years about theological inquiry. The main differ-ence, I concluded, between God and the average clergyman is that God does not take himself nearly so seriously.

In the comfort of our home we discussed with a theologian the subject of the need to reach out and help these oppressed victims of the Pol Pot regime. He responded by informing me of the big problem that we have with unemployment in our own country. "These people will only be taking jobs that other Americans need," he told me. I muttered something about them only taking unskilled jobs; the kind that often pay too little to provide adequate incentive to get our people off public assistance. My ideas seemed so secular and he was, after all, a theologian. I wondered if I should quote to him any of the myriad statements from the Bible about the obligation to meet the needs of the widow, the orphan, the oppressed, the alien. But I supposed it to be a bit presumptuous for a commodities trader to quote the scriptures to a theologian.

His view, however, was hardly uncommon. One Christian leader was reported to have said, "I think this Cambodian resettlement thing has gone way too far." A number of churches were happy to have a report on the difficult situation in Southeast Asia, showing pictures of the destitute people, starving children, and so forth. Everyone seemed happy to do the highly visible. But when people of a different culture group, different body odor, different language, different table manners began to intrude on our subculture, that was different. A bunch of Cambodian refugees in one's group did nothing to enhance one's status in a wealthy community.

The general feeling was, "I've got nothing against them being poor, I just wish they'd be poor somewhere else." It would, after all, be so much easier on the property values. Like an idiot, I had overlooked these realities.

I tended to respond by saying, "I thought your theology said you were going to leave all this stuff behind, remember: 'this world is not my home, I'm just a passin' through,' and all those nice ideas?" The bottom line is that it's so much easier to send a check off to a foreign country.

The squabble climaxed in a distasteful meeting in which I basically found myself a minority of one against the established authority. My opinion didn't amount to much, the powers that existed got what they wanted, and Nancy and I breathed an enormous sigh of relief that at least we had stopped giving when we did. We reasoned that if God would entrust us with these large amounts of money, He certainly would expect us to put them into causes consistent with our conscience.

"Maybe we should consider leaving this church," I told Nancy, and we argued about it all the way home. "We'll be older and wiser next time."

(As it turned out, we were only older the next time. A well-known Christian organization took our money and funded projects that they were also able to fund from a foreign government. The projects were therefore double funded and the extra money channeled into a secret corporation in a third country. The off-shore funds were controlled by the head of the Christian organization that had raised the money from us. I made a special trip to the headquarters and called for an investigation. They called me self-righteous. The money was, after all, doing God's work. Hmm, how does God keep getting himself dragged into all these deals? I left town.)

But a congregation dispute is different. You can't just leave town. It was a painful dilemma. We had made such dear friends at this church. But how could we continue to pour ourselves and our money into a place that was clearly going in a different direction than we?

So it was a sleepless night. At 5:00 A.M. I finally dozed off, woke a short time later, and couldn't decide whether or not to go in to work. On any other such day I would have taken off. Nancy begged me to stay home, but being a glutton for punishment I wouldn't listen. Besides, I figured I would only sit around home feeling sorry for myself anyway. I stared out the window of the Northwestern commuter train, half asleep, wondering what kind of mess God had allowed me to get into this time. I certainly wasn't looking to make trouble. The next place I get involved I'm gonna keep my mouth shut, I decided. I didn't need all this grief, I thought, more to God than to myself. I had made a fool out of myself at the meeting last night because I believed I knew what the right thing was. "All right, God," I thought to myself, "if you're there, I could sure use some kind of encouragement today." I desperately needed something to drag me out of my depression.

The grain market had been down for a record ten days in a

row, and I was betting there were some farmers who could have used something to help them with their depression at about this time. This day would extend that record to eleven and was one of the wildest and strangest trading days I had ever experienced.

A number of inexplicable market phenomena took place that day which could only be characterized as extremely fortunate. No one likes to think that he earns money by sheer luck, but on this day, honesty would demand the use of that word. It reminded me once again, of the statement "You can make a lot more money being lucky than smart."

Through a variety of accidental events, I became the beneficiary of enormous windfall profits that totaled exactly the amount of money we had donated that year. I had never seen a day like it before, nor would I again. Somehow or other, between that morning's train ride and the closing bell, I had forgotten my depression.

That settles it, God, I thought, next time I ask for relief from depression, this is precisely the kind of answer I'm looking for. A little more dramatic than I had anticipated, but I wasn't about to start complaining.

Looking back over the church squabble from the vantage point of some hindsight, I was surprised how easy it was to use the word "hypocrite" in place of "disagreement." That is not to suggest that hypocrisy is not alive and well. It is. But my quest was to see if Christianity really works. I wondered if it would work as well for the poor as it had in my marriage? Even if the church were packed with hypocrites, it should be no concern of mine. Christ himself had many followers who weren't really serious.

If the church's lack of concern for the poor troubled me, those outside the church were even worse. One of the major commodities exchanges announced the generous giving of their membership to the needy at Christmas time. Five thousand dollars; a whopping ten dollars per member. Generosity of this sort demanded an official announcement? I pictured a person throwing a peanut to a herd of starving elephants.

It was not surprising to find plenty of hypocrisy outside organized religion. Finding it inside was what was so frustrating. But many churches *were* resettling refugees. Some of our friends took a family all by themselves. I did some more mental calculating: If one out of every 500 families in America could resettle a refugee family, I reasoned, the problem could be totally eradicated. A neat numeric solution to a global problem, but who would be crazy enough to step up and make such a small contribution to such a big problem. Certainly the realists aren't going to do it, they know it can't be done. The atheists aren't going to do it, they need evil in the world to support their world view. That only leaves us idealistic theists who are foolish enough to think that for each problem there must be a solution.

I mentioned the idea to Nancy. "Y'know," I said cautiously, almost hoping she wasn't listening. "Just because we aren't able to get the right people interested in helping us doesn't mean we can't resettle them ourselves."

"Do you have any idea," she answered, "of the number of people who ask me how I can stand living with you?" I knew that this came up from time to time but I was unaware of the precise frequency. "Oh, yeah, 'How do you take him?' they ask, 'What's it like living with someone like that; inquiring minds want to know?'" I really hoped for a much more negative answer, something like, "No way, you're outta your mind!"

"I'm trying to be a little serious here," I went on. "Just think about it. Are we asking other people to do something that we are not willing to do ourselves? If it's a reasonable alternative for all of America to resettle refugees, then is it a reasonable alternative for us?"

She summarized the issue for most of the West. "The resettlement of Southeast Asians by the Western world is a fantastic theory. A lot of people can make wonderful careers for themselves by talking about it, writing about it, singing about it, and doing whatever else they do to give people neat little ways of dealing with their guilt. But when you start talking about bringing a bunch of people out of the jungle who don't know so much as what to do with a toilet, certainly they don't know how to use toilet paper, just think about it. Then you stick them into our home, to eat off of our dishes, to rub disease-filled noses with our little boys—well, that's where all that cool theory comes to a screeching halt."

Now that's just the sort of articulate speech I was looking for. Obviously my conscience had jumped the gun a bit when I came up with this idea about taking a family into our home. How much easier it would be to just go on the stump, to preach about the obligation of the church to meet this need, and to point out the hypocrisy of the clergy. I was already gaining some notoriety as a social critic, why not develop that. The public seems to get some mysterious enjoyment out of having guilt trips laid on them. In any case, I am certainly not going to bring any refugee family into my home without Nancy's 100 percent support. She's going to be the one who gets stuck with most of the work.

A few nights later, at the dinner table, I had already forgotten the subject when out of the blue Nancy said, "The love of God compels us."

"Huh?" I said, and paused, looking at her over my forkful of food.

"Well, doesn't it?" she asked.

"Doesn't it what? Doesn't what, what?"

"Doesn't the love of God compel us to have a refugee family in our home, to give them a new life in this country." By now I had forgotten all that Statue of Liberty, give-me-your-tired rhetoric. I was the one who was getting tired. Besides, I was back in my job and had my concentration on the making of money.

"I thought we had settled that issue. I'm busy making money now. We'll be giving the lion's share of it to help the refugee situation. I'm sure they need the money we can generate a lot more than they need our home."

"The love of God *compels* us." The way she emphasized the word "compels" made me uncomfortable. The glory of being self-employed was that no one *compelled* me to do anything. This conversation called for a change of pace.

"Whose idea was this in the first place?" I asked.

"Yours."

"So now I regret ever having brought it up. Why don't we just forget the whole thing?" Hypocrisy, it had been so easy to recognize in everyone else.

She thought about that for a moment. "The love of *God* compels us." This time her emphasis on the word "God" made me realize she was serious.

"Look, I'm the seminary grad in this family, I'll handle the God-talk if you don't mind."

The following evening at dinner I said, "You know you're the one who is going to get stuck with all the work, all the running around?"

"Oh, yeah! That's what you think, mister! You'll be in this just as much as I will. All the money in the world doesn't mean a hill of beans if a person can't get his hands dirty once in a while."

It was one of those typical Chicago summer days when Nancy and I put Dani and his three-month-old baby brother, Joey, into our Dodge Maxivan and drove to O'Hare to meet our refugee family. We really needed our little sons now; we knew they would provide more cross-cultural understanding than we ever could.

Our refugee family was smaller than we had anticipated. They had nine children but would only be bringing four: an infant, a boy of five, and two teenage boys. The other five had been lost.

Nancy and I stood with Dani and Joey watching six short refugees stumble up the walkway into a new world. It wasn't the same as entering New York harbor and passing under the lifted lamp; the lady of liberty inviting the world to give her its huddled masses. Even apart from the drama of the harbor, I could remember the strains of that old hymn, "Give me your tired, your poor." And here they were, headed straight at us; the wretched refuse, the homeless, tempest-tossed. And we, their statue of liberty.

No, it wasn't so dramatic—well, maybe it was for them. One could see their faces bright with that unmistakable yearning to breathe a breath of freedom. They were thrilled to see us even if our initial meeting was about as awkward as one might expect, salvaged only by the fact that the boys were able to give and take loving greetings so much better than we.

The next few months would be an incredibly different experience for us. Satisfying, fulfilling, and gratifying, but mostly characterized by long hours of hard work, rat race, frustration, and wondering just how we got ourselves into this thing.

Saran, their youngest boy, registered in kindergarten where Dani was attending first grade, and we began the difficult task of finding jobs for Mr. Tauch and his two teenage sons. There was also an ongoing list of government offices that had to be visited, English classes to attend, medical check-ups for each member of the family, dental problems to be solved—the list was endless. But these people's courage was amazing in the face of the most unfair odds stacked against them in their brand-new world.

One of the teenage boys had learned some English in the refugee camp, and so was able to secure a job pushing a broom in a small factory near our home. His work there was so good that the management decided to hire his brother and father to work on their lathes even though they didn't speak English. Keara, who was too young to work machines, would have to translate for his older brother and father.

Within a few weeks the owners of the company were called into the shop to see how these ignorant, uneducated Southeast Asians who didn't know any English were able to produce more knife handles than had been thought possible. These three workers began piling up money, paying for all their own food, and even making a rent payment to us.

Mr. Tauch had been a truck driver in Cambodia, so we thought it would be easy for him to secure a license here. This would take a great deal of the driving strain off Nancy and myself. A non-English speaker is allowed to have a translator with him to take the written section of the test, he needs to be able to recognize all the road signs, and then take the actual driving test. Mr. Tauch was obviously an experienced driver, so we set out to teach him the rules of the road and show him how to recognize road signs. Every day we went over all the signs in the book and on the highway we pointed to every road sign and said, "Mr. Tauch, what's that say?"

"Caution," he'd say. Or, "pass with care." Finally he knew them all and was ready for his first big test in America.

Four of us sat in the back of the testing area at the license center; the examiner who read the questions, the translator, Mr. Tauch, and myself. While they went through the test, I noticed another foreigner taking the test without an interpreter. She had numbers and letters written all over her left arm. When she turned in her test, the examiner observed how odd it was that she had all the questions right on the front, but all wrong on the back. Apparently, when she turned the page over, her coded cheat notes got confused. The examiner read a correctly answered question from the front page to see if she could answer it, but she didn't understand English.

There was a group of people who resettled Cambodians and put them on welfare. They had contacted Mr. Tauch, telling him that he need not work in his new country. It confused him. "This not Cambodian way," he had told us. "People in Cambodia all *want* to work."

After passing the written test, we proceeded to the other side of the center where the examiner would check to ensure that he understood the meaning of all the road signs. I had been over these signs a thousand times with Mr. Tauch, and I knew he understood them as well as I did. The first sign was the school zone.

"Twenty mile per hour—school zone," Mr. Tauch said proudly in his strong oriental accent.

"What else does it say?" the examiner asked. It had never occurred to me that they would expect him to be able to read the fine print at the bottom.

Mr. Tauch squinted at the lettering at the bottom of the sign and finally formed the word "On." Looking for another fifteen or twenty seconds, he slowly uttered the word "School." Next came the word "Days." Up to this point I had no idea that Mr. Tauch's English classes were coming along so well. Over approximately the next 120 seconds, Mr. Tauch was able to get the whole sentence out. "On school days when children are present." This is the end, I thought. He'll never get a driver's license.

I muttered something about him being a slow reader but even a slower driver. The examiner didn't seem too impressed. "He'd have to be driving awful slow in order to get a sign read at that rate." He thought a moment, then looked at me with an approving nod and smiled. We both started to laugh.

I looked at Mr. Tauch while we laughed at the thought of him trying to read this sign while driving down the street. In stature alone he was dwarfed by us. In status he was at the mercy of the kindness of my family; now at the mercy of a laughing driving examiner. Only a few years before he led a quiet life on another continent, in another time zone, another world. He knew his way, he held his head high, he was the proud father and sole provider of nine children. He drove a truck in a country where a person has to be truly talented to drive anything. Now, with only four children left and without knowing whether the other five are dead or alive, he finds himself in a country where he is considered stupid for his lack of linguistic skill. With no marketable talent and no means of gaining any of the respect he once had, he is, through no fault of his own, at the bottom of life, the punch line to a joke because he is slow to read the fine print on a traffic sign. How could I have been so slow in deciding to resettle his family? I had set out to solve the problem of the world's poor, and now found myself concentrating on Mr. Tauch. For some strange reason, this was more satisfying.

The Tauchs eventually located some of their relatives on the East Coast and wanted to relocate to be close to them. They didn't want to offend us by leaving, just needed to be close to a relative. We understood. The day they arrived, we would have had no problem at all with their leaving. But now we had become attached. They had become real people, real friends.

We all drove together, our family and theirs, to the Amtrak station in Chicago. Keara looked in awe at the Sears Tower. "Who lives in that house?" he asked in shock. In all the time they had been with us, we never had enough extra time to bring them to the big city for a visit. His English had greatly improved by now and he was the official translator for every member of the family.

Dani was in charge of the collapsible luggage carrier and we piled up their bags and all moved like a small tour group toward the train. We boarded the train with them, got them settled, told the conductor what town to put them off in, and began saying the good-byes.

Dani looked up at me with a puzzled look and whispered, "I think I'm about to cry." He didn't understand this new kind of tears. I knew exactly how he felt. It was an emotional parting. We would miss these people from a foreign land. I had a tear of sorrow myself.

Mr. Tauch said something to Keara and he translated to us. "He says to tell you that it was you who saved us from a horrible, horrible place and as long as we live, we will never forget what you have done for my family."

I had my tears pretty well under control until then. Surely we have been doing a job that God himself wanted done, I thought. Could this be what those Fundamentalists meant when they used to talk about serving the Lord? "Serving the Lord," another irrelevant phrase that had always prompted the response, "what a drag, what a bore." The sacrifice involved here (and it was substantial) was hardly worth mentioning by comparison to the inner satisfaction of knowing that I had been used by the creator of the universe to help relieve the suffering of a few of his humble creatures. What great honor I felt to be considered worthy to help God do his job, to help him make right the immeasurable evil inflicted by the wicked on the innocent.

We waved as the train pulled out of the station and I shed a few more tears. Dani folded the luggage carrier and put it in his right hand. I carried Joey in my left arm with my right arm around Nancy. She put her left arm around my waist and held Dani's hand with her right. Together we made our way out of the station. We contemplated the difficulties, the sacrifices, and the resulting gratification as we made our way across Jackson Boulevard and the icy sidewalks toward the van. "So the love of God compels us does it, huh?" I suggested.

Epilogue

The shrill clang of the bell spelled an end to another trading day in the grain market. But this was not an ordinary day, it was a special, magical day, a once-every-twenty-years day. I wouldn't hang around to estimate the day's profit, or figure what position I might be exposed to over the weekend, or shoot the breeze with the traders as we carded our last trades.

No, today was different. Not at all like the crazy days of a few years ago when we made and lost fortunes the way the big money is made and lost in this business, with mistakes.

This day was different because I was about to make a trip back to the past. In my pocket was a United Airlines ticket to the West Coast. I would board a plane, fly to Portland, rent a car, drive the scenic route south to central Oregon, turn west through the mountains to the coast, and arrive at my hometown. Ah, just the thought of the place put a smile on my face. The thought of leaving the big city and arriving a world away in a different subculture all in the same day created a rare euphoria in me.

I handed my cards to the desk and made my way across the grain floor to the exit. Down the escalators, I exited the Chicago Board of Trade, crossed under the Van Buren Street elevated tracks, entered One Financial Place, and rode the express elevator to the thirty-third floor. CRT now occupied two whole floors of the new Financial Plaza. I hung up my trading jacket and went back down the elevator for the short walk to the garage. I applied some of my adrenaline to the accelerator and the intercooled turbo shot me down the ramp and onto the Kennedy Expressway. In minutes, I thought, I will relax in that plane seat and be done with big-city tensions for a whole weekend.

I pushed the button that automatically dialed Nancy and put her on the car's speakerphone, told her "good-bye" and I would see her on Monday, hit the express lanes and a short time later pulled into the O'Hare parking lot. Grabbing my bag, I made my way through the tunnel to Terminal Two.

After twenty years I wondered what they could be like? Would they still be the people who were intent on impressing each other? Would they be driving the most impressive cars they could get their hands on? I wondered if I should have rented that exotic sports car? Or maybe have one of my rare Ferraris shipped to the coast to drive. Hardly my style. Besides, Nancy would have disowned me.

Like the engines on this 727, the memories raced as we taxied onto the runway. I had finally put my life together— it's what we all intended to do as we walked down the aisle that graduation day in June. How had the others fared? Would they have found happiness?

What a twenty years! I never thought, while growing up either in that small town or the variety of other places in which my family had lived, that life could be as fulfilling as it was. It was really strange, I thought, as I felt the power of the plane's acceleration push me back into my seat, that I would still feel such an affinity toward a town in which I had lived for only five years. Yet it was this little town that I considered to be my own, my hometown, my Lake Wobegone.

Within minutes I saw beneath me the unmistakable meandering of the Mississippi and thought about the boyhood years of Huck Finn. I had always planned to duplicate his raft journey, but as of yet the pace of life has not allowed it. As I looked I wondered if I have allowed the pace of life to change me. This weekend will help me to find out. I am actually going back in time—back twenty years—maybe more really; back where people think $20 for a weekend celebration is too much. These are truly small town folk; a different culture, somehow separated from the rest of the world. And it is that separation that I look so much forward to. That special something which says, "You can't change us, world. Nope, not us." How I missed it.

Ah, this was it; the beginning of a whole weekend with nothing to do but taste again the fresh breezes blowing in off the ocean and remember. Remember and enjoy. I said good-bye to the river, reclined my seat, relaxed like I hadn't in a long time, and started in on some of those memories.

Some of them were painful. We had all graduated and were gone that summer Jo Lynn died. This would be the first time we would get together without her. And I would visit the graves of Danny and Jimmy, too. I kept my face turned toward the window to keep the people around me from seeing the tears that these memories forced upon me. I saw scattered clouds blurred by tears and they reminded me of the flight from Copenhagen to Delhi en route to Dad's funeral. It felt funny to grieve after so long, and I was thankful that when Nancy and I had the twin girls three months ago, we named one of them in Jo Lynn's memory.

I recalled my struggle with morality in the decade of the sixties, and Mr. Ketchum's style of discipline. I couldn't help wondering if the ACLU had found Reedsport and sued Ketchum. Poor Mr. Ketchum wouldn't make it in the big-city schools, where a recent survey showed rape to be the number-one disciplinary problem. Cuff a student for raping his classmate? Ridiculous. Thankfully, our big-city value system protected our children from the likes of Mr. Ketchum.

I suppose we could just say that boys will be boys. My mother never said that to the poor little old lady next door, the target of my dirt clods. I remembered my favorite grade-school poet, Ogden Nash:

MARK A. RITCHIE

The trouble with a kitten is
THAT
Eventually it becomes a
CAT.

My mother, and Mr. Ketchum, too, I suspect, understood a lot more about kittens and boys than did the people who helped us structure our big-city educational systems. While the authorities on human behavior were asking "How long will it take this child to outgrow his urge to throw dirt clods?," my farm-raised mother asked simpler questions of almost no scholastic merit. Questions like, "I wonder how big a dirt clod Marky will be throwing next year?" For fear of the answer, she applied the rod of Solomon to the back of the fool and Mr. Ketchum cuffed the back of every head that got out of line.

They actually appeared to think that a child left undisciplined might actually become undisciplined. Maybe that's why my mother didn't even have the common courtesy of letting me off on the first offense.

Somewhere along the line, someone suggested that we allow a kid to work his way out of his dirt-clod-throwing stage on his own. Give him some space. Let him grow out of his "difficult" stages. And certainly never, never use corporal punishment. It never occurred to them that the dirt clods just might get bigger.

I stared out the window thinking that what was needed was a God-Ketchum who would keep everyone in line; if he would only agree to do so without stifling free expression of thought and behavior. It wouldn't be much longer now before I would be back in a town where no one thought twice about stifling any and all behavior that infringed on the right of others.

The clang of the bell and the roar of the grain market were a memory by the time I saw the Portland skyline. The anticipation mounted as the first leg of this journey came to a close.

An hour south of Portland, on Interstate 5, I stopped for gas and called home to see how Nancy and the twins were doing.

252

Back out on the highway the sun was fading over my right shoulder as my thoughts turned toward the twins, the boys, and Nancy. No doubt she had seen this same sun set on our lake just a few hours ago. I recalled being told even in grade school how every decision we made would have a grave effect on our futures. It is odd how silent they were on the subject of the selection of a life mate.

When I passed the sign for the Eugene exit, I knew the driving part of my trip was half over. The sun had fully set and I turned on the headlights. A few miles south of Eugene I took the turnoff to Drain and was now passing through the small town of Elkton. It had not changed a bit; 9:45 on a Friday evening and not a soul on the street—and this highway is the only street. Now I was only a few more minutes from home; I would get there at exactly 10:30, as I had predicted.

Looking back from the vantage point of a gorgeous drive through the wooded mountains that sheltered Highway 38, I had a warm sense of satisfaction. When a deer on the highway startled me from my thoughts, I saw that I was about to enter Scottsburg—just sixteen more miles to Reedsport. I was already sensing the atmosphere of the place. The giant trees, the sound of the river, the mountains, the fresh air, the winding road, the lack of traffic; it all added up to one thing: home.

The first few miles curved through the mountains along the river, but five miles from Reedsport the river basin opens and the highway straightens. I came down the long hill toward the sand and gravel pits of the lower section of town. A left turn on Highway 101 and I would check into the Tropicana Motel, where a reservation had been made for me. Then straight on to the party. The anticipation was killing me.

When I opened the door of my motel room, it hit me. There on my mirror was a large sign, "Welcome Home, Mark," plastered with the signatures and well wishes of a variety of my classmates. I was overcome. What a grand feeling—being home. I started to cry and supposed it would be better to get this out of my system here than to make a fool of myself when

I met everyone. I dumped my bags and ran back to the car. A short drive across the slough and up onto the flat and I was back in my old neighborhood. I turned right on Twentieth Street, just one block from the Dairy Queen, and drove to the Severson home, now owned by two of my classmates.

It was 10:30, exactly nine and a half hours with the time change since my plane had lifted off from O'Hare. I rang the doorbell, but they were having too good a time to hear it. So I let myself in. And there was the mad scientist with a few extra pounds—the master of the sideways remark—no doubt about it, that had to be Mark McClain. Then there was Rod, the tailback and class president. And Rex, the tackle who lined up next to me. Dan, who threw me a shutout. And I recognized almost all of them, except Elaine, who no one recognized.

What a grand time to embrace, even if I wasn't always real sure who I was embracing. But after a sentence or two, a smile, or a laugh, they gave away their identity. I never realized how good it would be to be home, to be among friends, to feel their acceptance, to reach out and grab a piece of the past, my past, to feel those roots, embrace the atmosphere that had so shaped me.

The party broke up about 2:30 and a few of us went a few blocks up the street to Matt's house, where we continued talking for a few more hours. There was more catching up to do than could be done in a weekend. I mentioned a little bit about my twenty-year quest for truth.

"Well, what did you find," asked Mike, my long-distance-running partner in eighth grade. I began to explain about my religious upbringing and the continual questions I had about what it meant to know God. Though it deserved an answer, his question never really got one. These group discussions tend to evolve with all the direction of the blowing wind. But I proposed to answer it thoroughly even if I had to, perish the thought, sit down and write a letter.

It was 4:30 A.M. when I left Matt's and drove past the school and out the old highway to the cemetery. But I was too tired to spend any time there, so I didn't stay.

The next day, Saturday, the guys all met at the high school ball field for a softball game. Again I was encouraged, even delighted at the total lack of interest in social status. No one seemed to care who had been a success or failure, only interested in enjoying each other's company, having a good time, renewing old friendships. And that is precisely what we did.

We all met at a waterfront restaurant in the evening for dinner. To my pleasant surprise, my favorite teacher was there. He was my favorite in spite of the fact that he taught English, my least favorite subject. We had absolutely the grandest of times. There were more people with more stories than one had time to hear.

And it was uncanny the number of friends who had taken journeys similar to my own. I sat across the table from the tackle I used to line up next to and heard him tell me how he and his wife, another of our classmates, had strengthened their faith in God at a church close to where they live in another small Oregon town.

I learned from my English teacher, an Episcopalian, of the friendship he had formed with my father, who had visited him to inform him of the ways of the Lord. If one discounts loving God and following Christ, the Episcopalians have almost nothing in common with Fundamentalists. But he had become friends with my father in spite of it. Maybe Dad hadn't been as closed-minded as I had always believed.

A classmate recalled a number of the popular sayings from the sixties to help us reminisce. The line that brought the most groans was, "Never trust anyone over thirty." Now that we were over thirty, we knew precisely how true this statement was and found ourselves intrigued at the insight of our youth. (The youth of the eighties have their own saying: Never trust anyone earning under $30,000 a year.)

After dinner and a time of socializing, the dancing began. This would bring back some old memories. It was dancing that had kept me from becoming as close to some of these people as I would have liked. Once again I found myself invited onto the dance floor. I whispered a prayer of thanks to God that I was no longer plagued by the feelings of guilt associated with this worldly activity. Freedom from guilt, however, did not make me any more disposed to making a fool out of myself, so I politely declined, content just to sit, quietly renewing old friendships.

In the wee hours of the morning, those who could still see straight made our way back to Matt's again, and stayed until 4:00 A.M. As I had the previous night, I took the old highway out of town and turned right into the cemetery.

A couple hundred feet in, I stopped the car. I knew exactly where it was, right there by the road. And Jimmy's and Jo Lynn's were only a few paces away. In the moonlight I could make out those familiar words, "Blessed is Danny, who died in the Lord."

I sat on his headstone and started to remember. It had been twenty-five years ago almost to the day that I was right here putting him in the ground. "Died *in* the Lord," I thought. A strange way of talking to be sure, but Christians have made it fashionable to say things in special phrases that sound irrelevant even if they have real meaning.

I knew what it meant anyway. It meant "covered with the blood of Christ," another strange Fundamentalist phrase that many did not try to understand. Jesus himself had started the confusion when he said, "Unless you eat my flesh and drink my blood . . ." No wonder his following of 5,000 was quickly reduced to twelve.

I was still thinking about those funny little phrases as I rose from Danny's headstone and walked the few paces over to Jimmy's and Jo Lynn's gravesites. I paced the few steps between them, back and forth as I thought. I had by now walked too many miles with God to think him unreal, in spite of the unreal religious language commonly used to describe him. Had I now after all these years of searching, I wondered, finally come back to be a Fundamentalist? Certainly I accepted the main truths of Christianity.

But what about that most basic teaching of all, that question which brought me hauntingly back here to the graves of my friends wondering whether I would ever see them again, and if not, whether I was the sole blame for it? That claim so clearly at the center of every Fundamentalist dogma: Any person who does not know Jesus Christ as his personal savior is going to hell. To reject this claim would most certainly get one ousted from Fundamentalism in the twinkling of an eye.

Yet I had to say in all honesty that I would have to reject this one. One of the greatest heroes of the faith, King David, never so much as once mentioned the phrase "Jesus Christ personal savior." How could he have? He lived centuries before and never heard the name of Christ. Had the great king known of Christ, he certainly would have worshiped him just like the wise men from the east. But no one could ever suggest that he would go to hell because of his ignorance of that phrase. I therefore had to conclude the same about all the illiterate heathen around the world who would live and die totally unaware of this Fundamentalist phrase. God would be their judge to be sure, but on what basis would he make his judgment?

Of one thing I am confident, I thought. The God I know would never send my friends to hell because they were ignorant. But how would he judge these two dear friends whom I now grieved over after twenty years? And, of course, the real question to me: How would my friends have measured up against it?

I began to imagine what might have been; what if I had talked to Jo Lynn about a topic as serious as God? Maybe we'd have gone for a Coke some night after play practice, stayed out late, and walked down the beach on a night just like this one; moonlight broken by scattered clouds. She would look at the moon and say, "There must be a God up there somewhere to make a night so friendly and enjoyable. Don't you think?"

And I'd say, "Yep, he's out there all right. I keep him pretty busy lookin' out for me, keepin' me out of all the trouble I keep tryin' to get into."

And she'd say, "You talk like you know him or somethin'."

"Sure," I'd say, "I just talked to him this morning. It's pretty neat to be able to call up your own deity anytime you need help."

"You sound like you really know him," she'd say. "How did you manage that?"

"Like Christ said," I'd say, "with the faith of a little child saying, God I'm sorry for how I've been and I want you to forgive me and make me a child of yours. It's easy to say it, but murder to mean it. Maybe you'd like to be a child of God?"

And she'd say, "Yeah, Mark, I really would. Y'know I shouldn't tell you this because nobody knows it, nobody at all, but I've really been feeling guilty lately about some things."

Or maybe she wouldn't. Maybe she'd say, "You know how busy we are these days, Mark, taking care of all the spring activities, the play, getting ready for graduation and finals, and I'm trying to make sure I graduate valedictorian. I just don't see how I have time for a major change in my life-style. I'm havin' too much fun right now. There'll be time for that later. Besides, even though I'm not perfect, I'm just as good as the next person."

"Better," I'd say, "better." And we'd listen to the pounding surf for a while.

Finally she'd say, "I suppose you think I'll go to hell, if I don't confess to God."

"Well," I'd say, "let me put it this way: It would be awful mean of God to force you to go to heaven against your will."

"Well, I certainly don't want to go to hell."

Then I'd say, "People who are uninterested in God couldn't possibly go to heaven. Think how bored they'd be: spending all eternity with someone they think is a drag. My dad's run into a host of people who just aren't interested in God, even in this town, with its strong traditional moral values. These people would die of sheer boredom in heaven." Maybe we'd sit on a log and watch the moonlight reflect off the surf.

After a time she'd say, "I wish you hadn't told me all this stuff y'know."

"Why's that?"

"Because if you hadn't, God couldn't blame me for not knowing."

"It's an interesting idea," I might say after thinking for a bit. "But I doubt if he's dumb enough to buy the excuse. He must know what you would have done in a bunch of different situations you've never faced. Besides, now you know exactly where you stand with God."

I was pacing slowly back toward Jimmy's grave when the concept hit me, shaking me from my fantasy world. Of course, that's it, I thought. If God is so smart, he surely knows precisely which of my hypothetical responses Jo Lynn would have had. Why couldn't he simply judge my friends on the basis of how they *would have* responded? If they had no interest in knowing or hearing about God, how could they keep him from knowing it simply because they had never formally rejected him? God knows with infinite accuracy precisely what Jo Lynn and Jimmy would have done had they known as much about him as I do. He could judge them on that basis alone, quite apart from their ability to recite Fundamentalist dogma as if taking a final exam. This issue, after all my worrying, didn't depend on how much they knew, on whether or not I had failed to inform them, but rather on their own inner attitude toward God. They could come under God's scrutiny not based on what I knew about God, but based on what they knew.

It all seemed so obvious, so simple. And it wasn't even an original thought. I had read the words of the apostle Paul that the things which are available to be known about God have been clearly shown to every living person, that they have been personally shown to them by God and can be seen simply by looking at nature, that every man through all history has had this idea of God planted in his mind such that he is quite without excuse. I recalled Sartre, who made his decision to be an atheist as a young preschool arsonist. How consistent his attitude was with the 2,000-year-old writing of the apostle Paul. How could I have been so ignorant of this simple concept?

These dear friends of mine whom I grieved over in this fresh, Oregon night air had the same inner idea of God that Sartre had. What their response was to that inner voice of God I do not know. I only hope they didn't respond like Sartre. I sure hope they had the same attitude about God that I have. It's always sad when your friends don't like each other.

I had been taught as a youngster the words "Yea, though I walk through the valley of the shadow of death, I will fear no evil, for thou art with me." I was standing in the middle of that shadow and feeling the same comfort I had felt years earlier halfway around the world in Herat. I had the overwhelming sense that I knew a God who had his act together, who knew the end from the beginning, who was indeed in the process of putting all the little pieces of this puzzle of human drama together to form a big picture. And the picture was starting to make sense.

Following God had turned out to be nothing but a bargain for me. And the bargain was totally in nonfinancial terms. Of course, I could hardly complain about the financial end of things either. I could still recall the tough times: the old potato I had found and eaten in my college days; the old car with no alternator or reverse; a very pregnant Nancy pushing the car back out of an intersection. They were tough times to be sure, but I wasn't going to say that God hadn't done right by me. I know where I came from, who I am, and where I'm going.

Amazing, I thought to myself as I examined Jo Lynn's

gravestone more closely in the cool moonlight. The creator of all this majesty of the universe—I know him, he's my friend. I've felt his comfort in my distress. I saw his care that day in Afghanistan when a poor man reached into his pocket to offer me money. I remember well the incredibly comforting feelings he gave me when I had those awful financial setbacks.

And most of all, I had complete freedom from guilt. The carpenter-preacher had said that he could by his death on a cross make people free of their guilt. He had been so credible in other things, I tried him on this one and found he delivered. The same forgiveness he extended to his executioners, he now handed me. My lifelong quest for truth and meaning has truly been met. I have been literally saved by his life.

But I still don't know, as I pace between their graves, what has become of Jimmy and Jo Lynn. To my God, my closest friend, who has answered my journey for truth and meaning, I beg you now, with tears falling into the grass that covers them, I beg you God to let me see Jimmy and Jo Lynn again someday. I only wish that every person in this cemetery could have someone who cares as much about them as I care about my friends.

It was 5:30 A.M. when I finally collapsed on my bed. The exhaustion I felt was much more than physical.

The next day was Sunday and I was invited by some classmates to attend the baptism of their son. Donna had been our head cheerleader and Mike a brilliant math student who sat behind me in trig class. They had been married shortly after our graduation and now their daughter was a cheerleader at Reedsport. Mike was in engineering and they had just recently moved back to our hometown.

Attending church with them was like taking another enormous step back in time. All those phrases, so packed with meaning. Phrases that no one really understands. The old nineteenth-century hymns, rich in a theology that has not yet been translated into the vernacular of the eighties. All that irrelevant God-talk that made him seem so impractical, so unreal, so far away and uninterested in us.

It was all the same religious theory I had grown up with, inviting Jesus Christ into your heart as your personal savior and so on. I didn't question the theology for a moment. I knew full well that the lover of money carries God in his wallet while the poor man carries his god in his heart. I'd tried God in both places and no one needed to convince me. God in the heart—what a way to pack the most living into life.

In the afternoon, the class met for a cookout in the forest at the edge of the sand dunes. While we relaxed on a sandy floor sheltered by towering pines, I asked Mike and Donna about it. "How do you guys expect your kids to accept all that old religious jargon?" I asked them. "It's taken me years to figure out that it's true and they can still make it sound so anti-quated. How irrelevant must it sound to the children?" They saw my point. I proposed to write them and continue the discussion.

As the cookout broke up and people started to leave, saying, "See ya in five years," I knew that my weekend was drawing to a close. I dropped a few friends off in town and drove out to the beach, walked the shoreline, marveled at the sand dunes, and once again saw the sun slowly sink toward the water, a sight only visible on the West Coast.

It is a magnificent world. Short of heaven, there couldn't be a nicer place. I ought to come here every weekend, I told myself. What could be better than being one of God's kids, in God's country, sitting in the middle of his coastline, watching his sun fall into his ocean?

Catching the red-eye from Portland and losing two hours on the time change, I landed in Chicago at about 6:00 A.M., giving me just enough time to get ready for the 9:30 bell in the grain market and another day of yelling and screaming. Three days later, caught up on my sleep, I picked up the phone to attempt to contact Jo Lynn's mother. I wanted to tell her of our class reunion and that I had named one of my twin daughters in Jo Lynn's memory. I had gotten her phone number from the funeral home in Reedsport. We had a warm chat. She told me that Jo Lynn's sister, Peggy, had converted to become a Mennonite. Could this be true? This was the same girl whom I knew to be bitter against God for having taken her sister. I also knew the Mennonites; these people were so straight they made Fundamentalists look downright loose. You can't be a Mennonite without having a real encounter with God.

Curious, I called her up. What I suspected was correct, she had found personal forgiveness from Christ for herself much the same way I had. Obviously, this wasn't something that I alone had discovered. It seemed to be going around.

Our eldest son, named after my brother Danny, attended a private Christian school where he was allowed to work ahead at his own pace. The pastor of the associated church acted as the principal. Dani came home from school one day asking how we know there is a God. I gave him a few interesting points to stimulate his thinking on the subject. After some discussion, I mentioned to Dani that he should put this question to the pastor at school tomorrow.

"Oh, no," he reacted. "I'll get in trouble."

"C'mon," I said, "they don't have a rule against asking questions, do they?"

"No, but some things you just get in trouble for." Some things never change. Dani now studies at the public school.

We heard from the Cambodian family we resettled. They now own their home and drive a new car, both purchased without a mortgage. Keara is married, lives in Atlanta, and drives an eighteen-wheeler—successfully.

The Afghan man who had become a follower of Christ through the reading of a history textbook was able to escape the country, and through a miraculous chain of events got his wife and child out as well. They are now making a new life for themselves in a Western country. Others of his countrymen were not so fortunate. Some were drowned in their own excrement at the hands of the invaders from the north.

I sat down to write a letter to my classmate who had inquired of my search. The letter got kind of long and involved. I started a letter to Mike and Donna to express more of my thoughts about their church. I started letters to other classmates as well, but they all seemed insufficient to communicate how I really felt. So I decided to combine them all into one long letter and send a copy to anyone with the inclination to read it. The story would tell how twenty years had shown me that Christianity was true, that it worked for me, and could work for anyone else willing to try it. Maybe I would at long last attempt to package some of those feelings I had always wanted to sell to the world.

So that is what I did. And that is the story you have just read.

Index

INDEX